Voices of the Civil War

Voices of the Civil War · Vicksburg

By the Editors of Time-Life Books, Alexandria, Virginia

Contents

VICKSBURG BESIEGED

This watercolor shows Grant's army launching its first direct assault against Vicksburg on May 19, 1863. Although the unknown artist has romanticized the scene by adding a wagon-borne band and depicting Vicksburg as a gleaming city on a hill, his work does convey a realistic impression of the rugged terrain of ravines and ridges surrounding it.

Prime Prize on the Great River

Before the outbreak of the Civil War, Vicksburg, Mississippi, had become one of the most prosperous and sophisticated towns on the old Southern frontier. Built atop bluffs overlooking the Mississippi River, the city was a booming center of trade, its wharves crowded with boats carrying all manner of goods and commodities. It boasted a municipal orchestra, a Shakespeare repertory company, and an imposing courthouse in the Greek Revival style. To its proud citizens Vicksburg was the "Queen City of the Bluff" and a center, as one of them wrote, of "culture, education and luxury."

All this was to change with the coming of the war. By early 1862 the peaceful town had become one of the most strategically important spots in the entire Confederacy—and would soon be one of the most bitterly fought over. Vicksburg by its topography was a natural fortress: Its high bluffs, once they had been fitted

---

This river view of Vicksburg—the "Gibraltar of the West"—is dominated by the Warren County Courthouse. Rising high above the Mississippi, amid almost impenetrable hills and ravines, the town was a natural fortress.

out with batteries of big guns, made the city impregnable to frontal attack from the river and from across the broken plain to the east. To the north stretched the Yazoo River delta —a vast morass of bayou, river, and swamp no attacking army could march through. To the south lay more of the same.

Yet so important was Vicksburg that Union forces would hammer away at it for more than a year while the Confederates tried just as desperately to hold it. As the fighting wore on, the city would suffer bombardments by the Federal navy, then become the target of a powerful Union army led by the most tenacious of Northern commanders, Major General Ulysses S. Grant. By the time the campaign for Vicksburg was over, it had become one of the longest and most harrowing ordeals of the war, marked by a half-dozen battles and ending with a siege that would leave the city in ruins.

Vicksburg became a prime strategic prize largely because it was the key to a vital Confederate supply line bringing huge quantities of food and other matériel from the West. Cargo vessels loaded with cattle and cotton and grain from Texas and Arkansas could steam down the Red River across Louisiana, then turn north up the Mississippi to unload at Vicksburg's docks. From there the supplies were shipped east on the Southern Mississippi Railroad for distribution throughout the South on a network of connecting rail lines.

Just as busy was a new railroad that ran westward from the west bank of the Mississippi opposite the town, the Vicksburg, Shreveport & Texas. Its trains brought in thousands of tons of freight—including European-made rifles and other munitions that had been shipped to Mexico and then hauled northward through Texas, evading the Union navy's blockade of Southern ports. In all, Vicksburg was, said Confederate president Jefferson Davis, "the nailhead that held the South's two halves together." Abraham Lincoln agreed. Pointing to a White House map of the region in 1862, he stated, "The whole lower Mississippi region is the backbone of the rebellion."

Aside from choking off the Confederate supply line, there were other reasons to capture Vicksburg. Most important was to open the Mississippi River for Northern commerce. Before the war the farmers of the Midwest had floated huge quantities of wheat and corn down the river on flatboats and barges to New Orleans, where the produce was transferred to oceangoing vessels for shipment to the East Coast and around the world.

But Vicksburg, sitting on its high bluffs, dominated the central Mississippi, strangling this commerce. Unable to pay the high costs of sending their produce east by rail, midwestern farmers began grumbling against the war. Thus, for economic and political reasons, too, Lincoln's government had to free the Mississippi of Confederate blockage.

By mid-1862 Union forces already controlled parts of the river. In April of that year, Flag Officer David Glasgow Farragut had boldly sailed a Union fleet into the mouth of the Mississippi

and then blasted his way past two formidable enemy bastions guarding the approaches to New Orleans. Union troops had quickly occupied the great port city, closing it to all Confederate traffic.

At the same time Federal troops and gunboats had been fighting their way south down the Mississippi. Victories at New Madrid, Missouri, at Island No. 10, and at Columbus, Kentucky, gave the Union a tight grip on the great river at the northern and southern ends of the western Confederacy. It remained for the Yankees to take the middle, centered on Vicksburg. That would prove to be an exceedingly difficult task.

First to try was Farragut, who had been ordered to steam up the Mississippi and take Vicksburg immediately after capturing New Orleans. Move Farragut did, taking his big, deep-water warships upstream through the river's twisting channels—and forcing the surrender en route of Baton Rouge, Louisiana, and Natchez, Mississippi.

On reaching Vicksburg, however, Farragut got a rude surprise. To a demand that the city capitulate, one of Vicksburg's defenders, Colonel James L. Autrey, sent back a succinct reply: "Mississippians don't know, and refuse to learn, how to surrender."

Worse, it was clear that while Farragut's ships had been slowly winding between the Mississippi's snags and sand bars, Vicksburg had been reinforced with both infantry and heavy artillery. Also, the guns of Farragut's warships could not be elevated enough to fire at the enemy batteries high on the bluffs, whereas the Confederate cannon were ideally sited to fire down on the Union fleet. Further, the 1,400 troops Farragut had brought along were far too few to attack the Rebel garrison of 4,000. Judging the situation hopeless, Farragut headed his ships back toward New Orleans.

There he received a still nastier surprise— a direct order from President Lincoln to try again. Some Federal gunboats were steaming downriver toward Vicksburg. Farragut's fleet was to join them, and together the two flotillas would use their "utmost exertions to open the Mississippi." On June 8 Farragut set out upriver once more.

This time he had brought along some mortar schooners that could lob shells into Vicksburg, which they did, subjecting the city to the first of many bombardments. Then, on the night of June 28, Farragut daringly steamed his fleet upriver past Vicksburg's guns. The ships blasted away at the town while the batteries of Rebel cannon poured a thunderous fire down on the Union vessels. Three ships were forced to turn back and others were damaged, but the fleet managed to run the gantlet with only 15 dead and 30 wounded.

Still, it was a hollow victory, as Farragut admitted. Except for a few lucky shots that had exploded near Confederate positions, the Federal fire had achieved little or nothing. Clearly, even with gunboats and mortar ships the navy was powerless to dislodge the enemy cannon, which still commanded the river. Again, the troops Farragut had brought along, a single brigade of 3,200 men, had no hope of storming the place. "I am satisfied," Farragut wrote Secretary of the Navy Gideon Welles, "that it is not possible for us to take Vicksburg without an army force of twelve or fifteen thousand men."

With that Farragut put the troops ashore on the west bank of the river under their commander, Brigadier General Thomas Williams, and anchored his ships nearby, safely out of range of Vicksburg's guns. The ships were badly shot up nevertheless—by a single armored Confederate ram called the *Arkansas*. The Rebel ship boldly steamed down the Missis-

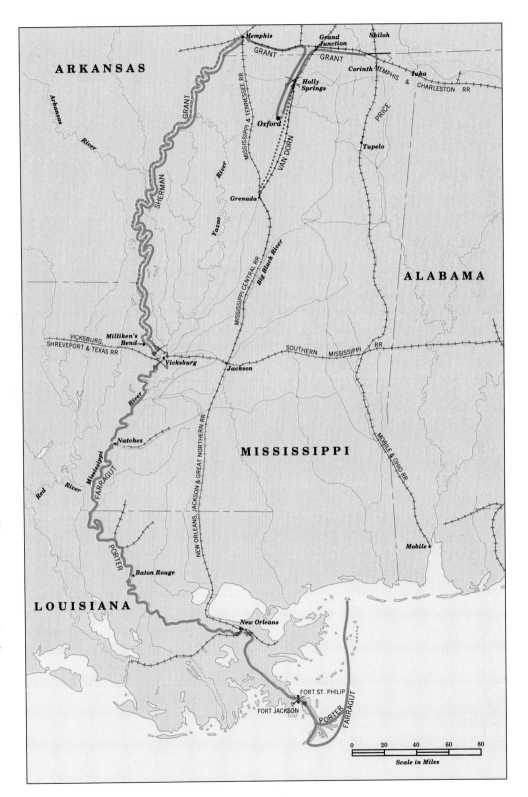

sippi and right through the middle of Farragut's fleet, all guns firing.

The *Arkansas* ended up badly battered, but the Federals fared worse, with every vessel hit and 17 men killed, 42 wounded. A furious Farragut attempted to take revenge by twice sending ships to attack the *Arkansas* at its Vicksburg mooring, but the ram refused to sink. With that, Farragut had had enough, and in late July he headed back down the river again. The navy's three-month attempt to take Vicksburg was over, with nothing accomplished. It would now be the turn of the army—with help from the inland navy's gunboats and transports.

The nearest Federal army was a force of about 100,000 men led by Ulysses S. Grant. For the moment, though, Grant was immobilized, his troops dispersed in a half-dozen places in northern Mississippi and western Tennessee, guarding rail lines and other strategic spots against attacks.

But in early October, after stopping suicidal attacks by the Confederates on formidable

Capturing New Orleans in April 1862, Farragut quickly secured most of the lower Mississippi. He then sailed upriver and in June attempted unsuccessfully to bombard Vicksburg into submission. In December Grant moved on the city from the north along the Mississippi Central Railroad while Sherman advanced downriver to attack Chickasaw Bluffs. Grant pulled back after Rebel cavalry under Van Dorn (red arrow) destroyed his supply base at Holly Springs, and, in late December, Sherman was repulsed at Chickasaw Bluffs. When McClernand captured Arkansas Post on January 12, 1863, Federal control of the upper Mississippi was complete. Grant then began massing his forces near Milliken's Bend.

Union earthworks outside Corinth, Mississippi, Grant was able at last to go after Vicksburg. His plan: to march south along the Mississippi Central Railroad, maintaining his supply route, and, outflanking Vicksburg, force the city to surrender.

Soon, however, everything began to go wrong. First, Grant was informed to his astonishment that a wholly separate Federal force led by Major General John A. McClernand was also being readied to advance on Vicksburg. Somehow McClernand, an ambitious and politically powerful former Illinois congressman appointed general in 1861, had persuaded President Lincoln to let him form an army in southern Ohio, float it down the Mississippi, and make his own attack.

Outraged that a vain and amateurish political general was about to mount a campaign in his own department, Grant moved to forestall McClernand, sending his friend and favorite subordinate, Major General William Tecumseh Sherman, marching with 30,000 troops to Memphis. From there Sherman was to steam down the Mississippi and assault Chickasaw Bluffs, a few miles up from the mouth of the Yazoo River and only three miles north of Vicksburg. At the same time, Grant would continue south and be ready to come at Vicksburg from the direction of Jackson.

But while Grant was maneuvering, the Rebels were making some moves of their own. In the course of strengthening Vicksburg's defenses, the Confederate government had named the stolid but reliable Lieutenant General John C. Pemberton commander of the city's garrison and then had sent one of the South's top generals, Joseph E. Johnston, to be overall commander in the West. The two leaders, it turned out, could not agree on strategy, Pemberton arguing that Vicksburg be turned into a fortress, Johnston holding that their

forces should remain mobile, ready to fight the Federals in open battle. Those differences were never settled, with dire results for the Southern cause.

For the moment, however, Pemberton devised a brilliant double strike to cut Grant's supply lines. General Earl Van Dorn would take his cavalry and hit Holly Springs, Grant's supply depot in northern Mississippi. At the same time the great Confederate cavalry raider Nathan Bedford Forrest would strike the vital rail lines near Jackson, Tennessee.

Both attacks were hugely successful, Forrest tearing up miles of track and Van Dorn capturing the entire Holly Springs garrison while destroying, by his own estimate, $1.5 million worth of Federal stores. Grant realized the raids had dealt his plans a critical blow. Caught in enemy territory with no way to get supplies, he had to fall back rapidly toward his main base at Memphis.

As he retreated, Grant tried to warn Sherman that half of their two-pronged attack was off. But the raiders had cut the telegraph wires, and the message never got through. Sherman, starting down the Mississippi from Memphis with three divisions on December 20, was unknowingly left to plunge ahead on his own—against a strengthened enemy and one, moreover, warned of his approach by Rebel spies upriver using a private telegraph line.

Reaching the mouth of the Yazoo the day after Christmas, the flotilla of Federal gunboats and transports bearing Sherman's force moved seven miles up the river. There the troops landed and, after a cautious advance, approached Chickasaw Bluffs on December 28. Immediately, 20,000 Confederates sent by Pemberton to meet the attack began hammering the Yankees as they struggled through swampy stretches of bayou and bog, stopping them cold.

Dismayed, Sherman called off the first assault but decided to try again the next day, sending two brigades to hit the Confederate left, where the ground looked passable. The attack was met, one Federal officer recalled, with "a flaming hell of shot, shell, canister and minie balls." Still, the Federals fought their way to the foot of the bluff—only to be pinned down there by more ferocious fire from above. Slowly, grudgingly, the Federals fell back, their units disorganized. In all the Union force lost 1,776 men to the Confederates' 187.

Sherman wanted to try again farther up the Yazoo at Haynes' Bluff and asked the gunboats' commander, the equally combative Admiral David Dixon Porter, to shift the brigades upstream. But then an impenetrable fog blanketed the swamps, followed by a driving rain. Fearful the water might rise and drown his army, Sherman had to withdraw, Admiral Porter ferrying the troops back down the Yazoo and across the Mississippi to Milliken's Bend.

Yet another humiliation was in store for Sherman. McClernand and his forces arrived at Milliken's Bend in the first week of January 1863, and since McClernand held superior rank, Sherman had to turn command over to the politician turned general. Fearing that McClernand might launch an attack of his own, Grant moved from Memphis to Milliken's Bend to take direct control. He arrived on January 29, bringing more troops and a huge flotilla of gunboats, mortar schooners, transports, and supply vessels. To McClernand's irritation, Grant immediately incorporated both him and his force into the main army as its XIII Corps. With Sherman's XV Corps, and the XVII Corps commanded by the exceedingly able James B. McPherson, Grant could now call on enough manpower, it seemed, to take Vicksburg at last.

How that was to be done from the Federal

base on the west bank of the Mississippi was another matter. Farragut had proved that river bombardments did not work, and Sherman had demonstrated the perils of attacking through the swamps to Vicksburg's north. Nevertheless, through the first months of 1863 Grant would stubbornly try every conceivable trick to get at or by Vicksburg—each new one, it seemed, more bizarre than the last. If nothing came of them, Grant figured, they would reassure Washington and the public that he was at work. That work would also keep the men busy and fit until a more feasible approach came along.

Oddest of all these schemes, perhaps, was the first—digging a canal across the base of the fingerlike peninsula formed by the river's 180-degree horseshoe bend opposite Vicksburg. Work on this had been started by General Williams' troops, put ashore the previous summer by Farragut. Now Sherman's corps was assigned the muddy task. Just possibly the Mississippi could be diverted through such a canal, causing the river to bypass Vicksburg—and simultaneously opening a safe route for Union shipping.

It proved grinding, nasty work, the troops perpetually soaked, and even Sherman often finding himself hip deep in mud and slime. In the dampness only insects seemed to thrive, the air becoming, one soldier complained, "a saturated solution of gnats." Still, the digging went on—until a Mississippi flood washed away much of the work and the Confederates planted a battery of guns opposite the canal's exit that could have blown to smithereens any boat trying the route. With that, Grant halted the project.

He was not through, however. Forty miles north of Milliken's Bend was a bayou called Lake Providence, left behind years after

one of the Mississippi's many course changes. South from the lake stretched 470 miles of interconnected waterways ending up at the Red River, far below Vicksburg. Again, if the Mississippi could be diverted, the Federals could bypass the city. Assigned the unenviable digging job this time was General McPherson, an experienced engineering officer, and his XVII Corps. Amazingly, McPherson's troops managed to trundle a 30-ton steamer overland from the Mississippi to Lake Providence and also perfected a rotary saw that could slice through huge submerged tree stumps. But mercifully for McPherson's weary men, Grant realized after two months that this scheme, too, had no chance of success and called it off.

Grant next turned his eyes to the intricate maze of waterways across the Mississippi north of Vicksburg. Long before the war much southbound river traffic had turned eastward about 150 miles above Vicksburg into Yazoo Pass and proceeded from there across a body of water called Moon Lake and then down several streams to trade at ports on the Yazoo itself. Boats going on to New Orleans had only to continue down the Yazoo to reenter the Mississippi just above Vicksburg. If Federal troops could be ferried down the Yazoo, they could, Grant figured, be put ashore on the eastern side of the Yazoo delta and, bypassing the bluffs that had frustrated Sherman, fall on Vicksburg from the northeast.

The first problem was that the Yazoo Pass was no longer open. A huge levee had been built across its mouth in the 1850s as a flood control measure. To deal with this, Grant sent a young West Point-trained engineer, Lieutenant Colonel James H. Wilson, sailing north with bags of explosives.

On February 2 a segment of the levee erupt-

ed skyward, and the flood-swollen waters of the Mississippi, rushing through the gap, demolished the rest. On February 7 a small flotilla of gunboats and transports carrying the first contingent of 4,500 men went swooshing through the pass and, bobbing frantically in the turbulent water, emerged into Moon Lake.

Grant had hoped to take the Confederates by surprise. But Pemberton had foreseen the move and had sent Rebel work parties to fell huge trees across the waterways. To proceed at all, the Federal troops had to disembark and, with 500 men at each hawser, tug and wrench the trees out of the way.

As the flotilla struggled on, the channels became painfully narrow and so thickly bordered by trees that the branches interlocked overhead to form a tunnel. In short order the branches had ripped away the transports' high pilothouses and smokestacks, knocking them overboard. "The vessels were so torn to pieces," Admiral Porter wrote, "they had hulls and engines left and that had to suffice."

Worse was to come. At the juncture of the Yazoo with the Yalobusha River the Confederates had sunk old ships, blocking the channel, and had also built a breastwork of cotton bales and sandbags defended by 2,000 men and eight cannon, which they named Fort Pemberton. More critical, the stronghold was surrounded by marsh so impassable the Federal infantry could not get at it.

After pondering for several days what to do, Lieutenant Commander Watson Smith sent ahead a pair of gunboats—which were immediately hit by enemy fire and forced to draw back. Two more attempts to rush past Fort Pemberton met with the same results. At that the Federals gave up and the entire expedition turned tail, heading back the 100 miles to the Yazoo Pass and the Mississippi and ending what one soldier aptly called "a picturesque farce."

Still another attempt to get through the bayous north of Vicksburg was to come. General Grant, worried that the Yazoo Pass expedition might become trapped, asked Admiral Porter to explore the waterways at the lower end of the Yazoo and to stage a rescue mission if needed. Explore Porter did, taking Grant along on his flagship *Black Hawk*. Steaming into the mouth of the Yazoo, they then turned into Steele's Bayou. From there, Porter explained to Grant, gunboats and transports could weave through a succession of flooded streams with names like Black Bayou, Deer Creek, and the Sunflower River and outflank the Chickasaw Bluffs fortifications. The whole thing involved making a 200-mile loop to reach a point only about 25 miles from their starting point at Milliken's Bend, but it just might work.

Grant approved, and that night, back at his headquarters at Milliken's Bend, ordered

Maintaining offensive pressure, Grant began a series of expeditions aimed at closing the ring around Vicksburg. Two efforts—a canal cut across Young's Point opposite the city and the opening of a 400-mile route from Lake Providence south to the Red River —were sabotaged by the unpredictable river. Then engineers holed a levee near Moon Lake to flood the Yazoo Pass, allowing boats to reach the Yazoo River. Yankee forces floated as far south as the Yalobusha River, where they were stopped by Confederates at Fort Pemberton. In support, Sherman and Porter pushed up the lower Yazoo into Steele's Bayou, but low water nearly bottled up Porter's fleet. Thus, these forays all failed, but Grant had one more plan.

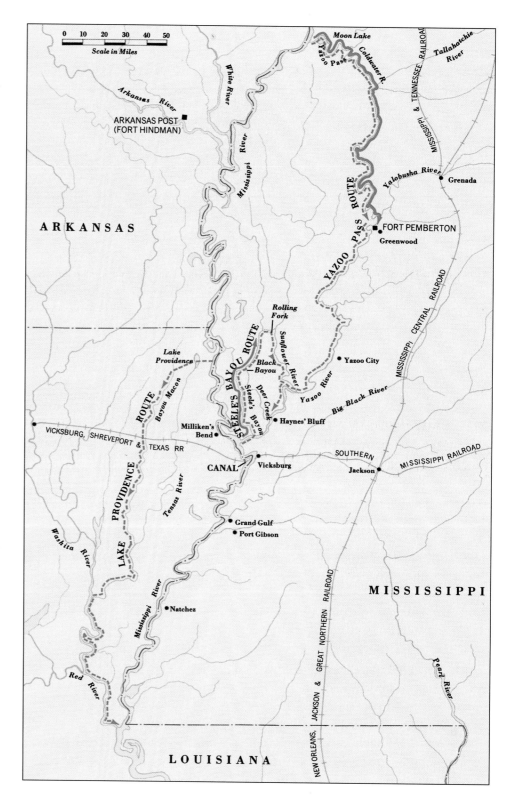

Porter to give his plan a try. Eleven vessels began to push through the tangled waterways, while Sherman's troops followed on foot.

But again, the farther the boats went, the narrower the channels became. This slowed the whole procession, and then crewmen spotted Confederate troops landing on a levee on a nearby bend in the Sunflower River. Porter's lead boats were immediately hit by artillery fire, and on May 19 he sent a message to Sherman to hurry forward a rescue party of supporting infantry.

This Sherman did, the troops, many with lighted candles in their gun barrels for the daring night march, groping along as best they could on narrow fingers of high ground. When they arrived a day later, however, they found Porter already trying to back his gunboats away from the fierce enemy fire. At last, with the infantry's help, Porter managed to extricate the boats from the watery maze before they were destroyed or captured. By May 27 they had reached relative safety through Steele's Bayou and the Yazoo, coming out into the Mississippi and back to Milliken's Bend. Another—in fact the last—of what Grant called his "experiments" had failed.

Grant now knew for certain that trying to hit Vicksburg from the north would not work. Clearly the best plan, risky and difficult though it might be, was to take his army down the Mississippi well south of Vicksburg, cross the river, fight his way in a wide semicircle to the east and north, and come at the city from the east. But April had come, and the spring sun was drying the terrain and making full-scale army movements possible. Grant had some 60,000 men. The experiments were over. Now Grant would gamble his entire army in one of the most dangerous movements of the Civil War.

CHRONOLOGY

1862

April 25	*Federals capture New Orleans*
May 18-July 26	*Farragut bombards Vicksburg*
June 6	*Federals capture Memphis*
December 27	*Confederates destroy Holly Springs*
December 27-29	*Sherman repulsed at Chickasaw Bluffs*

1863

February & March	*The Bayou Expeditions*
April 16 & 22	*Porter's gunboats run the Vicksburg batteries*
April 17-May 2	*Grierson's Raid*
April 29	*Porter's gunboats bombard Grand Gulf*
April 30-May 1	*Sherman makes his feint at Haynes' Bluff*
May 1	*Battle of Port Gibson*
May 12	*Skirmish at Raymond*
May 14	*Battle of Jackson*
	Farragut bombards Port Hudson
May 16	*Battle of Champion's Hill (Baker's Creek)*
May 17	*Battle of Big Black River*
May 18	*Siege of Vicksburg begins*
May 19	*First frontal attack on Vicksburg*
May 22	*Second frontal attack on Vicksburg*
May 27	*Siege of Port Hudson begins*
June 25	*First mine at the 3d Louisiana Redan*
July 1	*Second mine at the 3d Louisiana Redan*
July 4	*Vicksburg surrenders*
July 9	*Port Hudson surrenders*
	Second siege of Jackson begins
July 16	*Confederates evacuate Jackson*

GENERAL WINFIELD SCOTT
GENERAL IN CHIEF, U.S. ARMY

Scott foresaw that the Civil War would be drawn out and costly. Two weeks after the fall of Fort Sumter, he outlined a long-term plan to blockade Southern ports and seal off the Mississippi River. Northern newspapermen like Horace Greeley, who expected a quick resolution to the rebellion, mockingly referred to Scott's approach as the Anaconda Plan after the snake that slowly squeezes its prey to death.

We rely greatly on the sure operation of a complete blockade of the Atlantic and Gulf ports soon to commence. In connection with such blockade we propose a powerful movement down the Mississippi to the ocean, with a cordon of posts at proper points, and the capture of Forts Jackson and Saint Philip; the object being to clear out and keep open this great line of communication in connection with the strict blockade of the sea board, so as to envelop the insurgent States and bring them to terms with less bloodshed than by any other plan. . . . In the progress down the river all the enemy's batteries on its banks we of course would turn and capture, leaving a sufficient number of posts with complete garrisons to keep the river open behind the expedition. Finally, it will be necessary that New Orleans should be strongly occupied and securely held until the present difficulties are composed.

> "Let us get Vicksburg and all that country is ours. The war can never be brought to a close until that key is in our pocket."

REAR ADMIRAL DAVID DIXON PORTER
COMMANDER, MISSISSIPPI SQUADRON

Porter's fleet would play a crucial role in winning control of the Mississippi. A loner, he nevertheless got along quite well during the Vicksburg campaign with his army counterpart. He later wrote, "So confident was I of General Grant's ability to carry out his plans that I never hesitated."

See," said Mr. Lincoln, pointing to the map, "what a lot of land these fellows hold, of which Vicksburg is the key. Here is Red River, which will supply the Confederates with cattle and corn to feed their armies. There are the Arkansas and White Rivers, which can supply cattle and hogs by the thousands. From Vicksburg these supplies can be distributed by rail all over the Confederacy. Then there is that great depot of supplies on the Yazoo. Let us get Vicksburg and all that country is ours. The war can never be brought to a close until that key is in our pocket. I am acquainted with that region and know what I am talking about, and, valuable as New Orleans will be to us, Vicksburg will be more so. We may take all the northern ports of the Confederacy, and they can still defy us from Vicksburg. It means hog and hominy without limit, fresh troops from all the States of the far South, and a cotton country where they can raise the staple without interference."

THE SOUTHERN ILLUSTRATED NEWS.

Vol. I.—No. 9.   RICHMOND, SATURDAY, NOVEMBER 8, 1862.   PRICE 15 CENTS.

VICKSBURG, MISSISSIPPI.

Below we present a beautiful view of the gallant little city of Vicksburg, Miss., accompanied by a carefully prepared sketch furnished us by Mr. H. C. CLARKE, of that city. Vicksburg is situated in the county of Warren, State of Mississippi, on "the East bank of the great Father of Waters," about four hundred miles above the city of New Orleans, in the very heart of the cotton-growing region. At the time of its foundation, perhaps four thousand bales of cotton were the full extent of the shipment. In 1860 she shipped about two hundred and seventy-five thousand bales, brought from the great Yazoo valley and from the interior of the State by the Southern railroad. The town, at the time of its incorporation, (20th of January, 1825,) numbered about one hundred and fifty inhabitants, and now, with its suburbs, is estimated to have about eight thousand. It is justly celebrated for raising fine fruits, such as peaches, apples, pears, plums, apricots, nectarines, grapes, &c., together with the usual crop of vegetables, suited to such an admirably adapted climate. The city contains five elegant churches, with large congregations—namely, the Methodist, Catholic, Presbyterian, Baptist and Episcopal; also, a Jewish synagogue. It has also a large public school, numbering five hundred pupils, male and female.

The new court-house, lately completed, is one of the finest buildings in the State of Mississippi, and cost nearly one hundred thousand dollars. It is situated on a high hill, (shown on the left hand in the picture,) about two hundred feet above the Mississippi river at low water, and is the admiration of all packing up or down the river. The Catholic church is [...] in the [...] the picture, is a fine and tasteful structure, commanding a fine view. To the right and in front of the river, on a hill rising nearly four hundred feet above the river, called "Sky Parlor." There are many fine brick and other buildings, such as hotels, (the principal being the "Washington," of McMackin renown,) commission and produce-houses, hospitals, theatre, concert-saloons, &c. The city can also boast of its many fine and beautiful dwellings, ornamented with garden-shrubbery, &c., which, placed upon our lofty heights, make this "city of a hundred hills," exceedingly picturesque. It has two large foundries, besides factories, mills, &c.

If all the cotton arriving at that port could be sold there, in a few years Vicksburg might well aspire to rival most of her sister cities on the Mississippi river, for no place of its size has greater facilities naturally for trade and commerce than Vicksburg. Having an extensive cotton-growing region North, South, East and West, and lying on the 32d degree of latitude, where many of the tropical, as well as Northern plants are cultivated with great success, she needs but energetic and persevering action to insure her steady and active progress to prosperity, wealth and power. The health of the city is unsurpassed by any, excepting occasional and infrequent epidemics. The benevolent institutions (F, and A. Masons and I. O. O. F.) are well-represented and remarkably prosperous. The press comprises two highly popular newspapers, "The Whig" and "Citizen."

The natural and commercial position of Vicksburg must inevitably secure to it a splendid and glorious trade, population and wealth. With the Vicksburg, Shreveport and Texas Railroad extending immediately from the opposite bank of the Mississippi through the fruitful and teeming cotton-fields of Louisiana to the Texan border, there to be connected with the great "Southern Pacific Railroad" to California, and the Southern railroad stretching Eastward to the Alabama line, and forming a connection that will unite the Atlantic seaboard with the Mississippi at Vicksburg.

When the war-clouds which now dim our horizon shall have cleared away, a new and extensive trade looms up before the people of Vicksburg that must accelerate powerfully the car of our progress, and laden it with abounding prosperity.

The name of Vicksburg will hereafter be better known on account of the brave and remarkable defence made against the combined Federal fleets of the Mississippi river. The siege of Vicksburg lasted from May 18th to July 25th. The lower fleet, comprising 18 gun and mortar-boats, and three first-class and two second-class frigates-of-war, under the command of Com. Farragut, arrived below the city on the 18th of May. The surrender of the city was immediately demanded. Gen. Smith and Col. Autry, who were in command of the military post, replied that "Mississippians never surrender."

The fortifications around the city were commenced on the 29th of April, five days after the fall of New Orleans.

Gen. Smith arrived in Vicksburg on the 9th of May with a force of less than 1,000 men, incompletely armed. The work on the fortifications was pushed rapidly ahead by Gen. Smith, who had the assistance of experienced artillerists from New Orleans. On the 18th of May Gen. Smith's force was increased to about 20,000 effective men, principally composed of Louisianians. At the time of the refusal of Gen. Smith to surrender the city, but 12 guns were in position and ready for its defence. The bombardment commenced on the 26th of May, and lasted about two hours.— The siege lasted from that time to the 22d of July. The bombarding would generally take place at regular hours during the morning and afternoon—sometimes, to vary the monotony of the scene, the firing would be given during the night, from 8 to 10 o'clock. The greatest bombardment during the siege occurred on the 28th of June, when three of the war-frigates and four gun and mortar-boats passed up above the city, running the gauntlet of all the forts. The scene in the city during the passage of the boats was wild and terrific beyond description. Up to this time, but few of the residents had left the city. No person expected that such a feat would be attempted by the Yankees.

The boats commenced moving toward the city about half-past 3 o'clock in the morning, when the people were awakened from their sleep by the terrific firing, and were compelled to seek safety in flight. The battle lasted two hours and a half—no damage whatever being done to the forts. The boats suffered severely, being almost riddled by shot from our batteries.

On the 15th of July the celebrated "Arkansas" succeeded in defeating the whole upper fleet of gun-boats and rams, (30 in all,) passing by them all, and arrived safely under the batteries at Vicksburg on the evening of the same day July 15th. Several boats of the upper fleet came down, and attacked the Arkansas, and attempted to cut her out from the batteries, but it was a failure. On the morning of July the 22d, another great effort was made to capture or sink the

Arkansas. Three of the enemy's best iron-clad gun-boats came down and attacked the boat, and were again defeated, the Arkansas proving her invulnerability.

The bombardment of the forts and city was kept up till the 22d of July. On the 24th and 25th of July, the siege was abandoned, and the fleets left their scene of action.

The casualties during the whole bombardment amounted to the killing of one woman and one negro man in the city, and among the soldiers at the batteries and those on guard throughout the city, the loss was 20 killed and 7 wounded. The forts and fortifications sustained no damage whatever. The damage to the buildings and houses in the city, considering the very large number of shells thrown, (estimated at 25,000,) was very inconsiderable. Twenty thousand dollars will probably cover the damage done.

The loss to the enemy was very heavy in the several engagements with the "Arkansas," being estimated at 70 men killed and 97 wounded, while the Confederate loss on board the Arkansas was only 5 killed and 7 wounded.

In the engagements between the batteries and gun-boats, 27 Federals were killed and 25 wounded. It is also estimated that 500 died from sickness, and were buried in the swamps opposite the city.

The upper batteries are situated about half a mile above the city proper, on the river bank. The lower batteries are about one mile below the town—these are the most formidable, and extend along the river for several miles.

The history of this gallant little city before the war is also full of interest. Her attack upon the combined Yankee fleet is but in keeping with the onslaught she made some years ago upon the thieves, gamblers and assassins that infested the place.

In 1835, she made an onslaught on a notorious establishment, at that time known as the "Kangaroo," and totally demolished it, thereby ridding the community of an intolerable nuisance, and deterring the vicious from re-establishing anything of the kind for many years.

In 1835, she hung the gamblers, which caused great consternation throughout the whole country, particularly the towns on the Mississippi river, and followed up the good work until the light-fingered gentry who infested the State were entirely driven out. Gambling has never been carried on so openly, or to the same extent throughout the South, since that period.

When Secession came floating along on the autumn breeze of 1860, Vicksburg was for the Union, or more properly speaking, for co-operation. But when the State severed the ties that once bound her to the Union, Vicksburg cast aside her affection for the Stars and Stripes and linked her destiny with the new-born government which the love of freedom and aversion to tyranny had, in a few months, created.

Vicksburg has furnished 23 full companies, organized and fitted up in the city during the first year of the war. She has also voluntarily contributed as much money to carry on the war as any city of equal population in the Southern Confederacy. And lastly—she has conquered and driven back two combined Yankee fleets, one of which conquered and subdued New Orleans, the largest city in the Confederacy, and the other, the rising and prosperous city of Memphis. Vicksburg has established the fact that iron-clad gunboats are not invulnerable.

CITY OF VICKSBURG, MISS.

Vicksburg's strategic importance to Northern war plans was equally obvious to those in the South, as shown by this feature article in a Richmond newspaper. In the third column, the reporter describes the seamier side of the river town's early history. But by the outbreak of war in 1861, the city of 3,500 residents presented a genteel, cosmopolitan appearance all out of proportion to its size and location. Bustling trade, especially in cotton, which was transferred from steamboats to railcars at the depot pictured in the inset below, made all this possible.

"Gen. Grant faced his army north. I had not yet got a shot at a rebel. We were disappointed."

PRIVATE STEPHEN C. BECK
124TH ILLINOIS INFANTRY, J. E. SMITH'S BRIGADE

Beck enlisted at Otterville, Illinois, on August 11, 1862, and four months later was in Mississippi on Grant's first march on Vicksburg. The confident 20-year-old served with Grant's army throughout the campaign. He had originally been detailed by his regiment to drive a wagon, but one day his mule team spooked and bolted. "I would never try it again after that experience," he wrote with relief. "I enlisted to carry a gun so my mule 'whacking' ended right there and then."

The rebel army had retreated South, and as they would not come to us we would show them we were down there to "do business" with them, if they would give us an opportunity. The next day we marched into Hollysprings, Miss. All were gone but women and children and negroes, and how it did rain. Our tents were in the wagons somewhere in the rear and we were without shelter, wet as water could make us. We moved on the next day in the mud to somewhere; some were jolly and happy and some were not.

We thought we were gaining on the Rebels for could hear canonading in the distance when we would holler "give it to them" and we took longer steps anxious to get to them, even with our old condemned guns. The next day brought us to the Tallahatchie river where rebel Gen. Price had made a stand for a short time, and had burned all the bridges then retreated. We soon replaced the bridges and were on after them and continued to follow them for about a week. Every day we saw rebel soldiers come to our lines and surrended, had had enough of war. The thought came to us if they all do that we won't get to fight any. The trains in our rear were keeping pretty close up with supplies. Rebel Gen. VanDorn with a few thousand Cavalry swung around to our rear and captured Gen. Grant's supplies for his army. What VanDorn could not use he burned. Gen. Grant faced his army north. I had not yet got a shot at a rebel. We were disappointed.

A native of Port Gibson, Mississippi, General Earl Van Dorn was hardly beloved in his home state, which was "dense with horrid narratives of his negligence, whoring and drunkenness." In December 1862 he gave Vicksburg a crucial respite with his victory at Holly Springs. In May 1863 Van Dorn was shot and killed by a jealous husband who claimed the general had "violated the sanctity of his home."

BRIGADIER GENERAL STEPHEN D. LEE
BRIGADE COMMANDER, ARMY OF VICKSBURG

Lee, a West Point graduate and Charleston native, reluctantly resigned his U.S. Army commission and became a captain in the South Carolina artillery. By December 1862 he commanded a brigade in the defense of Vicksburg. Lee deployed his outnumbered troops in strong defensive positions atop Chickasaw Bluffs and stopped Sherman's attack there cold. Shown here in the uniform of a major general, Lee eventually, at age 30, became the youngest lieutenant general of the war.

These two large armies were to act in conjunction, Grant moving down what is known as the Illinois Central railroad, and attacking the Confederate army in his immediate presence, so no reinforcements could be sent to the relief of Vicksburg, while Sherman was to go in boats with his army, and land and take the city before its small garrison could be reinforced. The gunboat fleet which accompanied the transports bearing Sherman's army, and including them, made up the large number of about 120 river boats.

It looked as if the city could not escape this time, as these two large armies moved from different directions, co-operating with each other, and toward Vicksburg as the objective point. But the campaign was a short and decisive one, and both movements were defeated. Before Sherman started the Confederate cavalry, under General Forest, about December 11th, destroyed sixty miles of railroad between Jackson, Tenn., and Columbus, Ky., and soon after Sherman left Memphis the Confederate cavalry, under General Van Dorn, dashed around the flank of Grant's army, attacked and seized his depot of supplies for his army at Holly Springs, burned them up or utterly destroyed them (December 20th), necessitating the falling back of Grant's army to Memphis for supplies.

Sherman appeared in the Yazoo river on Christmas day, his transports, guarded front, flank and rear by Porter's gunboat fleet, disembarked his army on the banks of the Yazoo at the mouth of Chickasaw Bayou, eight miles from Vicksburg. When he landed General Smith did not have 5,000 effective men in the city, including the troops manning the heavy batteries. The infantry brigade, 2,500 men, protecting the batteries, was at once pushed out of the city to confront Sherman's army of 33,000 men and sixty guns, covering a line of thirteen miles, between the city and Snyder's Bluff, on the Yazoo river, where not a spade full of dirt had been thrown, nor were there fortifications of any kind, except at Snyder's Bluff.

By the morning of the 27th, three infantry brigades had arrived to assist in defending the city, and were moved out to cover the ground from the race course to Chickasaw Bayou. No others arrived till December 29th. The bayous and low lands where Sherman was operating presented great obstacles to his progress, but on December 29th he attacked the Confederates, the main attack being delivered at Chickasaw Bayou, six miles from Vicksburg, by two of his divisions numbering 20,000 men. This attack was signally repulsed by one Confederate brigade and eight light guns, with a loss to Sherman of 1,439 killed, wounded and missing, and seven stands of colors. This single trial decided the second attempt, as Sherman imagined he saw the bluff's fortifications, where none existed, but really only a few rifle pits hurriedly thrown up by the troops after arrival on the ground.

He re-embarked his army on his transports, and disappeared from before Vicksburg about the 3d of January, 1863.

MAJOR GENERAL WILLIAM T. SHERMAN

COMMANDER, XV CORPS,
ARMY OF THE TENNESSEE

During the war, Sherman maintained a regular correspondence with his brother, John, an Ohio senator. Well aware that he faced criticism at home for his failure at Chickasaw Bluffs, he seems to have gone out of his way in this letter to describe the bristling defenses and impenetrable terrain as justification for his defeat.

Steamer Forest Queen, Jan. 6, 1863.

Dear Brother: You will have heard of our attack on Vicksburg and failure to succeed. The place is too strong, and without the co-operation of a large army coming from the interior it is impracticable. Innumerable batteries prevent the approach of gun boats to the city or to the first bluff up the Yazoo, and the only landing between is on an insular space of low boggy ground, with innumerable bayous or deep sloughs. I did all that was possible to reach the main land, but was met at every point by batteries and rifle pits that we could not pass, and in the absence of Gen. Grant's co-operating force I was compelled to re-embark my command. My report to Gen. Grant, a copy of which I sent to Gen. Halleck, who will let you see it, is very full, and more than I could write to you with propriety. Whatever you or the absent may think, not a soldier or officer who was present but will admit I pushed the attack as far as prudence would justify, and that I re-embarked my command in the nick of time, for a heavy rain set in which would have swamped us and made it impossible to withdraw artillery and stores.

This contemporary engraving incorrectly depicts Sherman's troops struggling hand to hand with Confederate defenders at the crest of Chickasaw Bluffs. In fact, withering Rebel fire kept the Federals pinned down at the foot of the hill. "Balls came zip-zip into the trees and the ground around us," wrote an Ohio captain, adding, "Occasionally, thud, a bullet takes some poor fellow and he is carried to the rear." Heavy rains that night turned the already swampy ground into a bottomless quagmire and persuaded Sherman to abandon the offensive.

HARPER'S WEEKLY.

A SCENE IN ONE OF THE BATTLES BEFORE VICKSBURG.—[See Page 195.]

"The river below the city was again free."

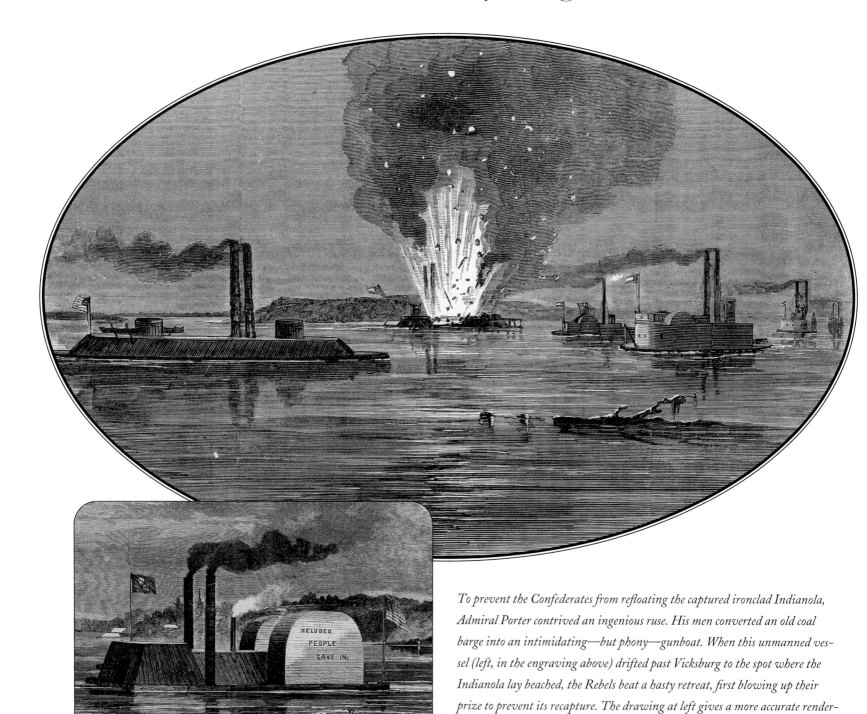

To prevent the Confederates from refloating the captured ironclad Indianola, Admiral Porter contrived an ingenious ruse. His men converted an old coal barge into an intimidating—but phony—gunboat. When this unmanned vessel (left, in the engraving above) drifted past Vicksburg to the spot where the Indianola lay beached, the Rebels beat a hasty retreat, first blowing up their prize to prevent its recapture. The drawing at left gives a more accurate rendering of the fake gunboat and shows the derisive motto added by its builders.

COLONEL MANNING F. FORCE
20TH OHIO INFANTRY, LEGGETT'S BRIGADE

Force had fought at Fort Donelson and at Shiloh, after which he was appointed regimental commander. Here, with obvious but understated relish, he relates the story of the unsinkable ironclad with which the Yankees so completely flummoxed the Rebels. Force later became a general and won the Medal of Honor for his service at Atlanta.

On the night of the 13th the iron-clad Indianola, with its heavy armament of two 11-inch and two 9-inch guns, ran by. But on the night of the 24th it was attacked by the Queen of the West and another ram, aided by two smaller boats. The Indianola, leaking from the blows of the rams, began to sink, surrendered, and was towed near the shore, a few miles below Vicksburg, and grounded in ten feet of water. The enemy had control of the river below the city.

Some soldiers, taking an empty barge, placed on it barrels, in the likeness of smoke-stacks, and a hogshead for a turret, and set it afloat at 3 A.M. The semblance of a monitor, in the gloom of night, slowly passed by the batteries. All the guns of Vicksburg opened upon it. It could not sink, and placidly floated on. It rounded the point at daybreak, just as the Queen of the West was coming up stream. The appearance of a monitor in the Mississippi was to much. The Queen of the West, with its consort ram, turned down stream, took refuge in the Red River, and never returned to the Mississippi. The harmless barge, carried by an eddy to the lower mouth of the canal, rested there, just two and a half miles from the Indianola. A working party, busied in raising the iron-clad, watched uneasily the stranger. Some soldiers of the Fifteenth Corps pushed the barge out into the current. The working party, seeing a monitor coming for them, set the Indianola on fire, and blew it up, and the river below the city was again free.

SERGEANT W. R. EDDINGTON
97TH ILLINOIS INFANTRY, LANDRAM'S BRIGADE

The canal Eddington describes was a pet project of Lincoln's. "The President attaches much importance to this," General Halleck informed Grant. Eddington erred in stating that a cut levee doomed the plan; it was the rain-swollen waters of the Mississippi overflowing its banks that washed away three months of digging, as well as the threat of Rebel cannon. General Sherman, in a letter to his wife, admitted the whole enterprise was "a pure waste of human effort."

On the 22nd of January, 1863, we were put to work digging a canal across Youngs Point. It was about one and one fourth miles long and worked at it until March 6th. The object of the canal was to make a channel wide and deep enough so that boats could pass from one bend to the other and get below Vicksburg without running by the batteries the Rebels had built along in front of Vicksburg which extended for about 15 miles along the river front. We worked about two months at the job. We had it all done except opening up the ends to let the water in and let it out. The Rebels cut the levee above us and let the water run all in the woods behind us. It rained almost all the time and the river rose rapidly and that night it ran over the bank and filled our canal full. If we had one day more we would have been alright. They had to move us back up the river to Millikens Bend, 25 miles, before they could find ground to camp us on. When the last of us got away from Youngs Point there was not a bit of ground to be seen and the water was running over our shoes as we stood on the levee. All the time we worked on the canal the Rebels had one big gun they called it "Whistling Dick." It would shoot big shells in on us. Sometimes it would knock our staging, wheelbarrows and planks all over the place. We would sit down under the bank until they got in better humor and then we would get up and go to work again. It was the most mud I ever saw. I saw six mules hitched to a Government wagon with one barrel of pork in the wagon mired down so that they could not get out. They had to unhitch them and the men dragged them out with ropes and then dragged out the wagon in the same manner.

While we worked on that canal almost one half the men was sick and could not work. They were dying every day like mice and no wonder; just throwing their blankets down in the mud and lying down in it.

HOSPITAL STEWARD THOMAS H. BARTON

4TH WEST VIRGINIA INFANTRY, LIGHTBURN'S BRIGADE

One day while his regiment toiled on the canal, Barton, wearing common soldier's fatigues, paused to view the progress. He narrowly missed being set to digging by an indignant officer, who assumed he was a slacker from a work party. Barton finally convinced the man he was on legitimate army business. Later he wrote, "I was afterwards very careful to keep away from that locality."

While at Young's Point, sickness prevailed to an alarming extent among the troops, typhoid fever, diarrhœa and rheumatism, being the prevailing diseases. Typhoid fever was caused by using the surface water, which was contaminated with human excrement in a partially putrified condition, thus making the drinking water a fit nidus for the germs of this disease. It is my opinion that diarrhœa was occasioned partly from the same cause, and by exposure to the weather, which, as I have stated in a former chapter, was wet and inclement. Throughout February and March the rain was almost incessant. During part of the time it rained from morning till night, and it would be impossible to perform our culinary operations, and cook our "sow-belly." Rheumatism was caused by exposure to the weather, the troops having no shelter. The regiment lost thirty one men by sickness at Young's Point and Milikens Bend; at Van Buren Hospital, two; on board a steamboat, one; at the general hospital at St. Louis, Missouri, two; on board hospital steamer, R. C. Wood, one; making a total loss of thirty seven from January 20th, to the first week in May. Several died who were left at the convalescent camp at Miliken's Bend: one or two died who had been sent away sick, and four were discharged for disability at these places; at Charleston, West Va., two; at St. Louis, one; at Gallipolis, Ohio, two; at Columbus, Ohio, one; total ten. There were two desertions, making a total loss of forty nine men.

The R. C. Wood, named for the Union army's assistant surgeon general, served as a floating hospital. Built in 1857, it began life as the steam packet City of Louisiana, plying the Mississippi. Five years later the engine was removed to increase interior space, and it was outfitted with operating rooms and patient wards. Moored at the wharf in St. Louis, the Wood received Union casualties ferried upstream from Vicksburg.

Lake Providence La. Feb 24th 1863.

Another Federal attempt to circumvent Vicksburg involved opening a 400-mile route from Lake Providence, north of the city, through the swamps and bayous west of the Mississippi and finally linking up with the Red River well below Vicksburg. This sketch by Lieutenant Henry Otis Dwight of the 20th Ohio accurately depicts the sodden, desolate terrain through which the men tried to cut a ship channel.

SERGEANT SAMUEL H. M. BYERS
5TH IOWA INFANTRY, BOOMER'S BRIGADE

Another promising route was through the Yazoo Pass, 325 miles upstream from Vicksburg. It would allow Federal troops and gunboats to descend the Yazoo River to just east of the city and attack its landward side. In the mid-1850s a levee 100 feet thick and 18 feet high had been built across the pass as a flood control measure. Union engineers blew a hole in the levee, and the river poured through over a nine-foot cataract as Byers describes.

At just four in the evening our little steamer got the order to turn out of the river and into the rushing waters of the pass. We would have not been more excited at being told to start over Niagara Falls. Our engines are working backward and we enter the crevasse slowly, but in five minutes the fearful, eddying current seized us, and our boat was whirled round and round like a toy skiff in a washtub. We all held our breath as the steamer was hurled among floating logs and against overhanging trees. In ten minutes the rushing torrent had carried us, backward, down into the little lake. Not a soul of the five hundred on board the boat in this crazy ride was lost. Once in the lake we stopped, and with amazement watched other boats, crowded with soldiers, also drift into the whirl and be swept down the pass. It was luck, not management, that half the little army was not drowned.

Now for days and days our little fleet coursed its way toward Vicksburg among the plantations, swamps, woods, bayous, cane-brakes, creeks, and rivers of that inland sea. Wherever the water seemed deepest that was our course, but almost every hour projecting stumps and trees had to be sawn off under the water to allow our craft to get through. Sometimes we advanced only four or five miles a day. At night the boat would be tied to some tall sycamore. Here and there we landed at some plantation that seemed like an island in the flood. The negroes on the plantation, amazed at our coming, wondered if it was the day of Jubilee or if it was another Noah's flood and that these iron gunboats arks of safety. . . .

The Yazoo Pass, though not so crazy as the crevasse we had come through, was nevertheless bad and dangerous. Two of our craft sank to the bottom, but the soldiers were saved by getting into trees. All the boats were torn half to pieces. One day as we pushed our way along the crooked streams amid the vine-covered forests we ran onto a Rebel fort built on a bit of dry land. In front of it were great rafts that completely obstructed our way. An ocean steamer was also sunk in the channel in front of us. To our amazement we learned that it was the *Star of the West,* the ship that received the first shot fired in the war of the Rebellion. That was when it was trying to take supplies to Fort Sumter. Our gunboats shelled this "Fort Greenwood" in vain, and now Rebels were gathering around and behind us and guerrillas were beginning to fire on the boats. The waters, too, might soon subside, and our fleet and army be unable to get back into the Mississippi. We could not go ahead. Suddenly the orders came to turn about and steam as fast as possible to a place of safety.

The design of the U.S.S. Rattler, Admiral Porter's flagship for the Yazoo Pass expedition, was a wartime expedient to meet the need for fast, lightweight, shallow-draft vessels with just enough armor to protect the pilothouse and machinery from small-arms fire. These so-called tinclads proved to be a great success, navigating through narrow passages and over shoals where the heavier ironclads could not go.

SERGEANT JOHN V. BOUCHER
10TH MISSOURI (U.S.) INFANTRY, HOLMES' BRIGADE

This letter, written by Boucher to his wife after his return from the Yazoo Pass expedition, accurately expresses the sentiments of the average soldier regarding the miserable 1,400-mile journey by transport. Boucher also described the rich agricultural panorama he observed from the railing of his steamer, as well as the "many fine plantations evacuated and left to grow up in weeds" and "thousands of acres of the best land I ever saw . . . rendered useless." About the latter he said, "This much good is done any how if no more it has broke up hundreds of the most welthy planters in the south."

April 12th 1863
Mrs. J. V. Boucher
Old Sand Bar, Arkansas

. . . to which we returned yesterday after a long and tedious voyage of 18 days in the Grand Yazoo Pass expedition and a grand expedition it was too. . . . Well this Yazoo expedition beats the devil oll hollow so far as I can see in to it. Twenty steamers loaded down with men munitions cannon horses & mules artilery hard crackers fat meat and no place to hook it only as we could croud round the furnace now and again passing rite through the woods twenty five miles not wider than your door yard the channel bottoms all overflowed of course thus we went tearing and smashing boats saplins and other timber at a woful rate till we came in to a little river caled Cold Water about as big as Old Elkhorn in a freshet thence in to the Talihatcha a stream not as big as Okaw, and down it with in two miles of Greenwood a rebble fortification. there we halted after a eleven days voyge remained two days about-faced and on the eighteenth day landed back on the Old Sand Bar all safe and sound except one man died on the way. I said sound I mean as sound as could be expected And so ends the great Yazoo expedition that you have heard so much blow about. Now weather our commanders got skeard at the fort or the fort skeard them I can not tell. Or weather they found the enimy to strong for us and backed off or weather the enimy found us to strong for them and backed off I am not able to tell. Nor know mortal man connected with the private ranks can tell any thing about it.

THEODORE DAVIS
SPECIAL ARTIST, HARPER'S WEEKLY

Davis traveled with Grant's army throughout the Vicksburg campaign, often sketching while under fire. "To really see a battle, one must accept the most dangerous situations. It is only by going over the actual ground during the battle that one can decide what were its most interesting features." Davis was twice wounded during the war, once nearly losing a leg.

To reach Steele's Bayou it is necessary to construct corduroy roads and bridges, and these are being rapidly built; Stuart's division having already disembarked and begun their march into the interior. The distance to Steele's Bayou is not much over a mile, and our troops will very speedily be encamped upon the banks of the Yazoo. The road thither is naturally very difficult, as I myself experienced, and you will observe by the sketches I inclose. One is necessitated to wade, to cross logs, to build rafts, in short to convert himself into an amphibious animal.

Two of the Union transports of small size, the *Eagle* and *Silver Wave*, have already gotten into Steele's Bayou through the Yazoo, but not without serious damage to their upper works from the thick boughs and trunks of the impeding gum, cottonwood, and cypress trees. The exertion one is compelled to make in bayou navigation down here at this season, the thermometer ranging at 90° and upward, causes a copiousness of perspiration. . . . The season here is quite far advanced. The trees are green, the fruit trees and blackberry bushes all in bloom; the birds singing as merrily as if such a thing as secession had never been.

Stuart's Division are working hard, and the General himself has doffed his coat and toils like a Trojan with his men; believing very justly that a commander's example is necessary to animate and encourage his soldiers. Stuart is emphatically, as I have styled him, a "working general"; is energetic, patriotic, determined, and has already distinguished himself by his ability and gallantry on several hard-fought fields.

In this series of drawings, Harper's Weekly shows the labors and hazards involved in Grant's last attempt to sidestep Vicksburg's batteries. This was the 200-mile loop through Steele's Bayou, which would finish some 20 miles up the Yazoo River from where it had started—but in good position to set troops ashore for a landward attack on Vicksburg.

MAJOR GENERAL ULYSSES S. GRANT
COMMANDER, ARMY OF THE TENNESSEE

In his memoirs Grant wrote this statement about Vicksburg and his feelings concerning his army's early attempts to take it. Thwarted by nature and the Confederates, he was left with only one very dangerous choice. He would have to abandon his base and march down the west bank of the Mississippi to a point south of Vicksburg. There he would cross back to the east bank and make a very long overland advance on the city from the south and east.

Vicksburg was important to the enemy because it occupied the first high ground coming close to the river below Memphis. From there a railroad runs east, connecting with other roads leading to all points of the Southern States. A railroad also starts from the opposite side of the river, extending west as far as Shreveport, Louisiana. Vicksburg was the only channel, at the time of the events of which this chapter treats, connecting the parts of the Confederacy divided by the Mississippi. So long as it was held by the enemy, the free navigation of the river was prevented. Hence its importance. Points on the river between

"Then commenced a series of experiments to consume time, and to divert the attention of the enemy, of my troops and of the public generally."

Vicksburg and Port Hudson were held as dependencies; but their fall was sure to follow the capture of the former place. . . .

Vicksburg, as stated before, is on the first high land coming to the river's edge, below that on which Memphis stands. The bluff, or high land, follows the left bank of the Yazoo for some distance and continues in a southerly direction to the Mississippi River, thence it runs along the Mississippi to Warrenton, six miles below. The Yazoo River leaves the high land a short distance below Haines' Bluff and empties into the Mississippi nine miles above Vicksburg. Vicksburg is built on this high land where the Mississippi washes the base of the hill. Haines' Bluff, eleven miles from Vicksburg, on the Yazoo River, was strongly fortified. The whole distance from there to Vicksburg and thence to Warrenton was also intrenched, with batteries at suitable distances and rifle-pits connecting them.

From Young's Point the Mississippi turns in a north-easterly direction to a point just above the city, when it again turns and runs southwesterly, leaving vessels, which might attempt to run the blockade, exposed to the fire of batteries six miles below the city before they were in range of the upper batteries. Since then the river has made a cut-off, leaving what was the peninsula in front of the city, an island. North of the Yazoo was all a marsh, heavily timbered, cut up with bayous, and much overflowed. A front attack was therefore impossible, and was never contemplated; certainly not by me. The problem then became, how to secure a landing on high ground east of the Mississippi without an apparent retreat. Then commenced a series of experiments to consume time, and to divert the attention of the enemy, of my troops and of the public generally. I, myself, never felt great confidence that any of the experiments resorted to would prove successful. Nevertheless I was always prepared to take advantage of them in case they did.

Sweeping to Vicksburg's Doorstep

Grant's final plan of attack—to march his army south, float it across the Mississippi, and then move east—was desperately chancy. It called for an amphibious landing that, if met head-on by the Confederates, could turn into a disaster. Even with a beachhead secured, Grant would have to fight across more than 100 miles of enemy territory with at most 44,000 men to face two Rebel forces under Generals John Pemberton and Joseph Johnston totaling almost 60,000. If defeated, Grant might be pinned against the river.

Still, he plunged ahead, starting General McClernand's XIII Corps southward on March 29 down the west bank of the river from the old camps at Milliken's Bend. The first objective was the town of New Carthage, planned staging point for the cross-river leap.

Trouble came immediately. For his plan to work, Grant had to move fast, surprising Pemberton. But McClernand's troops were soon slogging through seas of mud left by the winter rains. For weeks the men struggled southward, building causeways and corduroying roads—and completing a 70-mile route good enough, though just barely, for the rest of the army to follow.

Next came the risky job of getting Admiral Porter's gunboats and transports south past Vicksburg's lethal batteries to the crossing point. Slipping downstream the night of April 16, the boats were pounded by the big Confederate guns. Miraculously, all but three got by, even though Rebel troops had lighted fires on both banks of the river, illuminating the scene, said one observer, "as if by sunlight."

Grant's next job was to stage diversions to keep Pemberton confused about where the Federals intended to strike. He first ordered a cavalry force in Tennessee to ride through central Mississippi causing as much trouble as possible—a brilliant, daring foray famous ever since as Grierson's Raid.

Its leader, Colonel Benjamin H. Grierson —a peaceable musician and teacher in civilian life—quickly proved himself one of the war's great cavalry commanders. Heading out of La Grange, Tennessee, on April 17 with

Illuminated by Confederate bonfires, Admiral Porter's flotilla runs the Vicksburg batteries on April 16. Once the ships made it through the heavy shelling, they were in a position to ferry troops and supplies across the river to support Grant's land campaign.

1,700 Iowa and Illinois horsemen, Grierson sped south, tearing up both the Mississippi Central and Mobile & Ohio Railroads as he went, while also sending detachments back north to confuse the Confederates.

By April 24 Grierson had reached the rail junction of Newton Station, 200 miles deep in enemy territory and just 100 miles east of Vicksburg. There he captured two trains, destroyed supplies, burned bridges, and cut telegraph lines. Then, instead of fleeing back to La Grange, he rode west and south, evading some 20,000 pursuers and finally taking refuge with his exhausted, ragged men in Federal-held Baton Rouge, Louisiana.

Then, on April 30 Grant sent General Sherman and 10 regiments left behind at Milliken's Bend up the Yazoo River to make a show of once more attacking the bluffs north of Vicksburg. "The gunboats and transports whistled and puffed," recalled one of Sherman's officers, "and made all the noise they could." The ploy worked; in near panic, Pemberton hastily called in reinforcements, including regiments he had just dispatched south to guard against a river crossing by the enemy.

Meanwhile, a hitch in Grant's main thrust occurred on April 29, when Porter's gunboats got into a battle with enemy guns on bluffs above the port of Grand Gulf, where Grant had intended to land his army. Grant swiftly shifted his planned landing point to Bruinsburg, eight miles farther south, and the next day sent McClernand's XIII Corps churning across the Mississippi on transports. To Grant's immense relief, the troops got ashore safely and unopposed. "Vicksburg was not yet taken," Grant later wrote, but "I was on dry ground on the same side of the river with the enemy."

Grant immediately ordered McClernand to head for Port Gibson. Once it was taken, the Federals would be able to outflank Grand Gulf, about eight miles away, and capture its guns and docks. A furious little battle erupted the next day when the Confederate commander at Grand Gulf, Brigadier General John S. Bowen, cleverly deployed his reduced force of 7,000 men along the heavily wooded ridges outside Port Gibson. For hours Bowen's men hurled back repeated attacks by four divisions, retreating only when outflanked by regiments from General McPherson's newly arrived corps.

With Port Gibson and Grand Gulf in hand, Grant quickly started his entire force marching inland toward Jackson. His aim: to slice between Pemberton's army and Johnston's force to the east, turn on and defeat Johnston, then take the city and, wrecking its rail yards, prevent any Confederate reinforcements from getting through.

Living off the land instead of waiting for supply trains, Grant's three corps raced toward Jackson, encountering little opposition until they reached the outskirts of the village of Raymond. There fighting erupted early on May 12 when McPherson's troops ran into 2,500 Confederates led by Brigadier General John Gregg, whom Pemberton had ordered up from Port Hudson. Emerging from dense woods near a sluggish stream called Fourteen-Mile Creek, Gregg's Texans and Tennesseans slammed into McPherson's forward units, throwing them back in murderous hand-to-hand fighting.

But then a fierce, swarthy Union general, John A. "Black Jack" Logan, led his 3d Division in a furious counterattack, smashing Gregg's thin line. After a last futile assault, the Confederates gave up, retreating through the town of Raymond and beyond.

Pausing only to wolf down a lavish meal the ladies of Raymond had prepared for Gregg's now fleeing troops, McPherson's men marched the last dozen miles to Jackson itself. The city's

As the Federal fleet ran Vicksburg's guns, most of Grant's army also moved south, marching down the Mississippi's west bank. Then, while Sherman feinted against Haynes' Bluff, Grant sent McClernand's and McPherson's corps east across the river below Grand Gulf, well south of Vicksburg. On May 1 they beat back a Confederate force at Port Gibson. Then Sherman's corps joined them, and Grant put the army between Pemberton's forces near Vicksburg and Johnston's army at Jackson. After skirmishing against Gregg at Raymond on May 12, Grant took Jackson. He then overcame Pemberton at Champion's Hill. By May 18 he had Vicksburg surrounded.

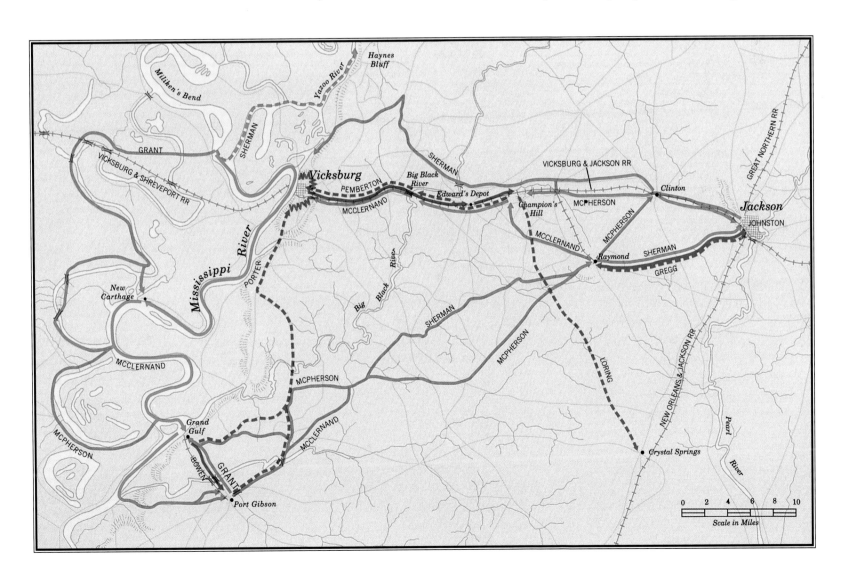

Confederate defenders numbered only about 12,000, but when a drenching rain slowed the Union advance, they were able to dig earthworks and, fighting stubbornly, to throw back McPherson's first assaults. But Colonel Samuel A. Holmes' brigade, attacking "at double quick, cheering wildly," as one officer recalled, broke through from the west while some of Sherman's regiments also smashed into the city. By the afternoon of May 14 troops of the 59th Indiana were jubilantly planting their flag atop the dome of Mississippi's capitol.

Grant immediately ordered the rail lines passing through Jackson torn up and everything of use to the enemy—arsenals, machine shops, warehouses—put to the torch. Then, with hardly a pause, he started McPherson's corps westward down the road to Vicksburg.

Pemberton, after much indecision and several false starts, moved west to meet the threat with about 23,000 men. By the morning of May 16 many of them were deployed on a wooded ridge dominated by a 70-foot rise named after a local farmer now serving in Pemberton's army, Sid Champion—Champion's Hill.

Fighting started on the Union left when troops of Major General A. J. Smith's division of McClernand's corps came under fire from General William W. Loring's Confederates. The battle began in earnest, however, with a charge by Brigadier General Alvin P. Hovey's two Federal brigades straight up Champion's Hill. Staggered by the rush, Major General Carter L. Stevenson's thin line gave way, and the Federals quickly reached the crest. There Hovey's men found a half-dozen enemy batteries lined up, but, by falling prone just as the first blasts of canister zinged overhead, they managed to keep going and capture the guns.

Pemberton, realizing his front was crumbling, frantically called for reinforcements from Loring and Bowen. Incredibly, Loring refused to move, but the combative Bowen acted fast, launching Colonel Francis M. Cockrell's and Brigadier General Martin E. Green's brigades in a ferocious counterattack. Hit hard in their turn, Hovey's Federals fell back down the hill.

At this point Grant ordered forward two brigades led by Colonels George Boomer and Samuel Holmes. Rushing at the Confederates, the Yankees were met, an Iowa sergeant recalled, by "a solid wall of men in gray, their muskets at their shoulders, blazing away in our faces and their batteries of artillery roaring as if it were the end of the world."

As the battle on the hill roared on, General McClernand moved, sending Brigadier General Peter J. Osterhaus' division slamming into Bowen's right flank. The Confederate defense began to disintegrate, the men flooding back off Champion's Hill. With the battle lost, Pemberton ordered a retreat, the troops trudging back down the road to Vicksburg—although Loring's division, too far south to begin with, became separated and never joined up. In all, Pemberton lost more than 3,800 men to Grant's 2,441.

Hoping to delay Grant, Pemberton ordered earthworks dug at the next natural obstacle, the Big Black River. But the weary Confederates quickly abandoned the trenches in the face of two headlong Federal attacks. Soon groups of ragged, dispirited men were straggling into Vicksburg, where the stunned citizens brought out water and food and frantically asked what was happening. One soldier's answer summed up the rest: "We are whipped."

Grant hurried after and by May 18 had thrown a cordon around the city, sealing it off. So far the operation had been, Sherman told Grant, "one of the greatest campaigns in history." But now came the siege of Vicksburg itself, which would prove in some ways an even sterner test for Grant's army.

Pemberton sent three divisions eastward to intercept the Federals at Champion's Hill. Alvin Hovey's Union brigade seized the hill on May 16 but was soon flung back in furious fighting by John Bowen's Confederates. Bowen was shortly in trouble, however, as William W. Loring failed to advance his troops in support. Federal brigades under John Logan and Marcellus M. Crocker smashed into Carter L. Stevenson's division on the Confederate left flank, and McClernand, though acting belatedly, sent Osterhaus' division forward on a successful assault on the Rebel right. By late afternoon, Pemberton's bloodied troops were in retreat toward Vicksburg.

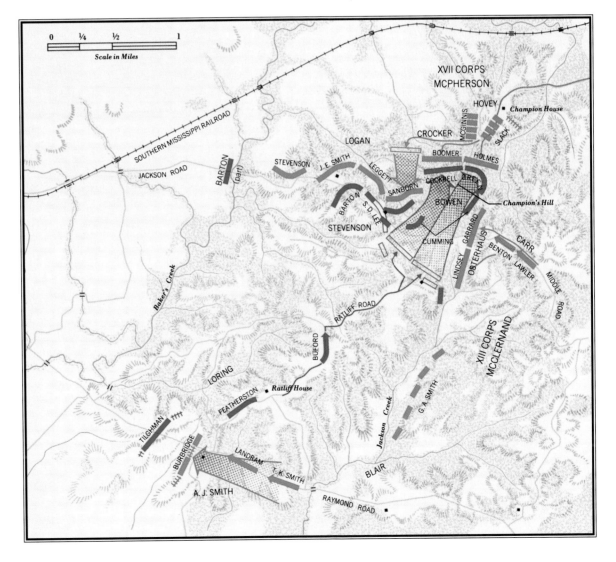

CORPORAL OWEN J. HOPKINS
42D OHIO INFANTRY, LINDSEY'S BRIGADE

One of 15 children, Hopkins volunteered for service over his widowed mother's strenuous objections "when the call for troops came after the battle of Bull Run." Although only 19 years old and poorly educated, he kept two highly detailed and literate pocket diaries of his campaigns with the Army of the Tennessee. Hopkins was mustered out as a regimental quartermaster sergeant on October 14, 1864.

As soon as the spring floods had sufficiently fallen to render it possible, we were ordered to advance by land, through the forests and threading the edge of the morass on the western shore of the river, entirely concealed from observation, and to march from Milliken's Landing, above the Rebel ramparts, to New Carthage, below. In this movement, Gen. McClernand with the Thirteenth Corps led the advance. It had been necessary to delay the enterprise until the waters in the river and the bayous should recede; still, the road was all but impassable. It lay through a vast bog, intersected by numerous bayous half flooded with water.

The heavy artillery wheels cut through the slime and the mud, making the path a perfect mortar bed through which we waded knee deep, and where the hubs of the wheels often disappeared out of sight. The advance of the army was found to be utterly impracticable, except by the building of corduroy roads, cutting outlets for the egress of the water, and bridging the bayous. The army had to build for itself, under the most difficult circumstances, a military road as it advanced. Twenty miles of levee had to be most carefully guarded, lest it should be cut by the enemy and the whole country flooded.

The vigilant foe got some intimation of the movement, notwithstanding it had been very carefully concealed. As we approached New Carthage, we found that the levee had been cut by the Rebels, and the surrounding country was so flooded that New Carthage was converted into an island. After ineffectual attempts to bridge the rushing waters or to cross them in boats, it was found necessary to march in search of some point farther down the river. Inspirited rather than discouraged by such obstacles, we pressed on, and after having constructed seventy miles of road and about 2000 feet of bridging, we reached our final destination.

SERGEANT WILLIAM PITT CHAMBERS
46TH MISSISSIPPI INFANTRY, BALDWIN'S BRIGADE

In February 1862 Chambers left his job teaching school to join the army. He served throughout the siege of Vicksburg and was captured when the city fell. Paroled two months later, Chambers rejoined his regiment. He later fought in the Atlanta campaign and was seriously wounded at the Battle of Allatoona. After the war he resumed his teaching career and wrote short stories, essays, and poetry on the side. Chambers died of influenza at the age of 76 in January 1916.

Between three and four o'clock next morning I witnessed an impressive scene. Being aroused by the pickets firing, I knew another battery running enterprise was on foot. Hastily climbing a high hill, I obtained a pretty fair view of the splendid panorama. Across the river two or three buildings were on fire, the flames leaping madly upward, lighting up the sky and the dense curtain of smoke that swung over the river with a livid glow. The whole surface of the stream was lighted up and far out on its broad bosom was a fleet of five or six steamers and two gunboats. The latter were firing as rapidly as their guns could be worked, while our batteries were sending forth a stream of shot and shell. The dense smoke that partially concealed the flashes of sulphurous flame, added to the wierdness of the scene.

One of the boats took fire. The flames carried upward losing themselves in a dense volume of smoke that shone like a rosy sunset cloud. The air was full of bursting shells and screaming shots, while through it all could be heard the wild hurrahs of our men. It was a sight never to be forgotten, and while a sensation of awe came over me to behold such a display of man's destructive energy, it awoke the savage in the heart and filled it with an enthusiastic desire to be in the thick of the work of death. Another bark went down, and the agonizing wails of the drowning wretches on the water were faintly heard amid the exultant tones of the victors' shouts.

The other boats ran past, the flames completed their work of ruin, the cannons were hushed and the gray streaks of the morning were stealing over the Eastern hills. Quiet once more reigned over the bosom of the "Father of waters."

This Harper's drawing accompanied a description of the Rumsey: "On the Vicksburg side she was protected by a barge filled with hay solidly piled to a height which completely screened the steamboat. On the other side another barge, containing a loose deck-load of cottonbales, protected the captain and his crew from rebel sharpshooters."

THE TUG "RUMSEY" ACCOUTRED FOR RUNNING THE REBEL BATTERIES AT VICKSBURG.

"I never understood before the full force of those questions—What shall we eat? what shall we drink? and wherewithal shall we be clothed?"

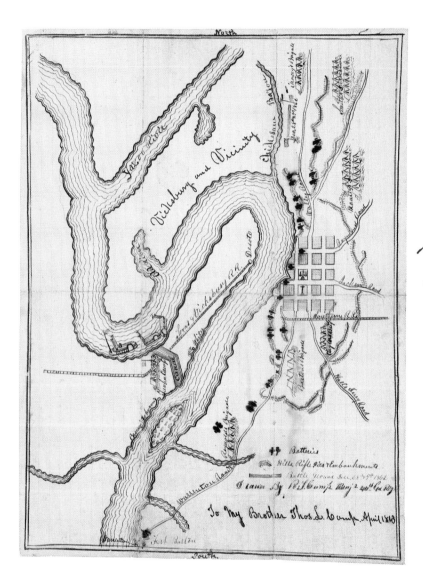

This map of Vicksburg, drawn by a Confederate officer, marks the positions of the numerous Rebel batteries ranging along the bluffs and clearly illustrates the perils faced by Admiral Porter's fleet. The vessels were under heavy fire from the moment they rounded the horseshoe bend above the city until they finally reached safety several miles south. The passage took an agonizing two and a half hours.

ANONYMOUS WOMAN
RESIDENT OF VICKSBURG

This remarkable diary was secretly kept by a woman who, along with her new husband, both Union sympathizers, had set up house in Vicksburg in January, a scant few months before the siege began. Despite her political views, she provided a compassionate portrait of the terrible hardships endured by Vicksburg's residents. Such was the depth of rancor over the war, however, that even 20 years afterward she insisted on remaining anonymous when this journal was published.

Vicksburg, April 28, 1863. I never understood before the full force of those questions—What shall we eat? what shall we drink? and wherewithal shall we be clothed? We have no prophet of the Lord at whose prayer the meal and oil will not waste. Such minute attention must be given the wardrobe to preserve it that I have learned to darn like an artist. Making shoes is now another accomplishment. Mine were in tatters. H. came across a moth-eaten pair that he bought me, giving ten dollars, I think, and they fell into rags when I tried to wear them; but the soles are good, and that has helped me to shoes. A pair of old coat sleeves saved—nothing is thrown away now—was in my trunk. I cut an exact pattern from my old shoes, laid it on the sleeves, and cut out thus good uppers and sewed them carefully; then soaked the soles and sewed the cloth to them. I am so proud of these home-made shoes, think I'll put them in a glass case when the war is over, as an heirloom. H. says he has come to have an abiding faith that everything he needs to wear will come out of that trunk while the war lasts. It is like a fairy casket. I have but a dozen pins remaining, so many I gave away. Every time these are used they are straightened and kept from rust. All these curious labors are performed while the shells are leisurely screaming through the air; but as long as we are out of range we don't worry. For many nights we have had but little sleep, because the Federal gunboats have been running past the batteries. The uproar when this is happening is phenomenal. The first night the thundering artillery burst the bars of sleep, we thought it an attack by the river. To get into garments and rush up stairs was the work of a moment. From the upper gallery we have a fine view of the river, and soon a red glare lit up the scene and showed a small boat towing two large barges gliding by. The Confederates had set fire to a house near the bank. Another night, eight boats ran by, throwing a shower of shot, and two burning houses made the river clear as day. One of the batteries has a remarkable gun they call "Whistling Dick," because of the screeching, whistling sound it gives, and certainly it does sound like a tortured thing. Added to all this is the indescribable Confederate yell, which is a soul-harrowing sound to hear. I have gained respect for the mechanism of the human ear, which stands it all without injury. The streets are seldom quiet at night; even the dragging about of cannon makes a din in these echoing gullies. The other night we were on the gallery till the last of the eight boats got by. Next day a friend said to H., "It was a wonder you didn't have your heads taken off last night. I passed and saw them stretched over the gallery, and grape-shot were whizzing up the street just on a level with you." The double roar of batteries and boats was so great, we never noticed the whizzing.

SERGEANT MAJOR CHARLES E. WILCOX
33D ILLINOIS INFANTRY, BENTON'S BRIGADE

Despite the five-hour bombardment described here, during which Union gunboats rained 2,500 shells on Confederate positions at Grand Gulf, one Rebel battery managed to hold out. The tenacity of these gunners forced Grant to alter his plans: Federal troops disembarked from their transports and marched eight miles down the west bank while the fleet ran the defiant guns. The next day, April 30, Grant's army crossed unopposed to the east bank at Bruinsburg.

The sun arose throwing an impressive splendor upon the exciting scenes of the early morn. Every boat—transport and barge— lies at the landing, about five miles above Grand Gulf, covered till they are black with troops. Every heart here is full of anxiety and emotion; wondering eyes and eyes not altogether tearless, gaze ever and anon upon the *Father of Waters* where lie the formidable fleet of gunboats and rams, transports and barges, the latter heavily loaded with troops whose courage and valor are sufficient when combined with that

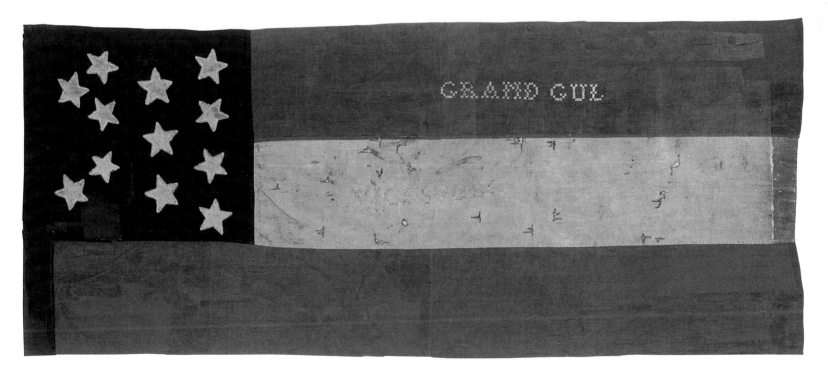

This flag flew over the battery of Company A, 1st Louisiana Heavy Artillery, at Grand Gulf. Most of the regiment had been captured at the Battle of New Orleans in April 1862 and paroled that fall. Captured again at Vicksburg and again paroled, the regiment finally surrendered for good at Citronelle, Alabama, on May 4, 1865.

of the rest of this mighty army, to redeem this lovely valley of the Mississippi from fiends and traitors who are desecrating it. Now it is 7 1/2 o'clock, a.m. Each gunboat and transport has gotten up full stream. The black smoke curls up from the blacker smoke-pipes, and moves towards the rebels, seeming to tell them of their black deeds and warns them of their portion when we attack them. It is like that which comes from the lower regions, scented with brimstone and issuing as it does from those gunboats, the traitors may well think, as they see it, that that fleet from which it comes has a portion of hell to give them, and that too, ere long, if they do not surrender or run. And now what means that? Every gunboat is steaming up the river. Can it be that the attack is not to be made? Every one is surprised. No; 'tis only the preparation for the attack. They are now "rounding to" and there they go. Thousands of eyes are looking upon. The first gun is fired by the enemy; the Benton, I believe, replies. 'Tis 8 o'clock. The contest has fairly begun; every gunboat is engaged. We all know when the enemy fires his heaviest guns as they make a sharper report than any of ours, though we have as large guns as he; this is probably accounted for by ours being on the water. Eleven o'clock, A.M. Several of the enemy's batteries are silenced. The gunboats ply around and close to his strongest battery which gives them a round every opportunity, but as they near that battery they, one after another, give him broadsides which are terrible and produce a marked effect. The Benton "lays off" nearly across the river and just opposite and within good range of this powerful battery; every few minutes she sends an 84 or 64 pounder with nice precision at it; the dust flies and the enemy is quiet for a minute. This boat makes the most of the best shots that are fired. It seems to me that the enemy shoots wildly. A few minutes after 12 M. The bombardment is over. Every one of the enemy's batteries save one, of three heavy guns are silenced, and we tried in vain to silence it. The fleet has retired; Gen. Grant who was in a messenger boat during the bombardment, has come ashore. A little while passes and we get orders to start immediately down the levee, past Grand Gulf. The transports are being unloaded. At two P.M. we started for below; all the boats are to run the gauntlet to-night.

The gunboat Benton, mentioned in Sergeant Major Wilcox's account, stands at far left in this drawing of the attack on Grand Gulf. Also at left, hidden behind the black smoke, is the position of Company A of the 1st Louisiana Heavy Artillery. The Federal boats, although close to the enemy shore, had great difficulty silencing the entrenched Confederate guns.

CAPTAIN GEORGE SMITH

33D ILLINOIS INFANTRY, BENTON'S BRIGADE

Smith writes almost frivolously about the fight between two Union corps and little more than three Confederate brigades on May 1 near Port Gibson. Although outnumbered nearly 4 to 1, the Rebels, by taking advantage of the terrain, held the Yankees at bay for most of a day before withdrawing under cover of darkness.

Addison Harvey, a resourceful young Confederate cavalryman, was detached from regular duty and ordered by his brigade commander to form a select company of 100 hand-picked scouts. In this capacity, wrote one of his sergeants in a postwar memoir, "Captain Harvey was unrestricted in his operations, and was authorized to scout when and where he pleased, and report to his General when he deemed expedient. These enlarged powers gave him full scope to his military genius." It was Harvey's unit, ranging up and down the east bank of the Mississippi below Vicksburg, that detected Grant's crossing at Bruinsburg. "The early discovery . . . gave warning in time for our Army to check his movement soon after landing and to keep from a complete surprise, which up to that time was unknown to our generals."

he boys were down side the road & asleep in 2 minutes. A great many "reflections" have been written on the eve of battle. I did not sleep for I saw it was near morning and was busy mentally with other things then reflections. I thought first of the Haversacks that had been left a mile back and resolved to have them up before daylight for I knew the boys would be hungry after their night march. So I got Saxie Steel to go with me and went after them, getting back just at daylight.

Well the fight began about 7 O'clock the enemy opening on us from all sides. They evidently under rated our numbers, and intended to surround & bag the whole concern. The ground was the best possible for a battle hills & open spaces cut up by woods & deep ravines. The action became general with infantry in about an hour. We were exposed to a cross fire of Artillery in the beginning of the action.

Shells grape & canister came Hot & Heavy.

That tries ones nerves, but is not very dangerous. For a few slight scratches was all the injury done us.

We "spread ourselves thin on the ground" and let them blaze away. Sam Fletcher was the first man touched in our Reg't. A canister shot bounced from a tree and raised a blood blister on the back of his hand. He was the only one scratched in our Company during the action. Although we were under a heavy fire of Musketry soon after.

We advanced soon after. The 18th Indiana done the heaviest fighting in our Brigade. They took one of the Secesh batteries with the bayonet. All honor to their gallant Col. Washburn. . . .

Some ten or twelve of Co. K. were wounded they being "skirmishers." I believe one of the 8th Indiana stopped a ball for me. We were just coming up the hill & filing in rear of the 8th who were in line. Just as I got up the hill a man on the left of the 8th exactly in front of me was struck & would have fallen on me had I not stepped aside involuntarily. The ball struck him right in the face & he was so close that the "clinck" made one shiver. I thought he was stone dead but he got up in a few minutes & walked off with the help of his comrade. The musketry fire at times was terrific beyond anything I ever conceived of before. About noon the enemy had got about enough and were falling back in every direction when they received large reinforcements from Vicksburg and renewed the battle fiercer than ever. Our Brigade was then moved into an open field and staid there until night. . . . Everybody expected a harder fight next day but all were dissapointed.

SERGEANT WILLIAM PITT CHAMBERS

46TH MISSISSIPPI INFANTRY, BALDWIN'S BRIGADE

Chambers' account of the battle at Port Gibson on May 1 vividly portrays the savage nature of the close-quarter fighting that day. The Confederates inflicted 875 casualties but suffered 832 of their own. Forced to retreat in the face of superior numbers, they were compelled within days to abandon the formidable works at Grand Gulf as well, leaving behind five large guns. Grant now had an open avenue to move on the state capital at Jackson.

It was an exciting time! The loud peals of artillery rent the sky and reverberated along the hills till their echoes blended with the sharp din of musketry that was rolling toward us from "Grindstone Ford." In the streets all was confusion. Men with pale faces were running hither and thither, some with arms and seeking a command, women sobbing on every side, children in opened eyed wonder clinging to their weeping mothers not understanding the meaning of it all, and negroes with eyes protruding like open cotton bolls were jostling each other and every body else and continuously asking about "dem Yankees."

The ladies cheered us through their tears, and besought us to drive the invaders from their homes. One lady while she prayed Heaven to protect us, said we felt as near to her as though we were her own sons going forth to battle. The wounded, too, were meeting us, some in vehicles and some on litters, and many a poor fellow with a shattered limb or a gaping wound would wildly hurrah for the "brave Mississippians."

We sped on! Louder roared the cannon and din of the musketry grew more deafening. We met our flying squadrons, regiments cut to pieces till a remnant only were driven from their position by a force fivefold greater than their own. Already we were in advance of our new line, and were going forward upon the run when we were ordered to "right about."

We rejoined the regiment and formed a new line of battle, our regiment occupying a small eminence to the left of the road with a small stream in our front. We had barely formed our line when the enemy open fire on us with artillery and small arms. Just at this time a sad accident occurred. Easterling being weak from recent illness, had been unable to keep up in our forced march. Coming up a little later utterly exhausted, he sat down by a tree. When the bullets began to whistle about us he took his gun by the muzzle to draw it to him. The hammer struck the tree, the cap exploded and the whole charge struck his right arm literally tearing it to fragments from the wrist to above the elbow. Never will I forget the horror-stricken face as he cried "Oh! Pitt, I have ruined my arm!" Seeing his clothes burning, I called Crawford [who] stood near him to extinguish the flame. Asking for water, he fell fainting as I reached him, but revived as the water was placed to his lips. He was placed on a litter borne to the rear, and I never saw him again.

But the screaming and bursting of shells, the whistling of shot, the ping of bullets, the shrieks of the wounded and the groans of the dying were calculated to strike terror to hearts unused to such scenes. I frankly confess that I was badly demoralized.

Co. "C" was deployed as skirmishers along the little Creek. The 4th Miss. on our left was soon hotly engaged, while further along the line the firing seemed to be heavier still. As we formed our line Col. Sears called out: "Fix bayonets, boys! and if they come bleed 'em!" With fixed bayonets, expecting a charge every minute, we held our line till about one o'clock when we were ordered to cross the narrow Creek on the opposite heights of which the enemy was posted. We did so and were met by a terrible fire of grape, canister and musket shot. In a few minutes, however, we were ordered to resume our former position. We left our dead across the creek, but brought most of the wounded away.

Resuming our position in line, our skirmish line was reënforced, and for the balance of the day the firing was mostly confined to the pickets with occasional artillery duels.

"By the 'right flank' we went into them with a will, striking them left and rear before they knew what was coming."

Confederate brigadier general John S. Bowen, shown in his prewar U.S. Army uniform, handled his vastly outnumbered forces so brilliantly at Port Gibson that he was promoted to major general within weeks. Holed up in Vicksburg during the siege, he contracted dysentery and died a few days after the garrison's surrender.

SERGEANT IRA BLANCHARD
20TH ILLINOIS INFANTRY, J. E. SMITH'S BRIGADE

In 1861 Blanchard had enlisted for a three-year term of service, even though, as he would later write, he "had no desire for the realities of actual warfare. Yet I had no wife, no little ones, was twenty-six years old, and what the world would call sound in body, and why should I not go?" He was wounded at Shiloh, fought throughout the Vicksburg campaign, and reenlisted in January 1864. Wounded again at Atlanta in July, Blanchard finally received a disability discharge.

The enemy was strongly posted on the opposite side of a large field behind a deep ravine. Across this ravine the main road ran on a sort of ridge which spanned the ravine as a natural bridge; and back of this defile was a large block house which was filled from cellar to garret with their "sharp shooters" whose deadly aim picked off many of our boys at long distances. On either side of this fortress their lines of infantry were posted, strongly guarding the narrow passage across the ravine. General Logan's third division was placed in the center and ordered to carry the block house, if possible. We formed in the center of the field and moved to the assault. The 45th Illinois attempted to force their way across, but the boys could not stand the withering fire, many were killed; they broke their ranks and fell back. Other regiments took their place but none could withstand the shower of lead that was hurled back upon them. Our Regiment being farther to the left, were battling with the enemy across the ravine while these assaults on the block house were being made and our loss was not heavy. . . . Finding the block house could not be carried by a direct assault of the infantry some heavy guns were ordered up, which shelled the citadel for more than half an hour, making logs and shingles fly in all directions but failing to set fire to the nest or dislodge the hornets within.

In the meantime General McPherson had dismounted, and throwing a blanket over his shoulders, that his uniform might not attract bullets, came to the front unattended, and being a good engineer, looked the ground carefully over; when he said he believed he had hit on a plan that would win.

Under a tremendous fire of artillery on the block house, he directed the 20th Illinois to crawl along the edge of the ravine, which we did without loss, then letting ourselves down by boughs or grapevines we finally reached the bottom unobserved. Then by the "right flank" we went into them with a will, striking them left and rear before they knew what was coming. Whole companies laid down their arms. One "reb" Captain, when he found himself cut off from escape and between two fires, was so terrified that he took off his hat and quietly walked up to Captain Stevens and delivered him his sword, supposing him to be the commanding General.

Thus in twenty minutes after the old Twentieth had reached the bottom of that ravine they had carried the block house which had been a bone of contention all day and taken nearly 300 prisoners.

Finding their block house gone and their position turned, they fled in all directions and left us masters of the situation.

MAJOR GENERAL ULYSSES S. GRANT
COMMANDER, ARMY OF THE TENNESSEE

Described here in dry fashion, Grierson's Raid, covering 600 miles in 16 days, helped to erase Confederate disdain for Federal cavalry. Grierson's troops killed, wounded, or captured more than 600 Rebels at a cost of "3 killed, 7 wounded, 5 left on the route sick . . . and 9 men missing." Grant, ordinarily stinting with his praise, was moved to write: "It has been one of the most brilliant cavalry exploits of the war, and will be handed down in history as an example to be imitated."

It was at Port Gibson I first heard through a Southern paper of the complete success of Colonel Grierson, who was making a raid through central Mississippi. He had started from La Grange April 17th with three regiments of about 1,700 men. On the 21st he had detached Colonel Hatch with one regiment to destroy the railroad between Columbus and Macon and then return to La Grange. Hatch had a sharp fight with the enemy at Columbus and retreated along the railroad, destroying it at Okalona and Tupelo, and arriving in La Grange April 26. Grierson continued his movement with about 1,000 men, breaking the Vicksburg and Meridian railroad and the New Orleans and Jackson railroad, arriving at Baton Rouge May 2d. This raid was of great importance, for Grierson had attracted the attention of the enemy from the main movement against Vicksburg.

Colonel Benjamin H. Grierson (inset) was the most unlikely of cavalry heroes. Kicked by a horse at the age of eight, he had hated the animal ever since. A musician, composer, and music teacher in civilian life, he had strenuously protested his appointment in 1861 to the 6th Illinois Cavalry. Yet Grierson soon proved so able a commander that Sherman told Grant he was "the best cavalry officer I have yet had." When Grierson's bedraggled soldiers and their worn-out mounts finally reached the Federal base at Baton Rouge (below), the commandant insisted on staging a parade, during which many of the exhausted troopers fell asleep in the saddle.

but taking only ten small regiments, selected out of Blair's division, to make a show of force. We afterward learned that General Pemberton in Vicksburg had previously dispatched a large force to the assistance of General Bowen, at Grand Gulf and Port Gibson, which force had proceeded as far as Hankinson's Ferry, when he discovered our ostentatious movement up the Yazoo, and recalled his men, and sent them up to Haines's Bluff to meet us. This detachment of rebel troops must have marched nearly sixty miles without rest, for afterward, on reaching Vicksburg, I heard that the men were perfectly exhausted, and lay along the road in groups, completely fagged out. This diversion, made with so much pomp and display, therefore completely fulfilled its purpose, by leaving General Grant to contend with a minor force, on landing at Bruinsburg, and afterward at Port Gibson and Grand Gulf.

The ironclad ram Choctaw, a converted side-wheel steamer, took part in Sherman's feint against Haynes' Bluff, during which it was struck by 53 Confederate shells.

MAJOR GENERAL WILLIAM T. SHERMAN
COMMANDER, XV CORPS, ARMY OF THE TENNESSEE

Sherman detested reporters, believing they had unfairly libeled him ever since Shiloh. Addressing Grant's concerns, mentioned below, he wrote: "As to the reports in the newspapers, we must scorn them, else they will ruin us and our country." His ruse at Haynes' Bluff worked; Pemberton diverted much-needed reinforcements from Grant's front to meet the illusory assault, while Sherman sent his corps south to rejoin the main army at Port Gibson.

I received a letter from General Grant, written at Carthage, saying that he proposed to cross over and attack Grand Gulf, about the end of April, and he thought I could put in my time usefully by making a "feint" on Haines's Bluff, but he did not like to order me to do it, because it might be reported at the North that I had again been "repulsed, etc." Thus we had to fight a senseless clamor at the North, as well as a determined foe and the obstacles of Nature. Of course, I answered him that I would make the "feint," regardless of public clamor at a distance, and I did make it most effectually; using all the old boats I could get about Milliken's Bend and the mouth of the Yazoo,

PRIVATE JENKIN L. JONES
6TH WISCONSIN BATTERY, CROCKER'S DIVISION

Although reared on a hardscrabble farm deep in the Wisconsin forests, Jones was not the typical backwoodsman. In his memoirs, written in 1913, he confessed to having a nonviolent nature: "As I approach my three-score-and-ten, I can say that I have never sighted a gun, or pulled the trigger on anything smaller than a cannon, and that only when ordered."

Near Black River, Sunday, May 3. Arose at 2 A.M. and as soon as practicable hitched up with one day's shelled corn in our bags. Did not leave until sunrise. Crossed a small stream on a chain-suspended bridge which the rebs had set afire, but was saved. Our way was disputed about a mile on by a rebel battery which threw shells at the advance, which formed line and moved on. At 10 A.M. the skirmishers were hotly engaged and sent back for a howitzer. The third (with which I was connected) piece moved out on a trot, took a position by direction of Colonel Powell within 200 yards of their sharpshooters, who were firing briskly in a thick wood. Opened on them with canister, which soon had the desired effect of "drying them up there." Advanced to the left a few rods and opened fire on a log house where the sharpshooters were working. Threw three shells, then retired to await orders, having shot ten rounds in all, four spherical case, three canister, three percussion shells. The litter-bearers report a rebel captain killed in front of the piece by canister cutting him nearly in two. In the meantime the

1st and 5th pieces took position on the right to prevent three pieces of artillery from taking position. Advanced about two miles when their pieces opened fire with shells on us. The howitzers went forward but were ordered back by Chief of Artillery, and two ten-pound Parrotts instead. A brisk firing on both sides for ten or fifteen minutes. The 1st Brigade in line on right, 2nd on left, when they pulled up stake and we marched without molestation within a mile of Black River; went into park. All very tired and needed rest. Passed about seventy-five prisoners during the day, many more being taken by Logan on the left. Pickets firing often during the night, once with artillery.

The days after the battle at Port Gibson saw a number of skirmishes, as the outnumbered Rebels did everything in their power to slow the Union pursuit. In the drawing above, General Logan's Federal division slogs through Bayou Pierre next to a blazing suspension bridge. Correspondent Theodore Davis recorded: "The yet burning structure and the often-clouded night moon lent 'aid and comfort' . . . and they pressed on in hot haste to reach, if possible, the fleet-footed chivalry."

they are all asleep, lying in their blankets under the trees, for in a quick march they leave their tents behind. Their guns are all ready at their sides, so that if they are suddenly called at night they can start in a moment. It is strange in the morning before daylight to hear the bugle and drums sound the reveille, which calls the army to wake up. It will begin perhaps at a distance and then run along the whole line, bugle after bugle and drum after drum taking it up, and then it goes from front to rear, farther and farther away, the sweet sounds throbbing and rolling while you lie on the grass with your saddle for a pillow, half awake, or opening your eyes to see that the stars are all bright in the sky, or that there is only a faint flush in the east, where the day is soon to break.

Living in camp is queer business. I get my meals in General Grant's mess, and pay my share of the expenses. The table is a chest with a double cover, which unfolds on the right and the left; the dishes, knives and forks, and caster are inside. Sometimes we get good things, but generally we don't. The cook is an old negro, black and grimy. The cooking is not as clean as it might be, but in war you can't be particular about such things.

CORPORAL OWEN J. HOPKINS
42D OHIO INFANTRY, LINDSEY'S BRIGADE

The foray Hopkins describes here precisely suited Grant's strategy. With his troops on the east bank of the river, the Union commander made the courageous decision to forgo maintaining a cumbersome and vulnerable supply line down the Mississippi to New Orleans, instead "boldly striking into the interior," as Dana wrote, "and depending on the country for meat and even for bread." On May 12 Grant's 44,000 men set out for the state capital at Jackson.

Captain Hutchins' company (which is *us*) was detailed on a foraging expedition, much to the delight of every man in it. Striking off across the country in the direction of Vicksburg, we came to a plantation where no Yankees had ever trod, and after putting to flight a pack of blood hounds and frightening half out of their wits a motly group of alternately black and white darkies, I discovered the *garden,* now full of early vegetables, while Jim W—— had the honor of discovering a well-filled *smoke-house,* and Don Van D—— accidentally fell over a barrel of dried peaches, Jake C—— in the meantime capturing three or four fat hens, while Adam D—— encountered a porker with such violence that Porker was killed and his hams amptuated with great skill.

CHARLES A. DANA
ASSISTANT U.S. SECRETARY OF WAR

When Dana arrived at Grant's headquarters in the early spring, the general's staff had treated him coldly, assuming him—correctly, as it turned out—to be a spy sent by Lincoln's secretary of war, Edwin M. Stanton. But their opinion soon changed, as Dana made clear in extensive communiqués to Washington his respect for Grant's abilities. Grant, he wrote, was "not an original or brilliant man, but sincere, thoughtful, deep and gifted with courage that never faltered."

All of a sudden it is very cold here. Two days ago it was hot like summer, but now I sit in my tent in my overcoat, writing, and thinking if I only were at home instead of being almost two thousand miles away.

Away yonder, in the edge of the woods, I hear the drum-beat that calls the soldiers to their supper. It is only a little after five o'clock, but they begin the day very early and end it early. Pretty soon after dark

Massa and the white folks having fled the premises, our search extended to the mansion and bureau drawers, where I succeeded in finding a dozen pairs of cotton socks, a welcome discovery as my only pair needed the tender care of a mother who could darn. I'll be darned if they didn't! Having secured all the provender on the premises, we "hired" a "colored individual" to hitch up the *ox and mule* teams, and hauled our prisoners and Wedgetables to camp, arriving tired but *not hungry* about dusk, receiving as a reward from our ravenous comrades a round of hearty cheers, and before morning chickens, turkeys, calves, pigs, and everything had become food for soldiers.

Captain Thomas L. Hutchins of Company K, 42d Ohio, led the foraging expedition described by Corporal Hopkins at left. Such tactics, later repeated by Sherman in Georgia, produced an unrelenting bitterness among the civilian population.

SERGEANT JOHN V. BOUCHER
10TH MISSOURI (U.S.) INFANTRY, HOLMES' BRIGADE

For a common soldier, Boucher had a rare grasp of grand strategy, perceiving that Grant, by moving quickly, hoped to put his army between Rebel reinforcements under General Joseph Johnston massing at Jackson and Pemberton's force at Vicksburg. It was a risky plan; if Johnston and Pemberton succeeded in joining up, they would substantially outnumber the Federals. Grant's only hope was to confront and defeat them separately.

On Sunday morning we came up with the enemys rear and they gave us a runing fight all day. Our artilery in front shelling the woods and we in supporting distance of our big guns they would return ocasional shots then run thus we chased them to Black River that night they crosed and burnt the bridge we have now got a pontoon up and our troops are crossing our fourses are somthing near fifty thousand strong on this side the river we have taken over one thousand prisinors among which are a great many Tennesee & Mo. troops and they say they don't want to fight us any longer nor wont if they can only get away. Gen. Austen has captured most all the Mo. 5th last friday after killing and wounding quite a number. we passed over their battle ground saw a number of the dead and their artilery horses were strewed for more than five miles. . . . we have entered the verry heart of their country. the old planters flea at our approch like the chased deer before the hounds leaving everything behind that they cant take along. . . . we are feasting fine at this time. I think we will march tomorrow . . . I think the design is to fall in the rear between Vicksburg & Jackson cut of their rail road and run them in we have already cut off their communications [with] Texas they cant get no more supplies from that direction we are above below and soon will be on each side of them.

"Duty to our Southland and our Southern homes, could be seen pictured on the faces of every member of our company."

PRIVATE B. F. HERRON
3D TENNESSEE (C.S.) INFANTRY, GREGG'S BRIGADE

Herron was shot in the right thigh at the Battle of Raymond. "Our command was repulsed," he later wrote, "and in a little while I was captured and sent to the field hospital where my wound was tenderly dressed by a Federal surgeon." During Herron's convalescence, Grant visited the hospital, and Herron personally overheard the Union chief tell the staff: "Give the wounded men every attention which it is possible and make no distinction between Federals and Confederates."

We arrived at Raymond early in the morning of the 11th of May, 1863, and next morning were ordered out to relieve a company which had been on picket the night before. Without breakfast, tired, hungry and with blistered feet, sadness was pictured on the faces of my companions as we were hastening on through the dust to the death of some of us and to great suffering of others. But our sadness was suddenly relieved when we saw on a porch of a palatial home, some beautiful girls waving the "Bonnie Blue Flag." We gave the old and familiar yell in return, and no sad faces were seen for a while, but on the other hand duty to our Southland and our Southern homes, could be seen pictured on the faces of every member of our company.

While on picket we could see our grand old colors, Third Tennessee, moving out to take its place in line of battle. In a very short time Gen. Gregg came up and ordered our Captain to move his company and take our proper place in the regiment. After taking our place in line we could see our skirmishers falling back. This proved to me that we would soon be in a hot engagement.

Never will I forget the picture of sadness that was on the faces of my comrades, the majority of whom were as still as death. Minutes seemed hours but we were not long in this suspense for as the Federal skirmishers came in sight our grand old Commander, Col. Walker, stepped out in front and calling "Attention," said, "We will soon be engaged in a battle and before we begin I wish to say that I do not command you to go, but to follow this old bald head of mine," and lifting his cap, gave the command, "Forward, Guide Center, March." In the twinkling of an eye sadness and despair vanished and in its place appeared a determination to conquer or die. Onward we went with the rebel yell, driving the enemy back through a cornfield and across a deep narrow creek. Here we were ordered to lie down and continue the fight in this position.

In the last charge which our regiment attempted to make I was wounded. When I was first struck I supposed I was killed and when I saw the blood running to the ground I was sure it was true. I did not seem to have any great fear of death but what worried me most was the thought of dying so far from home and loved ones.

Captain James S. Walker commanded Company H of the 3d Tennessee in the action Herron describes. In the regiment's bloody struggle with the 23d Indiana at Raymond neither side had time to fix bayonets before they collided, so they fought hand to hand with clubbed muskets, tree branches, and fists.

SERGEANT OSBORN H. OLDROYD
20TH OHIO INFANTRY, LEGGETT'S BRIGADE

On May 12 one Rebel brigade under John Gregg, deployed south of Raymond, held off McPherson's corps for most of a day. The battle centered on Fourteen-Mile Creek, mentioned in both Herron's and Oldroyd's accounts. The outnumbered Confederates initially gained the upper hand, pushing the 23d Indiana back from the streambed in hand-to-hand fighting. At that moment General John A. Logan, a former Illinois congressman beloved by his men, flung himself into the thick of the melee and by the force of his personality rallied the Federals and stemmed the rout.

Just here the firing began in our front, and we got orders: "Attention! Fall in—take arms—forward—double-quick, march!" And we moved quite lively, as the rebel bullets did likewise. We had advanced but a short distance—probably a hundred yards— when we came to a creek, the bank of which was high, but down we slid, and wading through the water, which was up to our knees, dropped upon the opposite side and began firing at will. We did not have to be told to shoot, for the enemy were but a hundred yards in front of us, and it seemed to be in the minds of both officers and men that this was the very spot in which to settle the question of our right of way. They fought desperately, and no doubt they fully expected to whip us early in the fight, before we could get reinforcements. There was no bank in front to protect my company, and the space between us and the foe was open and perfectly level. Every man of us knew it would be sure death to all to retreat, for we had behind us a bank seven feet high, made slippery by the wading and climbing back of the wounded, and where the foe could be at our heels in a moment. However, we had no idea of retreating, had the ground been twice as inviting; but taking in the situation only strung us up to higher determination. The regiment to the right of us was giving way, but just as the line was wavering and about to be hopelessly broken, Logan dashed up, and with the shriek of an eagle turned them back to their places, which they regained and held. Had it not been for Logan's timely intervention, who was continually riding up and down the line, firing the men with his own enthusiasm, our line would undoubtedly have been broken at some point. For two hours the contest raged furiously, but as man after man dropped dead or wounded, the rest were inspired the more firmly to hold fast their places and avenge the fallen. The creek was running red with precious blood spilt for our country. My bunkmate and I were kneeling side by side when a ball crashed through his brain, and he fell over with a mortal wound. With the assistance of two others I picked him up, carried him over the bank in our rear, and laid behind a tree, removing from his pocket, watch and trinkets, and the same little mirror that had helped him make his last toilet but a little while before. We then went back to our company after an absence of but a few minutes. Shot and shell from the enemy came over thicker and faster, while the trees rained bunches of twigs around us. One by one the boys were dropping out of my company. The second lieutenant in command was wounded; the orderly sergeant dropped dead, and I find myself (fifth sergeant) in command of the handful remaining. In front of us was a reb in a red shirt, when one of our boys, raising his gun, remarked, "see me bring that red shirt down," while another cried out, "hold on, that is my man." Both fired, and the red shirt fell—it may be riddled by more than those two shots. A red shirt is, of course, rather too conspicuous on a battle field. Into another part of the line the enemy charged, fighting hand to hand, being too close to fire, and using the butts of their guns. But they were all forced to give way at last, and we followed them up for a short distance, when we were passed by our reinforcements coming up just as we had whipped the enemy. I took the roll-book from the pocket of our dead sergeant, and found that while we had gone in with thirty-two men, we came out with but sixteen—one-half of the brave little band, but in a few hours before so full of hope and patriotism, either killed or wounded. Nearly all the survivors could show bullet marks in clothing or flesh, but no man left the field on account of wounds. When I told Colonel Force of our loss, I saw tears course down his cheeks, and so intent were his thoughts upon his fallen men that he failed to note the bursting of a shell above him, scattering the powder over his person, as he sat at the foot of a tree.

Although our ranks have been so thinned by to-day's battle our will is stronger than ever to march and fight on, and avenge the death of those we must leave behind. I am very sad on account of the loss of so many of my comrades, especially the one who bunked with me, and who had been to me like a brother, even sharing my load when it grew burdensome. He has fallen; may he sleep quietly under the shadows of those old oaks which looked down upon the struggle of to-day.

We moved up to the town of Raymond and there camped. I suppose this will be named the battle of Raymond. The citizens had prepared a good dinner for the rebels on their return from victory, but as they actually returned from defeat they were in too much of a hurry to enjoy it.

This drawing by Lieutenant Henry Otis Dwight (inset) of the 20th Ohio, entitled "A question of right of way," depicts the fierce struggle between his regiment and the 7th Texas along the banks of Fourteen-Mile Creek. At times the two regiments were so close, Colonel Manning Force recalled, that the "rifles of the opposing lines crossed while firing." Wounded men on both sides bore powder burns on their clothing from the point-blank fire.

May 12 1863   A question of right of way — 20th Ohio, vs. 7th Texas

"Captain Boone was killed while deploying his skirmishers. His death cast a momentary gloom over the regiment, but the circumstance was soon forgotten in the excitement of the hour."

PRIVATE W. J. DAVIDSON
41ST TENNESSEE (C.S.) INFANTRY, GREGG'S BRIGADE

Davidson's regiment was committed to the Battle of Raymond after Union general Logan had rallied his division and begun to drive the Confederate line back toward the town. But it was a case of too little too late for the Rebels; with McPherson's entire corps bearing down on him, Gregg was compelled to withdraw to Jackson. A sumptuous feast that Raymond's townsfolk had prepared for Gregg's troops was instead devoured by the victorious—and famished—Yankees.

John Gregg ably led his brigade in the Vicksburg campaign and later at Chickamauga, the Wilderness, and Spotsylvania. He was killed in 1864 at Petersburg.

At 12 o'clock the Forty-first, which had been held in reserve, was ordered to advance and support the left wing, which was said to be in danger of being flanked by the enemy. We advanced at a quick step, under a broiling sun, through a dusty lane, for nearly a mile, when a courier came up with orders for us to return to town and guard the ordnance. We had hardly reached our destination when a second order came to file off on a road leading to the center. After marching a mile in this direction, another order turned us back to town, which we had hardly reached before we were again ordered to return to the battle-field on the same road. On reaching this point we were formed in line in the center, and then obliqued across a field to the extreme left. Here we piled our knapsacks in a heap and double-quicked a mile and a half. Lieutenant Colonel Tillman performed a splendid maneuvre under the fire of the enemy's artillery, forming line of battle on the tenth company with great precision of execution and without the least confusion. We then advanced under fire to our position across a field, and gained the edge of the woods in which the enemy was concealed. Captain Ab. Boone's company was thrown out as skirmishers, while we formed along the road in an excellent defensive position. While waiting here for the advance of the enemy, we learned that Captain Boone was killed while deploying his skirmishers. His death cast a momentary gloom over the regiment, but the circumstance was soon forgotten in the excitement of the hour. We remained in position something over an hour, waiting for the enemy's advance, when an order came for the Forty-first to bring up the rear and cover the retreat of the rest of the brigade. It was now ascertained that Gregg's Brigade had been engaged all day, with a force eight or ten times its superior in numbers, and had successfully held it in check until it had orders to quit the field. The task assigned the Forty-first was performed in perfect order, though a Federal battery, on observing the movement, had advanced to within five hundred yards and opened fire on it as it crossed an open field. We fell back to a point four miles from Raymond and eleven from Jackson.

ANNE SHANNON
Resident of Raymond, Mississippi

To escape the indignities of Yankee occupation, Shannon and her husband, a disabled Confederate veteran, removed themselves first to Jackson, then finally found safe haven, along with many other Vicksburg families, in Eufaula, Alabama. Sadly, Anne Shannon never saw her home again; she fell ill and died in April 1864.

*I*magine our feelings when we saw them passing through town towards Jackson, and knew we were being left to the tender mercies of the yankees. Not more than fifteen minutes had elapse since the retreat of our troops, before the federals began to pour into town in quite an orderly Manner. Ma and the rest of us were sitting on the front porch when a party came up, looking around the yard and in the out-houses for "rebels." They were very common looking men. Then an aid of Gen. Logan dashed in on horseback to spy around. . . . We came to the conclusion that he was a dentist by the way he talked. Calm yourself, madam, be calm. I see you are nervous, be calm. Ma said she was afraid her house would not be safe from the pillaging of the soldiers. "Why madam, we come to protect you, our soldiers are gentlemen. Where have they pillaged?." That question being unanswerable, nobody said anything. Next came an aid to Gen. M'Pherson, wanted to pitch the General's tents in the front yard. Father in the meantime had arrived, having walked part of the way from Bolton's. "The General will be a protection," they said. Accordingly, the General's tents were pitched. Then began to throng in Aids, officers of all kinds guards, niggers and horses. Some of the aids, who all looked like spry New York clerks, came and seated themselves on the edge of the porch, and entered into conversation. Among them was a special artist of Harpers' Weekly, a tallow faced youth in enormous, high-topped boots, he had a regular down-eastern look. One of them was assuring Ma that "nothing on this place will be touched, your property is perfectly safe." When here came Aunt Esther with a most distressed air. "Mists, they are taking all my bedclothes and my clothes and everything I've got." Sure enough, there were the federal *gentlemen* flying with armloads of dresses, quilts, blankets andc. The aid who was administering consolation, seemed very much non-plussed. Springing to his feet, he dashed wildly after them, but too late.

THEODORE DAVIS
Special Artist, Harper's Weekly

Davis, the "tallow faced youth" of Anne Shannon's account at left, followed closely in the wake of McPherson's corps as it broke through the Confederate positions south and west of Jackson and raced into the town. The Union takeover was so sudden that many convalescing Confederate soldiers—and many deserters as well—were rounded up in the city's streets and hotels. That night, May 14, Grant slept in the same room occupied by Johnston the previous evening.

*O*n the morning of the 14th the troops of General McPherson's corps moved from Clinton, upon the direct Jackson road, and in a pelting rainstorm marched rapidly toward that place, the division under the command of General Crocker being in advance. At 10 o'clock, when within three miles of Jackson, the pickets of the enemy were driven in, and the column was at once advanced in line of battle. The enemy's "line of battle" was soon discovered posted in an excellent position to the right but reaching across the road. The character of the country, though mostly open, offered facilities for advancing, under cover of undulations, to within a short distance of the enemy's line, with but little exposure of our troops to their fire; and, in a drenching shower, the division did so. The skirmishers of the opposing columns were within less than one hundred yards of each other. The shower had just ceased. M. Battey, First Missouri Artillery, under Lieutenant McMurray, opened fire. At the same time the order was conveyed to General Crocker to "charge the enemy's line with his division, Holmes's brigade in the centre, Sandborne's to the right and rear, Boomer, with his brigade, to the left and rear." The division came steadily up the slope of the hill, over and down at a double-quick. They met a severe and effective fire; but never wavering, continued the charge with cheers up the second slope. Just at this moment the rebels broke. Flying in disorder, their exposed backs were a target for a fire until this moment reserved. At the crest of the last hill was posted the rebel reserve, who, as our men reached the line of fences and were breaking them down, opened a fire that sent to their long account too many of our gallant men. The 17th Iowa and 10th Missouri suffered principally at this point. Here the enemy could not stand, but joined the precipitate retreat of their advance. The guns of Dillon's battery had followed our charging troops in their advance, and were here speedily unlimbered, and one after the other, as they were brought in battery, opened with canister. Just at this moment General Crocker rode along the line of his advancing men, and was greeted with cheer upon cheer.

The division of General Logan was advanced and disposed to the left and reserve. Just at this time General Sherman, who, with his corps, was advancing, three miles distant and to our right, opened a brisk fire with his artillery.

General McPherson now steadily advanced his force, and occupied the enemy's works. Almost at the same time General Sherman's troops entered the town through the works, at some distance to the right, the division of General Tuttle forming his advance. The rebel cavalry was just leaving as the generals, with their escorts, dashed through the storm to the Capitol, over which was being raised the colors of the 59th Indiana, by Captain Cadle, of General Crocker's staff, and Captain Martin.

RAISING THE STARS AND STRIPES OVER THE CAPITOL OF THE STATE OF MISSISSIPPI.—[SEE PAGE 395.]

THE BATTLE OF JACKSON, MISSISSIPPI, MAY 14, 1863.—CHARGE BY GENERAL CROCKER'S DIVISION.—SKETCHED BY MR. THEODORE R. DAVIS.—[SEE PAGE 395.]

Davis sketched these illustrations to accompany the article (left) that he wrote for Harper's. Above he depicts the triumphant assault in the midst of a driving rainstorm by Union general Crocker's division that opened the gates to Mississippi's capital. At top Federal cavalrymen gallop jubilantly through the heart of Jackson as the American flag flies over the statehouse.

"Our lines were re-formed in that particular locality so as to avoid those Southern bees. They had no 'rebel yell,' but their charge on us was a successful one."

SERGEANT WILBUR F. CRUMMER
45TH ILLINOIS INFANTRY, J. E. SMITH'S BRIGADE

Although Crummer was able to look with humor on incidents such as the one described below, the Battle of Jackson was hard going for the troops involved. "The final charge made by the Iowa boys under Gen. Crocker . . . was one of the most superb and gallant of the war," Crummer recalled. "We are now 80 miles from Grand Gulf and 50 miles east of Vicksburg. Immediately the army is wheeled about and faced toward Vicksburg, and the march commences to that city."

During the battle at Jackson a rather amusing incident happened. We were in line of battle and had moved up to the vicinity of a plantation around which were scattered a number of bee hives. Now, had we not been engaged with the enemy, our boys would have liked nothing better than to have despoiled those bees and supped on honey, but for the present we had important work on hand. The bees were quiet enough until the minie-balls went crashing through their hives, when they came out and rushed at us with terrible ferocity. Men can stand up and be shot at, all day, with the deadly musket, but when a swarm of bees pounces upon a company of men in concert, it's beyond human nature to stand it, and so two or three companies retired from the field. In fact, our lines were re-formed in that particular locality so as to avoid those Southern bees. They had no "rebel yell," but their charge on us was a successful one.

Jasper A. Maltby (left), promoted to brigadier general after Vicksburg, commanded the 45th Illinois throughout the campaign and remained with the 45th on garrison duty for the rest of the war. In September 1867 he was appointed mayor of Vicksburg by General Ord, the department commander. Three months later he died of yellow fever; his body was returned to his hometown of Galena, Illinois, for burial.

When Union troops seized Jackson, they came across this makeshift Confederate prison camp, a dilapidated covered bridge over the Pearl River, and liberated 400 of their comrades. The prisoners, most of them captured four months earlier at Chickasaw Bluffs, had endured a wet, miserable winter of confinement. Their guards allowed no fires of any kind—not even candles—on the combustible structure, and many men died of disease or exposure. This pencil sketch on lined notepaper was drawn by Colonel Thomas C. Fletcher of the 31st Missouri Zouaves, one of 19 officers among the prisoners. Fletcher survived his captivity to become the first postwar governor of Missouri.

DESTRUCTION OF REBEL PROPERTY AT JACKSON, MISSISSIPPI, MAY 15.

This sketch by Theodore Davis depicts the burning of Jackson ordered by Grant. "Foundries, machine shops, warehouses, factories, arsenals and public stores were fired as fast as flames could be kindled," wrote a Northern journalist. It foreshadowed the devastating total warfare that would soon lay waste to large areas of the South.

PRIVATE CHARLES A. WILLISON
76TH OHIO INFANTRY, WOODS' BRIGADE

With his father's permission, Willison enlisted at the age of 16 in August 1862. The blue-eyed, five-foot-four-and-a-half-inch-tall teenager served for three years in the campaigns of General Sherman's XV Corps. After the war he married, had three children, and founded a bank in Wisconsin. But his idyllic civilian life was plagued with health problems—chronic indigestion, rheumatism, and hemorrhoids—which he ascribed to "exposure and bad food" encountered during his army days. Willison died in June 1915.

Arrived before Jackson, the capital of Mississippi, May 14. We struck it from the southwest, where the defense was comparatively feeble, but hard fighting was going on at our left in the neighborhood of the Jackson and Vicksburg road. The enemy soon left our front and our division immediately entered the city. Next day we under Sherman's direction, devoted to the work of destruction. The government buildings, arsenal, factories, warehouses, etc., all public property—were burnt, and the railroad for some distance out destroyed. Pearl river bridge having been burnt by the enemy, its abutments were battered down by our artillery. This ruthless destruction was necessary for the protection of our rear, as we turned to the hard task yet before us toward Vicksburg.

It was sad indeed to see great quantities of valuable supplies given over to the flames. They would have been a boon to our army, but there was no way to take them along. We were in the lightest marching order and they could not be left for the use of our enemy. What grieved me most I think was to see the sugar warehouses with their tiers upon tiers of sugar hogsheads, going up in fire and smoke. I loved sugar—it had always been a luxury with me, how great was evidenced by my carrying eight or nine canteens of it, hung to my shoulders, as we marched out of the city. But my endurance proved not equal to my zeal for sugar. One by one the canteens had to go as the straps cut into my shoulder. An immense amount of plug tobacco was brought out by the soldiers, their hankering for the weed evidently on the same scale as mine for sugar. I think enough was left strewed over the ground at our first camp to thatch a good-sized village.

"We saw the destruction caused by our battery, the ground being covered thickly with rebel grey."

SERGEANT OSBORN H. OLDROYD
20TH OHIO INFANTRY, LEGGETT'S BRIGADE

Oldroyd describes the action on the Federal right, positioned to the west of Champion's Hill. Logan's division pressed the Confederates so hard in this area that they were forced to divert troops from the high ground at the center of the battlefield. Union general Hovey was soon to take advantage by charging up and overtopping the crest of the hill.

May 16th.—We rolled out of bed this morning early, and had our breakfast of slapjacks made of flour, salt and water, which lie on a man's stomach like cakes of lead—for we are out of all rations but flour and salt, though we hope soon for some variety. We heard heavy firing about eleven o'clock. Our division reached Champion Hill about two P.M., and filed into a field on the right of the road. We were drawn up in a line facing the woods through which ran the road we had just left. It was by this road the rebels came out of Vicksburg to whip us. We had orders to lie down. The command was obeyed with alacrity, for bullets were already whizzing over our heads. I never hugged Dixie's soil as close as I have to-day. We crowded together as tight as we could, fairly plowing our faces into the ground. Occasionally a ball would pick its man in spite of precaution, and he would have to slip to the rear. Soon we got orders to rise up, and in an instant every man was on his feet. If the former order was well obeyed, the latter was equally so. The enemy charged out of the woods in front of us in a solid line, and as they were climbing the fence between us, which separated the open field from the timber, DeGolier's battery, stationed in our front, opened on them with grape and canister, and completely annihilated men and fence, and forced the enemy to fall back. Such terrible execution by a battery I never saw. It seemed as if every shell burst just as it reached the fence, and rails and rebs flew into the air together. They, finding our center too strong, renewed their charge on our left, and succeeded in driving it a short distance, but their success was only for a moment, for our boys rallied, and with reinforcements drove them in turn. We now charged into the woods and drove them a little ways, and as we charged over the spot so lately occupied by the foe, we saw the destruction caused by our battery, the ground being covered thickly with rebel grey. When we reached the woods we were exposed to a galling fire, and were at one time nearly surrounded, but we fought there hard until our ammunition was exhausted, when we fixed bayonets and prepared to hold our ground. A fresh supply of ammunition soon came up, when we felt all was well with us again. Meanwhile the right of our line succeeded in getting around to the left, when the enemy retreated towards Vicksburg, lest they should be cut off. . . .

. . . Several amusing incidents have occurred during the battle to-day. Company A, of the 20th, was sent out to skirmish, and moved forward till they could see the enemy. By this time General Logan made his appearance, when one of the boys who wished to go into the fight without impediments, approached Logan and said, "General, shall we not unsling knapsacks?" "No," was the stern reply, "damn them, you can whip them with your knapsacks on." This same company, in full view of a rebel battery, had taken refuge in a deep ditch, and when afterward the rebel captain cried out, "ready, take aim," Bryant, feeling secure on his position, interrupted the order with a shout, "shoot away and be damned to you."

This sketch by Lieutenant Henry Otis Dwight of the 20th Ohio Infantry shows Leggett's brigade of Logan's division lying prone at the foot of Champion's Hill awaiting orders to advance up the slope. At the first sound of firing that morning, Grant had galloped forward from his headquarters to take personal charge of the battle. Surveying the ground to his front, he remarked that the Confederate positions were situated atop "one of the highest points in that section, and commanded all the ground in range."

SERGEANT WILLIAM S. MORRIS
31ST ILLINOIS INFANTRY, J. E. SMITH'S BRIGADE

After having heard then congressman John Logan give a stirring call to service in the town square of Marion, Illinois, the 19-year-old Morris (left) had promptly enlisted. He served throughout the war and was mustered out as a first lieutenant. Afterward he practiced law, won election to both houses of the Illinois legislature, and enthusiastically backed his old division commander's successful bid for election to the U.S. Senate.

Passing rapidly to the right of the line, the brigade came to a front, looking across the Champion Hill farm house and the high ground where field batteries were in position to defend the extreme left of the Confederate line of infantry drawn up in double column. They crowned the hill, that with its abrupt northeastern face covered with timber, presented a formidable barrier to any force that might assail it. Behind the brigade was an open field; far off to the right the flat bottoms of Baker's Creek. The men here slung their knapsacks and lay flat upon the ground in line. Major Stahlbrand pushed his twenty-four pound Howitzers several yards in front of our position and opened at close range with shell and shrapnel, cutting his shell at a second and a half. The guns on the hill added their music and sent their missiles tearing across the narrow valley at Stahlbrand's guns. The Major observed from his position at the guns a line of infantry moving down the hill. He turned round and riding up to Gen. J. E. Smith, commanding the brigade, said: "Sheneral Schmidt dey are sharging you mitt doubled column. By damn it they vant mine guns." Smith looked to the right and left of his line and replied grimly: "Let 'em come, we're ready to receive them." He commanded, "Attention brigade," and the line stood upon its feet. Again he looked steadily up and down the line and bawled out "Fix bayonets." The bayonets flashed from the scabbards and the jingle of the steel rattled along the line. Logan and McPherson dashed up. The corps commander smilingly rode along the line, saying: "Give them Jesse boys, give them Jesse." Logan straightened himself in his stirrups and said: "We are about to fight the battle for Vicksburg." Appealing to his old regiment he cried out: "Thirty onesters remember the blood of your mammas. We must whip them here or all go under the sod together. Give 'em hell."

CORPORAL WILLIAM F. HOLLINGSWORTH

11TH INDIANA INFANTRY, McGINNIS' BRIGADE

McGinnis' brigade shared the unenviable task of charging straight up Champion's Hill into the teeth of the Confederate fire. As they reached the summit, the Federals came face to face with massed Rebel artillery loaded with canister. Before the gunners could pull their lanyards, McGinnis shouted to his men to fall flat. Thanks to his quick thinking, most of the deadly missiles flew harmlessly over them. Hollingsworth received a slight arm wound in the action.

We formed in line of batle and a bout 8 a.m. moved forward in line we had not went over a half of a mile untill our Skirmishers opened the fight. Hovey's hole division was to make the atact when we had advanced a bout three hundred yards of the rebels we found . . . a very strong forse and a . . . batry the ground was so ruff that our batries could take no part in the fight Our general saw that the only way to git at them was to charge them, so our regment was ordered to charg the Batry when we got within a bout 100 yards of the rebels batry we went forward at a charg Bayonetts double quick the greap and Canester and musket balls flew over our heds as thick as hale ever flew but as luck wold they hurt scarsly any of us

We did not fire a shot untill we got within a bout 20 steps of the rebels then we lit a volly in to them which kild a power of them and confused the Baline of them we then went in to them with the Bayonet we kild all there Batry horses with our Bayonets and captured a full Batry of artiliry we followed up the rebels nearly a mild killing and taking prisioners all the time and not without thining our ranks considerable

After we had followed up the rebels nearly a mild they got hevy renforements and returned the charge they came on to us 3 thousands out flankeds on all sid and we were forsed to fall back But not but a short distence when we got reinforcement and soon sent them flying a crost the field a gain they rebels was then persuid to Blackriver by fresh troops the loss of our regement in kild wounded and missing was 164 the Division loss was 1450 in kild wounded and missing.

Next in line of battle to McGinnis during the charge was the brigade of Colonel James R. Slack, including the 34th Iowa Infantry. Lieutenant William Rigby (left) recalled, "Our Regt. suffered severely they charged upon a Battery, carried it & pursued the Rebels some distance beyond. not being supported they were flanked on the right & obliged to retire." Rigby's field glasses and case are shown above.

CORPORAL EPHRAIM MCD. ANDERSON
2D MISSOURI (C.S.) INFANTRY, COCKRELL'S BRIGADE

At about 1:30 p.m., Confederate general Bowen's two brigades launched a counterattack on Champion's Hill and briefly swept the Federals off the heights. But, as Anderson describes below, Union forces rallied, and soon the opposing battle lines swayed back and forth along the crest as reinforcements from both sides poured in. Of this brutal contest a sergeant from the 24th Iowa noted afterward that "every human instinct is carried away by a torrent of passion, kill, kill, KILL, seems to fill your heart and be written over the face of all nature."

The battle here raged fearfully—one unbroken, deafening roar of musketry was all that could be heard. The opposing lines were so much in the woods and so contiguous, that artillery could not be used. The ground was fought over three times, and, as the wave of battle rolled to and fro, the scene became bloody and terrific—the actors self-reliant and determined; "do or die," seemed to be the feeling of our men, and right manfully and nobly did they stand up to their work.

Three times, as the foe was borne back, we were confronted by fresh lines of troops, from which flashed and rolled the long, simultaneous and withering volleys that can only come from battalions just brought into action. Their numbers seemed countless. Recoiling an instant from each furious onslaught of fresh legions, the firm and serried line of our division invariably renewed the attack, and, taking advantage of every part of the ground and of all favorable circumstances and positions, with the practiced eye of soldiers accustomed to the field, we succeeded each time in beating back these new and innumerable squadrons.

Once the enemy was driven so far back before fresh forces were brought up, that we were in sight of his ordnance train, which was being turned and driven back under whip. This could be seen where our lines were advanced through the woods to the edge of a large field in front, near which point was a small church or school-house. Though the force in front was vastly superior to ours, yet, if the fortunes of the day had depended upon the issue of the contest between us, as victory thus far was won, it might still have remained upon our side—Grant's centre was undoubtedly pierced.

By this time, however, the hostile columns were closing in upon our flank. . . . Our position was compromised, and the dense gathering lines of the enemy threatened us on three sides.

Francis Marion Cockrell commanded the Rebel 1st Missouri Brigade with distinction throughout the campaign. He later suffered a serious wound at the Battle of Franklin and was confined to garrison duty near Mobile, where he was captured on April 9, 1865. Nine years later, Cockrell succeeded Carl Schurz—a former Union general—as U.S. senator from Missouri, an office he held for 30 years.

PRIVATE A. H. REYNOLDS

19TH ARKANSAS INFANTRY, GREEN'S BRIGADE

After his capture, which he describes below, Reynolds was taken first to Camp Morton, Indiana, and then a month later shipped to Point Lookout, Maryland. On December 27, 1863, he was paroled and exchanged through Confederate lines at City Point, Virginia, and eventually rejoined his old regiment. Forty-five years after the battle, Reynolds returned to Champion's Hill. "I found the field well preserved and could locate all the surroundings," he wrote. "The tree where Billy Watts knelt when he killed that officer is green and still standing."

There was some heavy fighting going on near the center at this time, and occasionally a courier would come dashing up. By this time several officers had congregated near us, with Colonel Dockery in their midst. He had just ridden back to where we were when some fellow came down the road as if racing for life. He rode up to the little bunch and halted. Colonel Dockery was given orders to take his regiment and reeinforce in the center. As the adjutant rode off Colonel Dockery, as cool as an iceberg, gave the command: "Attention, load at will; load." My heart got right in my mouth, and I believe every other fellow was in like condition; but not a word was spoken by any one. The next order was: "Forward, double-quick, march." As we passed the squad of officers one of them said: "Turn in at those quarters." When we got there, Colonel Dockery had preceded us and was sitting on his horse as cool as ever and gave a ringing command, "Halt on the right; by file into line; double-quick march"; and quickly we were in line and facing a regiment of thoroughly routed soldiers. The next command was: "Fix bayonets and hold until ordered." With a forward march we passed those troops that were falling back, and then we were ordered to charge. We had caught the enemy with empty guns, and they gave way easily. We were charging up the long slope to the highest peak of Champion Hill and almost parallel with the public road to Bolton. At the top of the hill we met another long line of blues climbing the steep hill. They were within eighty feet of us when we gained the top of the hill, and without orders it seemed as if every man in our ranks fired at once. Never before nor since have I ever witnessed such a sight. The whole line seemed to fall and tumble headlong to the bottom of the hill. In a moment they came again, and we were ready and again repulsed them. And again and again for several hours in this way we held them at bay, when we charged them and gained the top of the next hill. . . .

After his distinguished performance at Champion's Hill, Colonel Thomas P. Dockery led the 19th Arkansas back to the prepared defenses at Vicksburg. On June 27 he took over Green's brigade after that general was killed. He became a general in August and was ordered to form a new brigade composed of paroled Vicksburg prisoners.

When we reached there we were ordered to fall back, as we were being flanked by Logan's Division. About twenty of us, mostly from my company were left to cover the retreat, being sharpshooters. We stopped in a hollow that headed up near the Bolton road. After waiting until the command was clearly out of sight six of our number . . . went out where we could see over the hilltop. A regiment of Federal infantry was just filing out of the big road to our right and about eighty yards away and advancing at trail arms in an oblique direction toward us, their commanding officer riding just in front and to our right. When they had covered about half of the distance between us, Billy Watts knelt beside a little oak tree and fired, when the officer fell as if dead or mortally wounded. Each of us singled out a man and fired. Immediately I primed my gun, a Springfield rifle, and was loading it and watching for another shot and walking backward down the hill, dragging my gun butt on the ground, intending to get my man when they came over the hill, and had just rammed the ball home when my foot came in contact with a root of a huckleberry bush that had been rooted up and I fell sprawling with my head down hill, and before I could recover they were upon us. They fired a volley just as I fell, and I have always felt that the fall saved my life. The next instant they were at us with bayonets. I raised on my right elbow just as a big fellow was in the act of thrusting his bayonet through me and fired. The muzzle of my gun was within four feet of his breast and loaded with a Springfield rifle ball and a steel ramrod.

I had fallen within ten feet of the hollow where we had previously been. With what strength I had left I sprang over the precipice . . . ; but before I could scramble down the lifeless corpse of my antagonist preceded me with a heavy thud in the slush below. In the next minute we were prisoners of war.

Private James Bell (above), a 31-year-old native of Scotland, served in Lieutenant Samuel H. M. Byers' Company E, 5th Iowa Infantry. He was killed in action on May 16 in the fierce struggle for Champion's Hill.

Lieutenant Colonel Leonidas Horney (right) had risen through the ranks of the 10th Missouri (U.S.) Infantry from captain to command of the regiment. The regiment's official history states that while moving his men across a road in preparation for a flank attack at Champion's Hill, Horney "fell, pierced by several balls, instantly killed falling from his horse."

LIEUTENANT SAMUEL H. M. BYERS
5TH IOWA INFANTRY, BOOMER'S BRIGADE

With Bowen's counterattack threatening the gains made in the initial Federal assault, General Grant rode up to the first brigades he could find, which included both Byers' and Horney's regiments, and ordered them up the hill. A private in the 10th Missouri wrote, "Although we had traveled 12 miles under the hot sun we started on the run; knapsacks, haversacks, blankets and everything except our guns and cartridge boxes were thrown to the side of the road. We started up the hill with yells and shouts that made the earth tremble."

We were met in a minute by a storm of bullets from the wood, but the lines in blue kept steadily on, as would a storm of wind and cloud moving among the tree-tops. Now we met almost whole companies of wounded, defeated men from the other division, hurrying by us, and they held up their bleeding and mangled hands to show us they had not been cowards. They had lost twelve hundred men on the spot we were about to occupy. Some of them were laughing even, and yelling at us: "Wade in and give them hell." We were wading in faster than I am telling the story.

On the edge of a low ridge we saw a solid wall of men in gray, their muskets at their shoulders blazing into our faces and their batteries of artillery roaring as if it were the end of the world. Bravely they stood there. They seemed little over a hundred yards away. There was no charging further by our line. We halted, the two lines stood still, and for over an hour we loaded our guns and killed each other as fast as we could. The firing and the noise were simply appalling. Now, I was not scared. The first shot I fired seemed to take all my fear away and gave me courage enough to calmly load my musket at the muzzle and fire it forty times. Others, with more cartridges, fired possibly oftener still. Some of the regiments in that bloody line were resupplied with cartridges from the boxes of the dead. In a moment I saw Captain Lindsey throw up his arms, spring upward and fall dead in his tracks. Corporal McCully was struck in the face by a shell. The blood covered him all over, but he kept on firing. Lieutenant Darling dropped dead, and other officers near me fell wounded.

I could not see far to left or right, the smoke of battle was covering everything. I saw bodies of our men lying near me without knowing who they were, though some of them were my messmates in the morning. The Rebels in front we could not see at all. We simply fired at their lines by guess, and occasionally the blaze of their guns showed exactly where they stood. They kept their line like a wall of fire. When I fired my first shot I had resolved to aim at somebody or something as long as I could see, and a dozen times I tried to bring down an officer I dimly saw on a gray horse before me. Pretty soon a musket ball struck me fair in the breast. "I am dead, now," I said, almost aloud. It felt as if someone had struck me with a club. I stepped back a few paces and sat down on a log to finish up with the world. Other wounded men were there, covered with blood, and some were lying by me dead. I spoke to no one. It would have been useless; thunder could scarcely have been heard at that moment. My emotions I have almost forgotten. I remember only that something said to me, "It is honorable to do so." I had not a thought of friends, or of home, or of religion. The stupendous things going on around me filled my mind. On getting my breath a little I found I was not hurt at all,—simply stunned; the obliquely-fired bullet had struck the heavy leather of my cartridge belt and glanced away. I picked up my gun, stepped back into the line of battle, and in a moment was shot through the hand. The wound did not hurt; I was too excited for that.

PRIVATE ALBERT E. QUAIFE
28TH IOWA INFANTRY, SLACK'S BRIGADE

Quaife had joined the 28th Iowa at the age of 20, serving as a fifer in the regimental band and, with his fellow musicians, as a litter bearer whenever the unit went into action. He wrote of the poignant encounter related below when he was in his fifties, concluding his account, "Almost 34 years has come and gone. . . . A few of us still survive, but the most of those who charged through those fateful woods have passed to that home where there is no more war and where no brother meets brother in deadly conflict."

The Musicians meanwhile stacking their knapsacks in rows & in a small patch of brush close to the regiment. We then reported to the Surgeons who tied a strip of white cloth around our left arms and ordered us to follow our regiment, and carry the wounded to the house. . . . As the hours passed away, the bloody work continued, and we were continually passing back and forth through the woods, carrying the poor boys on litters or blankets, as we happened to have them. It was on one of these trips, I came to a rebel lying under a tree, who called to me for a drink of water. Stopping only long enough to minister to his wants, I continued on my way. Passing the same place some time after, I heard a familiar voice say, "Al come here." Looking up I saw Wm. N. Bowen our drum Major . . . standing by the above mentioned rebel and calling me to come to him. Walking to where he stood, I told him I had given that same man a drink on my last trip and had no more time to waste on him. (our orders were to attend to the Union men first) "Well said he (with tears streaming down his cheek) waite a few minutes, this is my brother, what can we do for him." I found he was shot through the hips and very badly wounded. It was a sorrowful sight,—the brother in blue and the brother in gray, Foes to the death a few minutes before, now together weeping over their sad lot. The wounded brother was conveyed to the rebel hospital, while the loyal brother was compelled to the stern laws of war to march on. As I gazed on the trying scene, I thought—this is indeed a "Cruel War" when will it be over.

"A little further along, as we halted to give them a volley, my brother, John Henry Williams, was shot through the heart."

LIEUTENANT T. J. WILLIAMS
56TH OHIO INFANTRY, SLACK'S BRIGADE

Williams' brother was one of the regiment's 138 men lost out of 350 engaged. Years later Williams, shown here prior to his promotion, wrote about the action for an Ohio newspaper. Soon after a "grizzled veteran" approached him on the street to praise his article, adding, "I was there, but not on your side, but a member of the Virginia battery . . . that you men stormed, and one of the few that escaped."

The enemy, as was their custom, presented a stubborn resistance, and we had to fight for every foot of ground; we drove them, step by step, in our front, to a long corn field on top of the hill . . . ; across this field they fell back rapidly to the Raymond road. Here, behind a strong rail fence they poured into us a deadly fire. After entering the field a short distance, the first of our company, Henry Richards, fell, shot through the brain. A little further along, as we halted to give them a volley, my brother, John Henry Williams, was shot through the heart. He had his gun at ready, about to take aim, and as he fell in death, he pitched his musket toward the enemy; it fell with the bayonet stuck in the ground, the stock standing up. Captain Williams instantly grasped the musket and gave the enemy its load. I saw my brother fall, there being but one man between us in the front rank of the company. I stooped over him for an instant, but he never moved; the fatal ball, like an electric flash, had blotted out his young life. There was no stop. The comrade on my left had his arm shot off. Other comrades in the company were being hit, but there was no halt. Closing up ranks we pressed on. We drove them in our front to and beyond the Raymond road; our brigade captured the Virginia battery at the junction of the roads. For a short time there was no firing in our immediate front, and by permission of our Captain I returned to my brother's body, thinking it would be my only chance. I spread his rubber blanket over him, which had been folded across his shoulder, and was perforated through the several folds by the ball that took his life.

BATTLE AT CHAMPION HILLS.—COLONEL SLACK, WITH SOLDIERS OF THE VETERAN ARMY, DRIVING THE ENEMY THROUGH THE WOODS.—SKETCHED BY LIEUTENANT G. W. BAILE

357

LIEUTENANT JAMES HILL

21ST IOWA INFANTRY, LAWLER'S BRIGADE

Born in Somerset, England, Hill pursued a prewar career as a Baptist minister. His clever ruse during the closing phase of the battle won him the Medal of Honor. Hill resigned his commission after Vicksburg, returning to Cascade, Iowa, to look after his ailing wife, but then rejoined the 21st Iowa that fall as the regimental chaplain.

This drawing, sketched by a Union officer, depicts Federal reinforcements, having pushed the Confederates off the heights once and for all, pursuing them through the thick woods around the base of Champion's Hill. The scenes of carnage along the summit were so gruesome that to both armies this insignificant piece of Mississippi real estate was forever after known as the hill of death. Late in the day, with only one escape route to Vicksburg open, Pemberton's entire army was in danger of being cut off and captured. He ordered Brigadier General Lloyd Tilghman to defend the bridge over Baker's Creek at all costs.

took a pony belonging to the regiment and rode through some timber and brush in search of food, mules and horses. In following a path through the dense timber I unexpectedly rode right into the Confederate lines, and encountered three rebel pickets with their loaded rifles. I realized at once that I had gotten myself into a nasty position. Nevertheless, I did not lose my presence of mind, for as I emerged from the brush, I instantly and in the most natural manner, ordered the Johnnies to "ground arms!" They obeyed. Then slightly turning my head, I addressed an imaginary guard in the brush, with a hasty order to "halt." The under growth and brush were so heavy that the Confederates were prevented from seeing through and thus discovering the deception. I next gave the command: "Ten paces to the front, eyes to the center." Seeing my revolver in my hand ready for instant use, the three men complied with my command. I further added that if any of them turned his head to right or left I would shoot him down in his tracks. I frequently gave the order to "halt" to my imaginary guard, tending to frighten my prisoners into absolute obedience. This done, I deliberately dismounted and gathered up the three rifles, placed them against the neck of the pony, mounted, took the rifles under my arm and then gave the order to my prisoners: "Single file, march," and to my imaginary guard: "Forward, march." I hurried toward the command at good speed. Before it began to dawn upon my prisoners that I had fooled them, they found themselves within our lines. I turned them and their rifles over to Colonel Merrill who sent them to Major-General McClernand. When the prisoners saw that I had fooled them, their anger was vented in terms more strong than polite, one of them saying to me: "Lieutenant, you could never have taken us but for that devil of a body-guard we thought you had, from the way you kept halting them."

PRIVATE JAMES G. SPENCER
1ST MISSISSIPPI LIGHT ARTILLERY, MOORE'S BRIGADE

Spencer, a native of Port Gibson, fought this battle within 20 miles of his home. He survived the siege of Vicksburg and remained with his battery to the end of the war. Afterward, he returned to the family homestead and became a farmer. In 1892 Spencer was elected to the Mississippi legislature, and two years later won a seat in the U.S. House of Representatives, where he served one term. He died in 1926 and was buried in Port Gibson.

We were on the extreme right wing of the Confederate army & all morning lay in position waiting attack & listening to the terrible attack on Genl. Stevenson, who commanded our left wing & was gradually driven back towards Big Black bridge. About 3:00 P.M. the Federal force appeared in our front & Genl. Loring withdrawing his division rode up to our Battery & said to Capt. Cowan, "I intend to save my Division as I have been cut off by the defeat of Genl. Stevenson. I want your Battery to hold this position until sun down, or captured. If you suceed in holding until sun down, fall back, following my line of retreat." The Chicago Mercantile Battery had gone into position about 400 yds in our front, with 6 10 lb Parrot guns. We had 4 6 lb guns & 2 10 lb Howitsers. The Federal Battery opened on us, firing accurately. Genl. Tilghman & his staff rode up to Capt. Cowan & ordered him to open fire. The Genl. *dismounted* & said to Capt. Cowan, "I will take a shot at those fellows myself," & walked up to field piece No. 2 & sighted & ordered it fired & shell from the Federal Battery passed close to him while our gun was being reloaded. Tilghman remarked, "They are trying to spoil my new uniform." He then sighted the gun again & as he stepped back to order fire, a Parrot shell struck him in the side, nearly cutting him in twain. Just before he dismounted, he ordered his son, a boy of about 17 yrs. to go with a squad & drive some sharpshooters from a gin house on our left, who were annoying our cannoneers. The son had been gone 10 or 15 minutes on this mission before his father was killed. . . . After Tilghman was killed, we

were ordered to "fire rapidly at will" & in less than an hour it dismounted 4 Federal guns, silenced their Battery, killing nearly every horse & a great many of the men. Our Battery held our position until sun down & then limbered up & followed Loring's line of retreat, which swung around to our left away from Big Black bridge & headed towards Raymond. The Battery followed the line of retreat until 8 or 9:00 that night. When we got to Baker's Creek & could not get the guns across, Cowan ordered the guns to be spiked & thrown in the creek, & the cannoneers to mount double with the drivers on the Horses & continue the retreat. . . . Cowan & about 16 or 18 of the men detached from the column & struck out for Big Black River, which they swam that night & went on into Vicksburg & in the siege were assigned to guns on our line.

Brigadier General Lloyd Tilghman was a Maryland native and West Point graduate. His defense of the Confederate line of retreat from Champion's Hill saved the bulk of Pemberton's army but, as described by Spencer at left, cost him his life.

Major General William W. Loring commanded the right wing of Pemberton's army at Champion's Hill, where he incurred his superior's wrath by failing to attack when ordered. In the confusion of the retreat, Loring's division was cut off. Three days later, his 6,500 men—minus their artillery and supply train—linked up with Johnston's forces at Jackson and thus were spared capture at Vicksburg.

chase, scarcely any one came back without two or three prisoners and one little old Dutchman of our company by the name of Jahle came strutting back with eight. We "corralled" our prisoners, put a guard over them, and had a time of general rejoicing for the next half hour. After which we began to feel the pangs of hunger again, as we had had nothing scarcely for the last two days.

I picked out a clean looking "Reb" who had been shot down, and whose carcass lay stretched at full length on the grass, sat down beside him, and from his well filled haversack of corn bread and beef, made a sumptuous meal. When dinner was over I rolled the fellow over, unbuttoned his vest and took from the pocket thereof a copy of the New Testament, richly bound with pasteboard, and read, "If thine enemy hunger, give him to eat; if he thirst, give him to drink," etc. The poor fellow was now obeying the spirit and letter of that command; now, if never before in all his life. Little did that man think when he was so carefully preparing that haversack with 3 days rations, that a "blue-bellied yankee" would devour the contents thereof.

SERGEANT IRA BLANCHARD
20TH ILLINOIS INFANTRY, J. E. SMITH'S BRIGADE

The prisoners Blanchard mentions were among 3,839 Confederate casualties on May 16; Grant's army suffered 2,441 losses. Champion's Hill was thus the bloodiest engagement yet of the Vicksburg campaign. At the end of the day, General Hovey rode up to a handful of men gathered around the flag of his old regiment, the 24th Indiana, and asked plaintively, "Where are the rest of my boys?" A soldier pointed to the motionless blue forms littering the slope and said, "They are over there."

When we had chased them half a mile or more a halt was called, and looking round I saw we were far past the main body of the enemy, for the hill proper was yet literally coverd with them. But we had completely annihilated their left wing, and outflanked them so effectually that they made a hasty retreat from their stronghold on the hill and left us masters of the field with about 3000 prisoners.

Then the boys of our brigade brought in their prisoners from the

Lieutenant Samuel Denton, born in Ireland, was a comrade of Blanchard's in the 20th Illinois. He was wounded at Kennesaw Mountain and again at Atlanta in July 1864, where his actions later won him the Medal of Honor.

PRIVATE HENRY M. CHEAVENS

Lowe's Missouri (C.S.) Battery, Green's Brigade

Cheavens describes the action that took place on May 17 at the Big Black River, 10 miles west of Champion's Hill, as General Pemberton sought to delay Grant's advance on Vicksburg. But the overtired, disheartened Confederates were not in any condition to hold back the Federals, who were both determined and numerically superior.

We were soon ordered to our position in the entrenchments. We fixed our guns and rolled cotton bales to cover our caissons. Then a foolish thing was done, our horses were ordered off the field to the rear about 3/4 mile. We awaited until the sun was fairly on his road to the zenith when the enemy made a charge on our center, but our guns soon drove them back. Yet their shell came bounding around us, throwing dirt all around, while I was behind my cotton bale gouging spherical case. . . .

Col. Cockrell came to us . . . and said wait till you can do execution, then fire. But the Georgia Regiment on the extreme left ran, then one and then another till at last all deserted us. The Missourians were the last to leave. And Col. Gates' Regiment were mostly left behind and many were taken prisoner. Many swam Big Black. I had to go when my orders came. The field was half a mile across and you could see men flying across pursued by the Federals. Our guns, 4 in number, 2 10-pound Parrott guns, and 2 12-pound Howitzers, were left behind. All the other Missouri Batteries had to leave the guns except Landis', who got off one or two. Alack the day.

I took up my line of march as did the others. I ran some hundred and fifty yards, then thought I would prefer to walk, which I did, to the banks of the Big Black where we had a bridge across and were protected by some guns on the hill above. I picked up a gun, cartridge, and cap box, although we were under heavy fire all the time. Col. Cockrell was trying to bring his men into line. After crossing, I went to the first house, and finding a sauce pan I got a drink of water, quite refreshing after our run. I soon found some of our boys, and we went into the big road, where we found our officers and the artillery horses, one of which I mounted and soon was on my way. We soon came across some tents filled with clothing. I got a gun, coat, and pair of blankets in lieu of mine, which I had left with the guns.

We travelled on toward Vicksburg. We arrived in Vicksburg Sunday, May 17th, 1863, about 3 or 4 P.M. dispirited, weak, fatigued, and generally not in good humor.

CORPORAL EPHRAIM MCD. ANDERSON

2D Missouri (C.S.) Infantry, Cockrell's Brigade

Pemberton arrived on the battlefield just as his army was dissolving into the headlong retreat that Anderson describes below. In obvious distress at the scene before him, the Confederate commander turned to one of his staff and remarked bitterly, "Just 30 years ago I began my cadetship at the U.S. Military Academy. Today, the same date, that career is ending in disaster and disgrace." Pemberton was forced to withdraw his army the remaining 12 miles to Vicksburg itself.

The fighting was now becoming general on the inside as well as in front, and it only remained to retreat with as little loss as possible; our whole position was flanked, and we were ordered to fall back to the bridges. Many failed to reach either the pontoon or the railroad bridge, and were captured or compelled to swim the river. There were no horses to remove the artillery, and it was left behind; all the artillery of our brigade, and nearly every piece that belonged to the division, were lost.

The Federals now opened a battery from near the works and fired upon our men, as they were gathering in masses and crossing; fortunately their shot passed too high, and did no great execution. It was a long, hard run of a mile from our position at the lower extremity of the works to the bridge and a good many of the boys were unable to make it, and either swam the river, were captured, or killed in trying to get over; a considerable majority, however, succeeded in escaping. Most of the men near the bridge and the upper portion of the works made good their retreat. The whole army lost considerably, principally in prisoners; not a large number were either killed or wounded.

A line was formed on the opposite side of the river, which held the enemy in check; the railroad and pontoon bridges, and all the boats lying in the river, were set on fire and burned by the orders of our offi-cers. The pause of the army on the other side was only for a short time, and after seeing that the boats and bridges were consumed, and that there was no likelihood of the enemy's getting over immediately, the troops were withdrawn to Vicksburg.

THE BATTLE OF BLACK RIVER BRIDGE, MAY 17, 1863.—SKETCHED BY MR. THEODORE R. DAVIS.—[SEE PAGE 395.]

This sketch showing Federal troops scaling the Confederate parapets along the Big Black River was drawn by the ubiquitous Theodore Davis, correspondent for Harper's Weekly. "We had fought the battle of Champion's Hill," he wrote, "and at night lain down as tired as mortals ever are; yet the next day, finding the enemy, we, before dinner, captured his works, seventeen guns, and over two thousand prisoners."

CORPORAL OWEN J. HOPKINS

42D OHIO INFANTRY, LINDSEY'S BRIGADE

The Union success at the Big Black River, described here by Hopkins, was due mainly to Brigadier General Michael Lawler, a 250-pound Irishman whom Charles Dana labeled "as brave as a lion." Lawler had the men of his brigade fix bayonets, then led them in a charge through a knee-deep bayou and into the Confederate works. As Hopkins makes clear, the defenders had no choice but to leave their heavy equipment behind and make a run for it.

May 17th. Big Black. Sees us in motion early. By this time, the swift-flying Rebels have reached their dens at Big Black, and we will soon be stirring them with a hot stick. Stragglers from their scattered ranks are constantly being taken. Near noon, we are greeted with a volley from the Rebel 20-pounders at Big Black, it being a signal to prepare for warm work again. Our Column was soon deployed into line of battle, and the thrilling command of "Forward!" was given, and again the Rebel Batteries open with all their fury upon the ranks of our advancing line. The Fight soon became general and lasted with great Fury for six hours, when a charge was ordered, and Yelling like Demons, we went for the Rebel Breastworks, and were

greeted with one withering Storm of Grape and Canister, and the Rebels fled, leaving their Artillery Unspiked and loaded to the Muzzles with Grape-shot which we turned against them and paid them off in their own coin. The Forty-second captured the Twenty-sixth Tennessee Rebel Regiment with its colors and Officers. The Victory again is a complete one. The Rebs Fled across the Big Black, Destroying the Bridge and Firing the Railroad Bridge and Trusslework across the River. We have a Pontoon Bridge to build before we can follow.

Private Newell Fuller, shown in the tintype at right, joined the 42d Ohio in the fall of 1862 as a substitute for his father, who had been drafted. He was mustered out of the regiment not long after the surrender of Vicksburg, having completed his nine-month term of service. He kept his forage cap (above) as a souvenir.

"Colonel Lagow came dashing up and asked what was the matter. I promptly said, 'I am killed.' The Colonel presumed to doubt my word, and said, 'Move your toes'—which I did with success."

FREDERICK D. GRANT
CIVILIAN, GENERAL GRANT'S SON

The young Grant had joined his father at Bruinsburg, after running the Vicksburg batteries on a transport, and had remained at headquarters ever since. As the army pushed forward, living off the land, Fred often ate with the enlisted men—able foragers all—claiming their food was better than that in the general's tent.

The next morning we made an early start, and moved toward the Big Black River.

Our troops were now moving on the enemy's line at a double quick, and I became enthused and galloped across a cotton-field, and went over the enemy's works with our men. Following the retreating Confederates to the Big Black, I was watching some of them swim the river, when a sharpshooter on the opposite bank fired at me and hit me in the leg. The wound was slight, but very painful; Colonel Lagow came dashing up and asked what was the matter. I promptly said, "I am killed." The Colonel presumed to doubt my word, and said, "Move your toes"— which I did with success. He then recommended our hasty retreat.

MAJOR GENERAL WILLIAM T. SHERMAN
COMMANDER, XV CORPS, ARMY OF THE TENNESSEE

With the Federal crossing of the Big Black, the goal that had eluded Sherman and Grant for the last seven months was finally within reach: Vicksburg was isolated with no hope of relief. As the two commanders hurried toward the city, Sherman confessed to his friend that, up to this point, he had been dubious of Grant's overall strategy. "This, however," he acknowledged in homage to Grant's generalship, "was the end of one of the greatest campaigns in history."

We pushed on, and reached the Big Black early, Blair's troops having preceded us by an hour or so. I found General Blair in person, and he reported that there was no bridge across the Big Black; that it was swimming-deep; and that there was a rebel force on the opposite side, intrenched. He had ordered a detachment of the Thirteenth United States Regulars, under Captain Charles Ewing, to strip some artillery-horses, mount the men, and swim the river above the ferry, to attack and drive away the party on the opposite bank. I did not approve of this risky attempt, but crept down close to the brink of the river-bank, behind a corn-crib belonging to a plantation-house near by, and saw the parapet on the opposite bank. Ordering a section of guns to be brought forward by hand behind this corn-crib, a few well-directed shells brought out of their holes the little party that was covering the crossing, viz., a lieutenant and ten men, who came down to the river-bank and surrendered. Blair's pontoon-train was brought up, consisting of India-rubber boats, one of which was inflated, used as a boat, and brought over the prisoners. A pontoon-bridge was at once begun, finished by night, and the troops began the passage.

In a single night Federal engineers laid four floating bridges across the Big Black River, one of which is shown in the photograph below, to speed the army's passage to Vicksburg. They first inflated a string of India rubber pontoons with hand bellows (inset), then roped them securely in place to span the stream. Finally, wooden planking was lashed atop the pontoons, and the bridge was ready to carry troops, wagons, and artillery safely across the river.

"This may have been war, but to us of the rank and file it seemed somewhat deficient of common sense."

CAPTAIN JAMES H. JONES
38TH MISSISSIPPI INFANTRY, HÉBERT'S BRIGADE

Jones' comments reflected the widespread skepticism among the common soldiers regarding their commanding general. "The men learned to trust and to follow certain officers with blind confidence; while they distrusted others, often with disastrous consequences. I doubt if the soldiers of Lee and of Jackson ever entered into a battle with a thought of defeat; I doubt if the soldiers of Pemberton ever entered into one with a hope of success."

The battle of Big Black Bridge may have been planned accordingly to the most approved military rule, so far as I know, but we of the rank and file could not understand why a beaten and retreating army, more or less demoralized and facing heavy odds, should have taken position in a level plain, with a deep stream in the rear, and only a pontoon and a trestle bridge as a means of escape in case of further disaster. It was not surprising that some of the rank and file should have deemed it wise to withdraw to the other side of that stream while the way was yet open, and that the others should have followed after upon the first assault, leaving many guns and prisoners in the hands of the enemy. This may have been war, but to us of the rank and file it seemed somewhat deficient of common sense.

EMMA BALFOUR
RESIDENT OF VICKSBURG

The ragged soldiers that Mrs. Balfour describes were in no shape to hold off Grant's army. Fortunately for Pemberton, he still had 10,000 unbloodied troops available. As they marched out to bolster the city's defenses, another resident wrote, "The men, who were fresh and lively, swung their hats, and promised to die for the ladies— never to run—never to retreat."

I hope never to witness again such a scene as the return of our routed army. From twelve o'clock until late in the night the streets and roads were *jammed* with wagons, cannons, horses, men, mules, stock, sheep, everything you can imagine that appertains to an army—being brought hurriedly within the intrenchment. Nothing like order prevailed, of course, as divisions, brigades and regiments were broken and separated. As the poor fellows passed every house poured forth all it had to refresh them. . . . There were some visitors carrying buckets of water to the corner for the men. Then in the back gallery I had everything that was eatable put out—and fed as many as I could. Poor fellows, it made my heart ache to see them, for I knew from all I saw and heard that it was want of confidence in the General commanding that was the cause of our disaster. I cannot write more—but oh! there will be a fearful reckoning somewhere. This has been brooding, growing and many fears have been felt for the result. Gen. Pemberton has not the confidence of officers, people or men judging from all I am compelled to see and hear. I would rather not have heard if I could have helped it.

The Bloody, Bitter Siege

Marching into the outskirts of Vicksburg, Grant's troops, fresh from their string of victories farther east, found themselves facing the most formidable obstacle yet—a nine-mile-long arc of redoubts and log-reinforced trenches built by the Confederates on the steep hills east of the city. Worse, these defenses bristled with cannon and the rifles of 22,000 Rebel troops—the 12,000 or so that had managed to retreat from Champion's Hill plus two divisions of infantry that Pemberton had left in the city as a garrison force.

Despite the menacing earthworks, Grant—convinced that Confederate morale had been shattered—decided to attack immediately, sending his troops swarming forward at 2:00 p.m. on May 19. In minutes McClernand's and McPherson's troops had been blasted back by deadly Confederate fire. Sherman's XV Corps, assaulting the northeast corner of

....

Troops of the 22d Iowa Infantry attack one of Vicksburg's ring of formidable defensive posts, the Railroad Redoubt, on May 22. Heavy Union losses suffered in two failed assaults convinced Grant that his only hope for victory was a protracted siege.

the city's defenses, initially made some progress when troops of Colonel Giles A. Smith's brigade gained a ditch north of a strongpoint called the Stockade Redan. But they were soon pinned down by sheets of rifle fire, escaping only after dark. In the futile assaults, the Federals lost 942 men. "This is a death struggle," General Sherman wrote his wife, "and will be terrible."

Hoping to avoid a long, grinding siege, Grant tried again on May 22, this time preparing for the assault with a thunderous, hours-long bombardment, his own 200 field guns joined by Admiral Porter's mortar barges lobbing huge 200-pound shells from the river. At 10:00 a.m. precisely the guns fell silent and the infantry charged, aiming for salients in the enemy line. "Suddenly there seemed to spring almost from the bowels of the earth dense masses of Federal troops," recalled Confederate general Stephen D. Lee, the men rushing "forward at a run with bayonets fixed."

But the bombardment had merely churned the earth. Once the shelling had stopped, the Confederate riflemen let the Union troops get close, then "deliberately rose and stood in their trenches," Lee later wrote, "pouring volley after volley into the advancing enemy."

In minutes Federal dead were piled in windrows on the steep slopes leading to the enemy positions. Worst hit were the troops of General Michael K. Lawler's brigade of McClernand's corps, who attacked the Railroad Redoubt just south of the Southern Mississippi tracks. "It was a tornado of iron on our left, a hurricane of shot on our right," recalled one officer. "We passed through the mouth of hell. Every third man fell, either killed or wounded." A few survivors reached the redoubt but were then hurled back by the counterattacking 30th Alabama.

The fighting was just as ferocious to the north, where other XIII Corps troops assailed a lunette held by the 2d Texas. McPherson's attackers and Sherman's were also hammered back with heavy losses. By late morning Grant could see the attack was doomed—but ordered more assaults to support McClernand who, eager as always for glory, reported his men had captured two enemy strongpoints. This claim proved false, and the renewed attacks also failed, swelling the casualty lists and making May 22 the bloodiest day of the campaign, with 502 Union dead and almost 2,700 wounded or missing. Grant, glumly sitting his horse and whittling a piece of wood, was

heard to mutter, "We'll have to dig our way in."

Dig the troops did, first cutting a road north to the landings on the Yazoo River. Soon flotillas of steamboats were unloading huge quantities of food, ammunition, and other supplies floated down the Mississippi. Arriving, too, were a pair of fresh divisions, swelling Grant's force to about 70,000 men and tightening the ring around the city until, as one Confederate noted, "a cat could not have crept out of Vicksburg without being discovered."

Reconciled now to a siege—he would, he said, "outcamp the enemy"—Grant nevertheless kept pressure on the Confederate defenders, bombarding the Rebel works day and night. He also ordered his troops to dig interlocking systems of zigzag trenches within yards of the enemy redans. "The soldiers got so they bored like gophers and beavers," one said, "with a spade in one hand and a gun in the other."

Before long the opposing lines were so close together that the men could easily call back and forth, shouting jokes and insults. In time, in this strange brother-against-brother war, the troops began visiting each other's trenches in the evenings, chatting amiably,

playing cards, and trading coffee and tobacco.

As Grant's cannon and Porter's boats fired away at the Rebel entrenchments, hundreds of errant shells inevitably shrieked into the city and struck with deafening, nerve-shattering explosions. Many of the town's inhabitants quickly decided that their houses were death-traps and began digging burrows into the substrata of yellow clay. Eventually about 500 caves honeycombed the hillsides, turning the place, Federal troops said, into "Prairie Dog Village."

Many of the caves were simply small bombproofs. Others were large and even luxurious warrens furnished with beds and tables and rugs covering the dirt floors. Rounds often smashed into the underground refuges, but miraculously only about a dozen civilians were known to have been killed and three dozen injured in weeks of shelling.

Almost worse than the shelling was the hunger. By mid-June most of the supplies collected on General Pemberton's orders had been exhausted, and the people were reduced to eating a repellent gruel made of ground peas and horse meat or, for those who could stand it, grilled mule. The soldiers' daily ration was reduced and reduced again

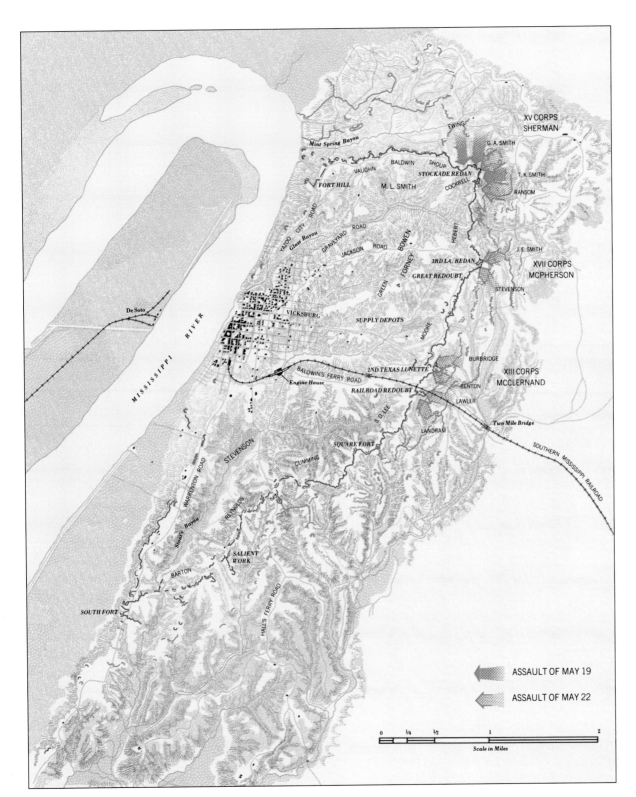

XV CORPS
SHERMAN

EWING

G. A. SMITH

Mint Spring Bayou

BALDWIN   SHOUP

VAUGHN

STOCKADE REDAN

T. K. SMITH

FORT HILL

M. L. SMITH

COCKRELL

RANSOM

Yazoo City Road

Glass Bayou

GRAVEYARD ROAD

JACKSON   ROAD

HEBERT

BOWEN

FORNEY

3RD LA. REDAN

J. E. SMITH

XVII CORPS
MCPHERSON

GREAT REDOUBT

GREEN

STEVENSON

De Soto

VICKSBURG

SUPPLY DEPOTS

MOORE

MISSISSIPPI RIVER

BURBRIDGE

2ND TEXAS LUNETTE

Baldwin's Ferry Road

Engine House

BENTON

XIII CORPS
MCCLERNAND

RAILROAD REDOUBT

LAWLER

S. D. LEE

Two Mile Bridge

LANDRAM

SQUARE FORT

SOUTHERN MISSISSIPPI RAILROAD

STEVENSON

CUMMING

Warrenton Road

Stout's Bayou

REYNOLDS

SALIENT WORK

Hall's Ferry Road

BARTON

SOUTH FORT

ASSAULT OF MAY 19

ASSAULT OF MAY 22

0   ¼   ½   1   2

Scale in Miles

Grant's army faced a powerful line of fortifications on Vicksburg's perimeter, but in the push-ahead style for which he would become famous, he tried to pound through it. Only after attacks were bloodily repulsed on May 19 and again on May 22 did he finally decide to settle in for a siege. Even at that, however, he wasn't quite willing to give up on trying to carry the city by assault. On June 25 the Federals detonated a mine beneath the Jackson road defenses, and troops charged into the resulting crater but were trapped there and had to withdraw at night with heavy losses. The siege resumed in earnest, and Vicksburg surrendered on July 4 after 47 days of shelling and near starvation.

until it consisted of one biscuit a day with a few scraps of stringy or rancid bacon.

The people of Vicksburg were buoyed through the ordeal, however, by the belief that a relief column was on the way. General Johnston, now back at Jackson, was said to be gathering an army of 30,000 or more men for a thrust westward. To meet the reported threat to his rear, Grant withdrew a division from each of his corps and, putting Sherman in command, formed what he called "a second line of defense facing the other way."

In fact, the cautious Johnston balked at moving. He had too few men, he complained when the Confederate high command tried to urge him on, and not enough equipment, supplies, or wagons. When at last he got in motion in early July, heading for the Big Black River, it would be too late to save Vicksburg.

Spurred to hasten the end of the siege, Grant in late June decided to try mining an enemy strongpoint or two and issued a call for all soldiers who had worked in coal mines before the war. Within days the 35 miners who showed up had completed a tunnel under a Rebel position called the Great Redoubt, north of the Jackson road, and packed it with 2,200 pounds of gunpowder.

The explosion blasted out a deep, smoking crater 50 feet across but killed fewer men than expected, as the redoubt's Louisiana and Mississippi defenders had heard the digging and fallen back to a new line. There they waited until the Federals of General Mortimer D. Leggett's brigade of John Logan's division stormed into the crater—to be hit, one recalled, with "a terrible volley of musketry" from the hidden Confederates, then raked with canister from Rebel batteries. So murderous was the fire that General Logan cried out, "My God, they are killing my bravest men in that hole." At last, after three days of struggle, the Yankees retired, leaving behind 200 casualties.

Hoping for better results, Grant ordered another, larger mine exploded on July 1. This one did worse damage to the Rebel trenches and took a heavier toll in men. But Union officers, now more cautious, decided not to follow up and run the risk of another bloody repulse.

In any case, the siege was showing signs of achieving its purpose. The Confederate troops, and Vicksburg's citizens, were increasingly exhausted and hungry. With starvation looming, Pemberton on July 1 asked his division commanders whether they thought that

a breakout was possible. All four replied that their ragged, hollow-eyed troops, who had been cramped in rifle pits for week after week, were too sick and worn down to try. Finally, on July 3 Pemberton sent a message to Grant, carried under a flag of truce by General Bowen—who was himself dying of dysentery. It proposed an armistice to prevent "the further effusion of blood."

Grant's reply was predictably unyielding: a demand for unconditional surrender. But at a meeting with Pemberton later that day Grant softened his terms, agreeing to parole the Confederate troops if they signed an oath not to fight again until Federal captives were freed in exchange.

It was a pragmatic decision. "Had I insisted upon unconditional surrender," Grant later wrote, "there would have been over 30,000 men to transport to Cairo, very much to the inconvenience of the army on the Mississippi." He also figured that, in any case, many of Vicksburg's defenders would be too war weary and disheartened to fight again. Pemberton accepted the terms, and the 47-day siege came to an end—on the same day, in a malign omen for the Confederacy, as the defeat of Robert E. Lee's army at Gettysburg.

ORDER OF BATTLE

ARMY OF THE TENNESSEE (Federal)

Grant 70,000 men

IX Corps Parke

1st Division Welsh	2d Division Potter
Bowman's Brigade	*Griffin's Brigade*
Leasure's Brigade	*Ferrero's Brigade*
	Christ's Brigade

XIII Corps McClernand/Ord

9th Division Osterhaus	10th Division A. J. Smith	12th Division Hovey	14th Division Carr
A. L. Lee's Brigade	*Burbridge's Brigade*	*McGinnis' Brigade*	*Benton's Brigade*
Lindsey's Brigade	*Landram's Brigade*	*Slack's Brigade*	*Lawler's Brigade*

XV Corps Sherman

1st Division Steele	2d Division Blair	3d Division Tuttle
Manter's Brigade	*G. A. Smith's Brigade*	*Buckland's Brigade*
Woods' Brigade	*T. K. Smith's Brigade*	*Mower's Brigade*
Thayer's Brigade	*Ewing's Brigade*	*Matthies' Brigade*

XVI Corps Washburn

1st Division W. S. Smith	4th Division Lauman	Provisional Division Kimball
Loomis' Brigade	*Pugh's Brigade*	*Engelman's Brigade*
Hicks' Brigade	*Hall's Brigade*	*Richmond's Brigade*
Cockerill's Brigade	*Bryant's Brigade*	*Montgomery's Brigade*
Sanford's Brigade		

XVII Corps McPherson

3d Division Logan	6th Division McArthur	7th Division Quinby	Herron's Division
J. E. Smith's Brigade	*Reid's Brigade*	*Sandborn's Brigade*	*Vandever's Brigade*
Leggett's Brigade	*Ransom's Brigade*	*Holmes' Brigade*	*Orme's Brigade*
J. D. Stevenson's Brigade	*Hall's Brigade*	*Boomer's Brigade*	

ARMY OF VICKSBURG (Confederate)

Pemberton 20,400 men

C. L. Stevenson's Division	Forney's Division	M. L. Smith's Division	Bowen's Division
Barton's Brigade	*Hébert's Brigade*	*Baldwin's Brigade*	*Cockrell's Brigade*
Cumming's Brigade	*Moore's Brigade*	*Shoup's Brigade*	*Dockery's Brigade*
S. D. Lee's Brigade		*Vaughn's Brigade*	
Reynolds' Brigade			
Waul's Texas Legion			

ARMY OF TENNESSEE (Confederate)

Johnston 29,300 men

Breckinridge's Division	French's Division	Loring's Division	Walker's Division
D. W. Adams' Brigade	*McNair's Brigade*	*J. A. Adams' Brigade*	*Ector's Brigade*
Helm's Brigade	*Maxey's Brigade*	*Buford's Brigade*	*Gregg's Brigade*
Stovall's Brigade	*Evans' Brigade*	*Featherston's Brigade*	*Gist's Brigade*
			Wilson's Brigade

"Bullets came thick and fast, shells hissed and screamed through the air, cannon roared, the dead and dying were brought into the old home. War, terrible war, had come to our very hearthstone."

ALICE SHIRLEY
RESIDENT OF WEXFORD LODGE

Despite the hardships visited upon her family as a result of the presence of Federal troops around her home during the siege of Vicksburg, Shirley maintained her Union sympathies and later married a Federal officer named John Eaton. She died on June 5, 1927, and was laid to rest next to her husband in Arlington National Cemetery.

The Confederates, knowing that they must soon retreat behind their fortifications at Vicksburg, began their preparations by destroying what they could outside, and burned all the houses in the vicinity; but my mother's persistent refusal to go out of hers, and her determination to prevent its destruction, delayed its being set on fire until the Federals made their appearance on the hills to the east of us. The poor fellow who was appointed to do the work, while holding the ball of blazing cotton to the corner of the house, was struck by a bullet of the pursuing vanguard, and crept away under the shelter of some planks, where he died alone. His body was found the next day and was buried under the corner of the house.

My mother and the old home were greeted with a shower of bullets and shell from the advancing army. One shot passed her as she stood in an open doorway. A piece of shell struck the top of a chimney and tore it away, and passing into an upper room, shattered a bedstead. She thought rapidly; the thing to be done was to hang out a flag of truce, and quickly she secured a sheet to a broom handle, and sending it by our carriage driver to the upper front porch where it might be seen from a distance, it was soon waving a truce to the bullets.

The first officers rushed in half expecting to find Confederates hidden away ready to betray them, and were not easily persuaded to believe that we were Union people, and my mother had some talking to do.

Now all was confusion and excitement. The great hosts advanced rapidly, and the house, the grounds, the road, and the woods behind were soon alive with Union soldiers, and that same afternoon the fighting began. Bullets came thick and fast, shells hissed and screamed through the air, cannon roared, the dead and dying were brought into the old home. War, terrible war, had come to our very hearthstone, and here my mother and brother remained for three days. The two house servants stayed by them. Household treasures were soon destroyed under the ruthless hand of the soldier. Daguerreotypes prized so highly by the family, letters, valuable papers, etc., etc., quickly disappeared. A dinner set of beautiful china which had been packed away in a box for safe keeping, was taken out, piece by piece, and smashed. Mother saved out of the set a teapot and several plates. . . . Choice books were carried off, furniture was destroyed, but through the kindness of some officers our trunks and the best of our furniture were saved; among these were the piano and melodeon.

With my books sent home from Clinton was a diary that I had kept for several years; and this, I suppose, was read by many a soldier, much to my mortification at that time; but it removed all doubts of our Unionism, for I had given there the truth about our sentiments.

Shortly after the siege began, the beautiful grounds and gardens of Wexford Lodge, also known as the Shirley House or White House, which had kept the Shirley family "bountifully supplied with vegetables and small fruits and a row of peanut hills," were destroyed by the spades of Union troops as they constructed bombproofs to protect themselves from Confederate artillery fire. In this photo the dugouts of the 45th Illinois Infantry can be seen covering the slope beneath the battered house.

CAPTAIN J. J. KELLOGG
113TH ILLINOIS INFANTRY, G. A. SMITH'S BRIGADE

Eager to take Vicksburg and hopeful that Pemberton's army was suffering from low morale, Grant quickly ordered a series of infantry assaults against the Confederate defenses on May 19. The pragmatic Union commander directed the heaviest of these charges to fall against the Stockade Redan, as it was located in a corner of the Rebel line and thus was vulnerable to attack from two directions at once. Kellogg describes the prelude to the assault.

Some time before daylight on the morning of the 19th we were quietly aroused and instructed to prepare our breakfasts without noise or unnecessary fire or light. Every man of my company proceeded, by the aid of twigs and dry leaves, to make just fire enough on the protected slope of the hill, to boil his tin cup of coffee and broil a slice of diaphragm um et swinum for the morning meal. We did not at first know what the program for the day was, but before we had dispatched our breakfast it was whispered to us by those who claimed to have access to headquarters that we were scheduled to charge the enemy's works in the early morning. I hadn't had a good view of the Vicksburg fortifications the day before, and now in the first faint light of the morning, while the men were eating and making preparations for the charge, I crept cautiously out on the crest of the hill, and so far as I could without exposing myself, contemplated the defenses against which we had to charge. Three strong bastioned forts on the right, center and left on high grounds within a line of entrenchments and stockades confronted us. It required but a brief inspection to satisfy me that more than likely we wouldn't go into town that day. I confess that my observations did not in any great measure increase my confidence in our ability to take the place by assault. When I returned to my company I saw many of the boys entrusting their valuables with hasty instructions to the few lame and sick ones, who must needs stay behind and care for the company effects while we were gone. I felt like turning over my stuff also, but happened to recollect I had no valuables. From the outlook I was satisfied very many of us would not answer to roll call that night, and I felt that I might be one of the silent ones. A more beautiful May morning than that of the 19th I had never seen. The pickets had ceased firing, the birds sang sweetly in the trees, and the cool morning breeze was fragrant with the perfume of flowers and shrubs. It was hard to believe that such a beautiful morning as that would bring such an eve as followed it.

CHAPLAIN WILLIAM L. FOSTER
35TH MISSISSIPPI INFANTRY, MOORE'S BRIGADE

Although Foster feared that his comrades, "dispirited by continual retreating," might not withstand a determined Yankee attack, the deadly fire of Moore's brigade broke up the dense Union ranks. Meanwhile, to the north, Confederate defenders were hammering Sherman's columns. Although Foster survived the carnage of the war to continue preaching the gospel in civilian life, he died of unknown causes in 1869, when he was just 39 years old.

Under cover of a heavy artillery fire they wind through the valleys until they come in a short distance of our works. In perfect order they form in a solid body, six deep. They begin their advance. They think of their late successes & on they rush with flying banners & glittering arms. Their numerous sharpshooters cover their advance. On they come. Our cannon pours forth the deadly grape into their ranks. They fill up the vacant gaps, without pausing a moment. They come now in startling proximity to our works. Not a musket yet has been fired by our men. They have received orders to wait until they can see the white of their eyes. Not a single head is seen above the works—except now & then a solitary sentinel, who stands ready to give the fatal signal. They come now in seventy yards of our lines. Now a thousand heads rise above. Above the earthworks, a thousand deadly guns are aimed & the whole lines are lighted up with a continuous flash of firearms & every hill seems to be a burning, smoking volcano. The enemies solid columns reel & totter before the galling fire—like grass before the moving scythe they fall. For a while they pause & tremble before this deadly storm of death, & then in confusion & dismay they fall back, behind the hills. They again rally & make another attempt. As before our men reserve their fire. But when they reach the fatal line the same murderous fire is poured into their bosoms—The same deadly tempest hurls them back—defeated, scattered & in utter disorder. Our Reserve reached the assaulted point in time—but their service was not required. The musketry during this charge was most furious. After the enemy retired & the smoke had been dissipated, an awful scene was spread before the eyes of our brave men. The hillside was strewn with the dead & dying. Some had fallen just in front of our works. Two stands of colors were lying in thirty steps of our ditches. There the colors lay while the brave standard bearer lies close by, cold in death. Bravely did the enemy charge & bravely were they repulsed.

During the attack upon the Stockade Redan, young Orion Howe of the 55th Illinois Infantry and his fellow musicians were given the task of retrieving ammunition from dead and wounded comrades and from ordnance wagons at the rear. After several trips through a "hailstorm" of Confederate fire, the lad was ordered to the rear to stay by his regimental commander, Colonel Oscar Malmborg, shown here with Howe. The colonel also implored him to have more ammunition sent forward. Struck in the thigh by a Minié ball on his run to safety, the youngster, reduced to a hobble, chanced upon General Sherman, whom he begged to "send some cartridges to Colonel Malmborg . . . right away!" Sherman complied, but not before ordering Howe to the hospital. Though primarily a drummer, Howe also played the fifes pictured here. He later received the Medal of Honor for his deeds.

"I Feel it my painful duty to write to you on this occasion with the sad inteligence of the Death of one of our bravest Boys your Son."

PRIVATE LEWIS LOVE
4TH WEST VIRGINIA INFANTRY, EWING'S BRIGADE

This simple note, hastily scrawled by Love as he hunkered down in a dirty trench on May 26—and representative of many such letters written during the campaign—irrevocably changed the Fog family's world. It brought them the devastating news of their son's fate. Clarkson Fog died in the attack on the Stockade Redan, where the 4th West Virginia suffered 137 casualties in a futile assault—more than half of the losses incurred by the entire brigade.

Near Vicksburg May 26/63
Mr Thomas P Fog
Dear Sir

I Feel it my painful duty to write to you on this occasion with the sad inteligence of the Death of one of our bravest Boys your Son. He was killed on the 19th while making one of the most galant charges of the war. in honor to him I must say that he died at his post many of our brave Boys fell by his side our loss is very great upwards of 150 killed and wounded

our regiment is laying with in one hundred yards of the enemies works and while I write the balls are whistling over my head The enemy is surrounded they can not get out without breaking our lines which will be hard to do Nothing more of importance to communicate I remain your obt Servant

Lewis Love
Co A 4th WVI

Though a native of Salem Center, Ohio, located near the Buckeye State's eastern border, Clarkson Fog had traveled to West Virginia to enlist—perhaps so he could go into the army with friends. His death at age 21 ended his promising career as a reporter for several newspapers in Cincinnati.

MAJOR GENERAL ULYSSES S. GRANT
COMMANDER, ARMY OF THE TENNESSEE

During his army's arduous campaign to reach the eastern, or "rear," approaches to Vicksburg, Grant had ordered the troops to cut loose from their supply trains and live off the land. Under these circumstances, one of his first priorities following the attacks of May 19 was to open supply lines through the Yazoo Pass to the north. While seeing to this urgent task, however, he made sure that his men kept inching their earthworks closer to Vicksburg's defensive positions.

The 20th and 21st were spent in strengthening our position and in making roads in rear of the army, from Yazoo River or Chickasaw Bayou. Most of the army had now been for three weeks with only five days' rations issued by the commissary. They had an abundance of food, however, but began to feel the want of bread. I remember that in passing around to the left of the line on the 21st, a soldier, recognizing me, said in rather a low voice, but yet so that I heard him, "Hard tack." In a moment the cry was taken up all along the line, "Hard tack! Hard tack!" I told the men nearest to me that we had been engaged ever since the arrival of the troops in building a road over which to supply them with everything they needed. The cry was instantly changed to cheers. By the night of the 21st all the troops had full rations issued to them. The bread and coffee were highly appreciated. . . .

The work to be done, to make our position as strong against the enemy as his was against us, was very great. The problem was also complicated by our wanting our line as near that of the enemy as possible. We had but four engineer officers with us. Captain Prime, of the Engineer Corps, was the chief, and the work at the beginning was mainly directed by him. His health soon gave out, when he was succeeded by Captain Comstock, also of the Engineer Corps. To provide assistants on such a long line I directed that all officers who had graduated at West Point, where they had necessarily to study military engineering, should in addition to their other duties assist in the work.

The chief quartermaster and the chief commissary were graduates. The chief commissary . . . begged off, however, saying that there was nothing in engineering that he was good for unless he would do for a sap-roller. As soldiers require rations while working in the ditches as well as when marching and fighting, and as we would be sure to lose him if he was used as a sap-roller, I let him off. The general is a large man; weighs two hundred and twenty pounds, and is not tall.

CAPTAIN PATRICK H. WHITE
CHICAGO MERCANTILE BATTERY, A. J. SMITH'S DIVISION

On May 22 Grant ordered another series of attacks. This time, however, the onslaught was preceded by a massive artillery bombardment. White claimed that by the end of the day one gun "was as hot as a live coal." He and five of his men won the Medal of Honor for their role in the attack.

The morning of May 22d, at 10 A.M., was set for the grand assault. At 3 o'clock A.M. the cannonading began from the land side. Every available gun was brought to bear on the works. The bombardment this day was the most terrible during the siege and continued without intermission until nearly 11 o'clock, while our sharpshooters kept up such a galling fire that the rebel cannoneers could seldom rise to load their pieces.

The artillery of McClernand's Thirteenth Corps had succeeded in breaching several points of the enemy's works, silencing five or six guns and exploding four caissons, and at 10 o'clock the column moved to the assault. About twelve o'clock I received a note from General Smith to bring two guns down the ravine, to go up to the breastworks and hammer down a fort. The general concluded his note with: "We shall be inside the rebel works in half an hour."

In order to ascertain the nature of the ground, I went up the gully to the fort and discovered a lunette in their works on the Balding's Ferry Road, with a twenty-four pounder covering that approach. On the top of the fort they had piled cotton bales. In building this fort they covered half of the road with earth, so there was space enough for only one gun. I got a detail from the Eighty-third Indiana Infantry, and with ropes we dragged one gun up to within a few feet of the breastworks by hand, the infantry carrying the ammunition in their arms. We used shrapnel, with fuses cut so close that the shells exploded almost as soon as they left the gun. The first discharge was simultaneous with that of the enemy, striking their gun in the muzzle and scattering death among their gunners. I never saw a gun loaded and fired so fast. Every man was at his best. They did not take much care in sponging, and once or twice the gun was prematurely discharged. We disabled the enemy's gun and set the cotton bales on fire, and they abandoned the fort for twenty minutes, thinking it was undermined. That was the time for our infantry to pass in, but we did not know it then. The rebels returned and threw water on the cotton bales, but our guns blew the latter to pieces. An Irishman of the Eighty-third called out: "Be gad, captain, there's not a pound of them left. I'll go and get you another load of ammunition." As he stepped off the road to go down the gully, a shot from the Seventeenth Ohio Battery cut off his right arm.

> "The rebels for a moment stood on the top of their rifle pits, pouring their deadly shot into us. Then was our sharpshooter's opportunity, and well they made use of it."

LIEUTENANT SAMUEL C. JONES

22D IOWA INFANTRY, LAWLER'S BRIGADE

A 24-year-old farmer from Iowa City, Jones, who was the only commissioned officer present in Company A for the regiment's attack on the Railroad Redoubt, commanded the company in the action. He came through unscathed, even though the 22d sustained a "loss of 164 killed, wounded, and missing" in the action.

men required action. Inaction under incessant fire demoralizes. Hundreds of guns and mortars opened their mouths and belched forth flame and missiles of death. For an hour or more the chasing shot and shell from both sides passed over us (as if we were not known to be there) with all their weird noises, hisses, and shrieks. About 10:15, our army arose at once as if by magic out of the ground. Then commenced the ordeal. The Regiment on a charge started for the Fort. At once the Confederates opened with grape and canister, plowing gaps through our ranks. Steadily, we pushed on up the slope into the ditch and over the parapet, placed the flag on the fort, and kept it there for some time. Thirteen prisoners were taken out of the fort, only a few of our boys got into the fort and they had to come out of it, and remained in the ditch outside. By this time the Confederates that fled or were driven away returned with re-enforcements, so we now had to protect ourselves the best we could. That was done by all kinds of devices. In the open we dug holes for our bodies in the ground, or in the wall of the ditch with our bayonets, or maybe a friendly stump protected us. As the Regiment moved forward, it was met with a torrent of shot and shell and minnie balls. The rebels for a moment stood on the top of their rifle pits, pouring their deadly shot into us. Then was our sharpshooter's opportunity, and well they made use of it. Many of the Confederates paid with their lives for their foolhardiness. The noise of battle was fearfully awful, with shrieking shot, exploding shells, and the groans of the wounded and dying. Missiles of all kinds, dust and powder-smoke filled the air. This state of things continued for hours, then quieted down. About three o'clock reenforcements were sent, and an attempt was made to follow up our victory, but it proved useless. By that time the few left of our Regiment had secured partial safety till darkness would assist us to fall back to the rear.

*M*ay 22nd finds us in line of battle along the edge of the ravine under the fort. We were awakened before day and moved a little to the left of where we were. Orders are given in a whisper. Company "A" . . . was ordered to the left, and deployed as sharpshooters. Company "B" . . . was ordered to the right with the same orders. The bugs and beetles, only, are allowed to make a noise. About 9 a.m., cannonading commenced all around our line simultaneously. The Confederates replied, but not vigorously. They knew this was a prelude to something more desperate and only fired when the

PRIVATE CHARLES I. EVANS
2D INFANTRY BATTALION, WAUL'S TEXAS LEGION

During the assault of Brigadier General William P. Benton's brigade on May 22, the bravery of Illinois colorbearer Thomas H. Higgins so impressed Evans and his fellow Texans that they refused to shoot the gallant Yankee. After the war, veterans of Waul's Legion successfully petitioned the Federal government for recognition for their ex-foe's deed. Higgins was eventually awarded the Medal of Honor.

After a most terrific cannonading of two hours, during which the very earth rocked and pulsated like a thing of life, the head of the charging column appeared above the brow of the hill, about 100 yards in front of the breast works, and, as line after line of blue came in sight over the hill, it presented the grandest spectacle the eye of a soldier ever beheld. The Texans were prepared to meet it however, for, in addition to our Springfield rifles, each man was provided with five additional smooth-bore muskets, charged with buck and ball.

When the first line was within fifty paces of the works, the order to fire ran along the trenches, and was responded to as from one gun. As fast as practiced hands could gather them up, one after another, the muskets were brought to bear. The blue lines vanished amid fearful slaughter. There was a cessation in the firing. And behold, through the pall of smoke which enshrouded the field, a Union flag could be seen approaching.

As the smoke was slightly lifted by the gentle May breeze, one lone soldier advanced, bravely bearing the flag towards the breast works. At least a hundred men took deliberate aim at him, and fired at point-blank range, but he never faltered. Stumbling over the bodies of his fallen comrades, he continued to advance. Suddenly, as if with one impulse, every Confederate soldier within sight of the Union color bearer seemed to be seized with the idea that the man ought not to be shot down like a dog. A hundred men dropped their guns at the same time; each of them seized his nearest neighbor by the arm and yelled to him: "Don't shoot at that man again. He is too brave to be killed that way." when he instantly discovered that his neighbor was yelling the same thing at him. As soon as they all understood one another, a hundred old hats and caps went up into the air, their wearers yelling at the top of their voices: "Come on, you brave Yank, come on!" He did come, and was taken by the hand and pulled over the breast works, and when it was discovered that he was not even scratched, a hundred Texans wrung his hands and congratulated him upon his miraculous escape from death. That man's name was Thomas J. Higgins, color bearer of the Ninety-ninth Illinois.

S. G. Van Anda
Lt Col 21st Iowa Vol

MAJOR SALUE VAN ANDA
21ST IOWA INFANTRY, LAWLER'S BRIGADE

Van Anda and the 21st followed the 22d Iowa during the rush on the Railroad Redoubt. Like their fellow Hawkeyes, they paid a dear price for their efforts in this "terrible charge" into the curtain of Rebel fire. On July 29 Van Anda was promoted to lieutenant colonel, taking the place of the slain Cornelius W. Dunlap. The Iowa attorney served through the rest of the conflict at this rank, mustering out in 1865 and returning to his legal practice.

The Twenty-first Regiment received orders to be ready to charge on the enemy's works at 10 a.m. At the hour precisely, I formed the regiment in the rear of the gallant Twenty-second Iowa, within 20 rods of the enemy's rifle-pits. In this position we were partially covered from the enemy's fire by the hill immediately in front of their works. I then gave orders to fix bayonets, and charge by the left flank over the hill and into the enemy's rifle-pits. During this charge, the fire of the enemy from both flanks, as well as the front, was terrific. Many of our officers and men fell on every side, but with a determination that knew no fear, the enemy's works were gained and they were routed from their stronghold. This position we held till after dark, pouring continually a destructive fire into their ranks. Being unable to hold our position longer, we withdrew under cover of darkness, carrying with us many of our killed and wounded. The loss of our regiment in this terrible struggle was severe; many of our officers were either killed or wounded. . . .

Lieut. Col. C. W. Dunlap was shot through the head and instantly killed. He was wounded at the battle of Port Gibson and was unable to keep up with the regiment, but came up after the charge. In the death of this brave soldier and gallant officer the regiment has sustained an irreparable loss. Our total loss is 12 killed, 80 wounded, and 13 missing—supposed to be killed or taken prisoners.

CAPTAIN JAMES H. JONES
38TH MISSISSIPPI INFANTRY, HÉBERT'S BRIGADE

Hébert's tough veterans from Louisiana, Mississippi, Alabama, and Arkansas were posted near the 3d Louisiana Redan, north of the Railroad Redoubt. Jones and his comrades were able to dig in and weather Grant's preattack bombardment with little damage. During the charge of the Union XVII Corps on May 22, they unleashed a torrent of lead on the hapless Yankee soldiers as they struggled toward the formidable Rebel earthworks.

On the night of the 21st of May preceding this assault, the fratricidal feature of the war was called to our attention in a most pathetic manner. Just on our left was Green's Missouri brigade, and, by the irony of fate, a brigade of Missourians, on the Federal side, was directly opposed to them. They discovered this in some way, and until late at night we could hear the Confederates calling to their old neighbors and asking of the loved ones in their far-away homes. . . .

Before daylight on the morning of the 22d the enemy began a tremendous cannonade on our front. It was the grandest and most awe-inspiring scene I ever witnessed. The air was ablaze with burning and bursting shells, darting like fiery serpents across the sky, and the earth shook with the thunderous roar. The scene recalled descriptions of the meteoric shower of 1833, only these meteors were too close and too solid for pleasant contemplation. I do not hesitate to assert that coarse print could have been read by the light of these blazing missiles. It would appear almost incredible that but little harm was done by such a fierce cannonade, but so it was. A ditch is almost a perfect protection against a shell fired across it, provided one sits against the side next to the battery. Its momentum carries even the fragments of an exploded shell forward, and there is little danger from it. It is only when the messengers of death are dropped from above, or when they enfilade a line of breastworks that they get in their deadly work.

Educated at Kentucky's Western Military Institute, Colonel Preston Brent commanded the 38th Mississippi at Vicksburg on May 22. On June 30 his face was disfigured when a Yankee bullet slammed through both his cheeks. After recovering from this wound he returned home to Pike County, Mississippi.

When the cannonade ceased the Federals formed three lines of battle, near the woods, and began a steady advance upon our works. Their lines were about one hundred yards apart. They came on as rapidly as the fallen timber would permit, and in perfect order. We waited in silence until the first line had advanced within easy rifle range, when a murderous fire was opened from the breastworks. We had a few pieces of artillery which ploughed their ranks with destructive effect. Still they never faltered, but came bravely on. It was indeed a gallant sight though an awful one. As they came down the hill one could see them plunging headlong to the front, and as they rushed up the slope to our works they invariably fell backwards, as the death shot greeted them. And yet the survivors never wavered. Some of them fell within a few yards of our works. If any of the first line escaped, I did not see them. They came into the very jaws of death and died. The two other lines of battle, when they recognized the impossible, sought refuge among the fallen timber, but held their advanced positions tenaciously during the day, and next morning were intrenched not far from our front, where they remained. Surely no more desperate courage than this could be displayed by mortal men. On our left a battle flag was planted upon the walls of a fort held by the 36th Mississippi, and it was waved there defiantly all day until it was carried off at night by its owners, who had found shelter in the ditch outside. This gallant deed was accomplished by an Ohio regiment.

SERGEANT OSBORN H. OLDROYD
20TH OHIO INFANTRY, LEGGETT'S BRIGADE

Aware of the strength of the 3d Louisiana Redan—known to the Yankees as Fort Hill—the 20th Ohio's soldiers stoically handed over personal effects as they prepared for battle. Manning F. Force, the 20th's commander, praised his men after Vicksburg's fall for "performing . . . every duty required" and for their "earnest and intelligent desire to . . . end the rebellion." The regiment served until the end of the war, losing 88 men in battle and 271 to disease.

May 22d.—Last night mortar-shells, fired from the boats on the river on front of the city across Point Louisiana, fell thick over all parts of Vicksburg, and at three o'clock this morning every cannon along our line belched its shot at the enemy. Nothing could be heard at the time but the thundering of great guns—one hundred cannons sent crashing into the town—parrot, shrapnell, cannister, grape and solid shot—until it seemed impossible that anything could withstand such a fearful hailstorm. It was indeed a terrible spectacle—awfully grand.

At ten o'clock we had orders to advance. The boys were expecting the order and were busy divesting themselves of watches, rings, pictures and other keepsakes, which were being placed in the custody of the cooks, who were not expected to go into action. I never saw such a scene before, nor do I ever want to see it again. The instructions left with the keepsakes were varied. For instance, "This watch I want you to send to my father if I never return"—"I am going to Vicksburg, and if I do not get back just send these little trifles home, will you?"—proper addresses for the sending of the articles being left with them. Not a bit of sadness or fear appears in the talk or faces of the boys, but they thought it timely and proper to dispose of what they had accordingly. This was done while we awaited orders, which at last came in earnest, and in obedience to them we moved up and took our place in the rifle pits within a hundred yards of Fort Hill, where we had orders to keep a diligent watch, and to fire at the first head that dared to show itself. The air was so thick with the smoke of cannon that we could hardly see a hundred yards before us. The line to our right and left was completely hidden from view except as revealed by the flash of guns, and the occasional bursting of shells through the dense clouds. About eleven o'clock came a signal for the entire line to charge upon the works of the enemy. Our boys were all ready, and in an instant leaped foward to find victory or defeat. The seventh Missouri took the lead with ladders which they placed against the fort, and then gave way for others to scale them. Those who climbed to the top of the fort met cold steel, and, when at length it was found impossible to enter the fort that way, the command was given to fall back, which was done under a perfect hail of lead from the enemy. The rebels, in their excitement and haste to fire at our retreating force, thrust their heads a little too high above their cover,—an advantage we were quick to seize with well aimed volleys. In this charge a severe loss was met by our division, and nothing gained. What success was met by the rest of the line I cannot say, but I hope it was better than ours. Thus ended another day of bloody fight in vain, except for an increase of the knowledge which has been steadily growing lately, that a regular siege will be required to take Vicksburg. This day will be eventful on the page of history, for its duties have been severe, and many a brave patriot bit the dust under the storm of deadly fire that assailed us.

Helping defend the line assailed by the Union XVII Corps on May 22 was New Orleans native Sergeant Joseph Corneille (above) of the 22d and 23d Louisiana Infantry. His regiment, consolidated because of heavy losses, sustained 58 more casualties in this battle. The battle honors on the 22d's flag (below), which was carried at Vicksburg, also attest to the unit's extensive service.

LIEUTENANT SAMUEL H. M. BYERS
5TH IOWA INFANTRY, MATTHIES' BRIGADE

Though a Union veteran claimed the "South could not have been worsted" without the "invaluable . . . services" of mules, he also admitted that the beasts "preferred to do military duty in the safe rear." Byers, rushing ammunition to his pinned down regiment, found himself in a situation with a mule that would have been considered comical were it not for the dire circumstances. Byers was captured at Missionary Ridge but managed to escape and was mustered out in 1865.

I had been detailed to bring cartridges to my regiment, which had advanced out of the hollow in which it lay and over the brow of the hill under a heavy fire. The firing was still going on, but the regiment lay down unharmed, when cartridges were called for. I went back, but found the boxes of a 1,000 "58s" too heavy to carry, and so strapped two of them over the back of a strong mule, and started to the front. I walked and led the mule, while a companion followed, administering a wagon-whip from behind. On emerging from the breastworks it was necessary to hurry over a little rise in full view of the enemy. It was but a dozen rods to a spot of safety in the hollow. We took a good start at a run, and emerged into full view of the forts, not a hundred rods away, when the beast, true to his instincts, took it into his head at this particular crisis to stop stock-still. Persuasion, pulling, whooping, separate or combined, helped nothing. There he stood, fixed as the general of the army himself, and apparently ten times as cool. What could be done? Bullets were whizzing about our heads and ears, two had skinned up the boxes on the mule's back, and the next moment some sharpshooter might, and certainly would, pick us off forever. We couldn't run; the ammunition was pressingly needed. It was too hot to remain there, and go we could not. Again my comrade whipped, both shouted, and I pulled and tugged till, suddenly, halter and bridle both slipped over the mule's head. Free from restraint, he was disposed to run, and run he did—but fortunately in the right direction. We, too, ran faster, possibly, than did the mule. He was caught in the right place, unloaded and tied to a bush, where, in a few hours, when the line fell back, he was left standing as an outpost, being probably seized upon and eaten by the hungry soldiers of Pemberton's army. I have often wondered since then how that mule was accounted for at Washington. Was he reported stolen, captured, or simply

"Died on the field of honor?"

As other Union forces attacked farther south on May 22, General Sherman's infantrymen once again tried to capture the Stockade Redan. After the battle, Sergeant Enos Seth Hall (left) of the 8th Iowa Infantry made this sketch of the rugged ground over which "Uncle Billy's" men had fought. Visible at the right center of the Rebel works are the palisaded walls of the impregnable redan; immediately opposite can be seen the 8th Iowa's position. Through the center of the drawing winds the aptly named Graveyard road, used by the Federals as an approach route for their hopeless assaults.

CAPTAIN J. J. KELLOGG
113TH ILLINOIS INFANTRY, G. A. SMITH'S BRIGADE

Although Union gunners pounded the Stockade Redan with an artillery barrage that "literally burdened the air" over the strongpoint "with hissing missiles of death," the bombardment could not save the men of Brigadier General Giles A. Smith's brigade from again being bloodily repulsed by the fort's defenders. Confederate colonel Francis M. Cockrell proudly stated that his Missouri brigade men "greeted every assault of the enemy with defiant shouts and a deliberately aimed fire."

Our brigade was formed in a ravine threatening the parapet, 300 yards to the left of the bastion, and we had connected with Ransom's brigade. From that formation we fixed bayonets and charged point blank for the rebel works at a double quick. Unfortunately for me I was in the front of the rank and compelled to maintain that position, and a glance at the forest of gleaming bayonets sweeping up from the rear, at a charge, made me realize that it only required a stumble of some lubber just behind me to launch his bayonet into the offside of my anatomy, somewhere in the neighborhood of my anterior suspender buttons. This knowledge so stimulated me that I feared the front far less than the rear, and forged ahead like an antelope, easily changing my double quick to a quadruple gait, and most emphatically making telegraph time. During that run and rush I had frequently to either step upon or jump over the bodies of our dead and wounded, which were scattered along our track. The nearer the enemy we got the more enthusiastic we became, and the more confidence we had in scaling their works, but as we neared their parapet we encountered the reserved fire of the rebels which swept us back to temporary cover of a ridge, two-thirds of the way across the field, from which position we operated the rest of the day.

HOSPITAL STEWARD THOMAS H. BARTON
4TH WEST VIRGINIA INFANTRY, EWING'S BRIGADE

Though outgunned, Confederate artillery in Vicksburg gamely replied to the Union salvos. Their fire tore huge holes in the attacking columns of Federals and ensured that Barton and his fellow hospital stewards would soon be busy with the frightful work of attending the wounded. After the war Barton built upon his military medical experience to enjoy a successful career as a physician in Syracuse, Ohio.

On the 22d I saw the Eighth Wisconsin regiment charge the enemy's works. They had a live bald eagle called "Old Abe," for a standard. He was carried on a platform supported by two men. The regiment was making a charge up the ridge on our left and front; and "Old Abe," unconscious of danger, was flapping his wings and croaking, and appeared to be as lively as any of the soldiers. They marched up the ridge and when within plain view of the Confederates, the enemy opened fire with several pieces of artillery. One shell burst in a wagon that was with the regiment, and at the same instant I saw something that looked like a man, or his clothing, about fifteen feet in the air, though I do not think that any one was injured. The regiment had one gun with them, but did not use it. I heard the iron hail falling on the ground, and the bursting of the shells sounded like replying cannon. My position was towards the front, and I stood watching the shells for a few minutes, and then looked across the ravine to see if any of my companions were in sight, they having deserted me. Surgeon Waterman was hiding behind a stump; comrade Mercer had found shelter behind the stem of a tree, and the rest of my comrades had sought safety elsewhere. In a few minutes the Eighth Wisconsin filed to the rear and were out of sight, leaving their gun and wagon on the ridge, but not within view of the enemy. After this regiment fell back everything was quiet along this part of the Union lines.

One of the more famous regimental mascots of the Civil War was the 8th Wisconsin Infantry's "Old Abe," an eagle that accompanied the regiment into battle while tethered to a special perch. Although Old Abe was wounded in several battles, he was able to "muster out" in September 1864, finding a home in a specially made cage in Wisconsin's statehouse. Here Old Abe lived an honored existence as a patriotic symbol until 1881, when he died in a fire.

CAPTAIN SEWELL S. FARWELL
31ST IOWA INFANTRY, WOODS' BRIGADE

Farwell's letter calmly points out the folly of Federal attacks on Vicksburg's fortifications. The 28-year-old from Bowen's Prairie, Iowa, enlisted in August 1862, and the soldiers of Company H promptly elected him captain. This election was a portent of Farwell's future—in the 1880s he served Iowa as a congressman and state senator.

On the hills near Vicksburg
5/24/1863
Dear Parents

. . . I have with the men been in places of considerable danger. I was knocked down thursday with a shell that killed a private & severely wounded three others. . . . Dawson was wounded severely in the hand & Herbert Kilgore also, both are doing well. Wm S. Johnson received a bruise from a piece of shell & several were grazed by balls.

The 9th were in the charge & were badly cut up. Alonzo Burdrick has a painful wound in the neck, but is in good spirits & expects to get along well. I saw him yesterday. The ball entered the neck about two and a half inches from the ear & passed out on the opposite side about as near the other ear. He thinks the bone was not touched. . . . Sutherland was wounded, the ball entering his back & remaining there. The charge was not successful & it is sad indeed to think that so many lives were thrown away & so much danger incurred when it was not necessary & no good accomplished.

We are sure to take Vicksburgh. We have them surrounded with an army that can't be whipped in a fair fight & Victory is sure to come sooner or later. Therefore all that is necessary is to wait patiently our time instead of charging upon works that have been built upon the best military knowledge & principles.

Yours S. S. Farwell

MAJOR GENERAL WILLIAM T. SHERMAN
COMMANDER, XV CORPS, ARMY OF THE TENNESSEE

Sherman relates here Grant's receipt of exaggerated reports of success from McClernand, which induced him to order another wave of attacks, also handily repulsed by Vicksburg's defenders. An Ohioan described the failures of the 22d as a "Slaughter of Human Beings in cold blood. We done our best; we struggled manfully; we fought desperately; all would not do, we were repulsed and with fearful loss."

After our men had been fairly beaten back from off the parapet, and had got cover behind the spurs of ground close up to the rebel works, General Grant came to where I was, on foot, having left his horse some distance to the rear. I pointed out to him the rebel works, admitted that my assault had failed, and he said the result with McPherson and McClernand was about the same. While he was with me, an orderly or staff-officer came and handed him a piece of paper, which he read and handed to me. I think the writing was in pencil, on a loose piece of paper, and was in General McClernand's handwriting, to the effect that "his troops had captured the rebel parapet in his front," that "the flag of the Union waved over the stronghold of Vicksburg," and asking him (General Grant) to give renewed orders to McPherson and Sherman to press their attacks on their respective fronts, lest the enemy should concentrate on him (McClernand). General Grant said, "I don't believe a word of it"; but I reasoned with him, that this note was official, and must be credited, and I offered to renew the assault at once with new troops. He said he would instantly ride down the line to McClernand's front, and if I did not receive orders to the contrary, by 3 o'clock P.M., I might try it again. Mower's fresh brigade was brought up under cover, and some changes were made in Giles Smith's brigade; and, punctually at 3 P.M., hearing heavy firing down along the line to my left, I ordered the second assault. It was a repetition of the first, equally unsuccessful and bloody. It also transpired that the same thing had occurred with General McPherson, who lost in this second assault some most valuable officers and men, without adequate results; and that General McClernand, instead of having taken any single point of the rebel main parapet, had only taken one or two small outlying lunettes open to the rear, where his men were at the mercy of the rebels behind their main parapet, and most of them were actually thus captured. This affair caused great feeling with us, and severe criticisms on General McClernand, which led finally to his removal from the command of the Thirteenth Corps, to which General Ord succeeded.

To the satisfaction of many in Grant's army, McClernand (above) was relieved of command of the XIII Corps when Grant tired of his penchant for inflating dubious battle achievements. Major General Edward O. C. Ord replaced McClernand.

PRIVATE WILLIAM H. TUNNARD
3D LOUISIANA INFANTRY, HÉBERT'S BRIGADE

By May 25 the bodies of hundreds of Federal dead lying between the opposing lines had begun to rot after three days under the hot Mississippi sun, adding an unbearable stench to the ghastly scene. Both sides finally agreed that the bloated, blackened corpses should be retrieved and buried; thus began the strange truce described here. Tunnard was taken prisoner at the conclusion of the siege and later reenlisted after being exchanged, serving until the war's end.

In the afternoon of May 25th, a flag of truce was sent into the lines, requesting a cessation of hostilities for the purpose of burying the dead, and the request was granted for three hours. Now commenced a strange spectacle in this thrilling drama of war. Flags were displayed along both lines, and the troops thronged the breastworks, gaily chatting with each other; discussing the issues of

"Now commenced a strange spectacle in this thrilling drama of war. Flags were displayed along both lines, and the troops thronged the breast-works, gaily chatting with each other, discussing the issues of war, disputing over differences of opinion, losses in the fights, etc."

war; disputing over differences of opinion, losses in the fights, etc. Numbers of the Confederates accepted invitations to visit the enemy's lines, where they were hospitably entertained and warmly welcomed. They were abundantly supplied with provisions and supplies of various kinds.

Of course, there were numerous laughable and interesting incidents resulting from these visits. The foe were exultant, confident of success, and in high spirits; the Confederates defiant, undaunted in soul, and equally well assured of a successful defense. The members of the Third Regiment found numerous acquaintances and relatives among the Ohio, Illinois and Missouri regiments, and there were mutual regrets that the issues of the war had made them antagonistic in a deadly struggle. Captain F. Gallagher, the worthy commissary of the regiment, had been enjoying the hospitalities of a Yankee officer, imbibing his fine liquors and partaking of his choice viands, and as they separated, the Federal remarked: "Good day, Captain; I trust we shall meet soon again in the Union of old." Captain G., with a peculiar expression on his pleasant face, and an extra side poise of his head, quickly replied: "I can not return your sentiment. The only union which you and I will enjoy, I hope, will be in kingdom come; good bye, sir." At the expiration of the appointed time, the men were all back in their places. The stillness which had superseded the uproar of battle seemed strange and unnatural. The hours of peace had scarcely expired ere those who had so lately intermingled in friendly intercourse were once again engaged in the deadly struggle. Heavy mortars, artillery of every calibre, and small arms, once more with thunder-tones awakened the slumbering echoes of the hills surrounding the heroic city of Vicksburg.

MAJOR RALEIGH S. CAMP
40TH GEORGIA INFANTRY, BARTON'S BRIGADE

Before joining the 40th Georgia, Camp had served with the 7th Texas Infantry. After Vicksburg he fought at Chattanooga and in the Atlanta campaign. Wounded near Marietta, Georgia, in 1864, Camp lost his left arm to amputation. After the war he resided in Texas, working as an insurance agent until dying there of "congestion of the brain" in 1867.

The Boa Constrictor is drawing his coils around us with all his strength. He has found that he cannot kill his victims at one stroke with his fangs, so he has concluded to crush us out by the Squeezing process. We have stood his *bite* and we will not be intimidated by his touch. Our men are determined to meet any shock they may bring against them; and if human effort can hold them in check we will hold them at bay till the day of relief. . . . On Wednesday the 27th we witnessed one of the grandest and most terrific scenes that had taken place lately. About 9 oc.A.M. Three of thier Iron Clads From below began to steam up the River. When they reached the point opposite our fortifications, they then opened upon us. Broadside after Broadside and the fire from thier for Guns as are now poured upon us with all the fury that human skill can invent and power execute. The Boats moved up slowly, keeping up a continuous fire. It seemed to me that the thunder of Heaven had broken up from the Bowels of the Mistress of waters that even Jove had taken this as his time to deal out the bolts he has been forging for centuries past. The air was filled with thier shells and the fragments. In fact each and every place was filled with thier missiles. This continued for three long hours and one, unaccustomed to such, would have said that no living flesh could survive this fiery ordeal. But strange to say not a life or a limb was lost, except for a few mules. Surely an All-wise Providence protected us with his Shield. And did not allow a hair of our heads to be harmd.

When they came within Range our Batteri's paid thier respects in a becoming manner. After many rounds a shot from one of large Guns entered the side of one of the ugly monsters and tore off a large part of the other side iron and all. They took the hint and steamd down the River out of range of our guns. Where they have remained up to this time; and I presume will for a while at least.

This sketch shows a naval action of May 27, when Union gunboats attempted, with little effect, to shell Vicksburg. Well-aimed shots from the heavy artillery of the Confederates' Battery Tennessee, posted in a dominant location overlooking the "Great Bend" in the Mississippi River above the town, ripped through the ironclad Cincinnati, causing it to sink with the loss of more than 40 lives. In the days following this incident, Battery Tennessee's gunners kept busy shelling Yankee workmen trying to salvage the Cincinnati's cannon.

This photograph of a "U.S. Quartermaster's Camp" behind the front lines gives evidence of how thickly the ground surrounding Vicksburg was honeycombed with Union trenches and earthworks. The works at the front were even more elaborate than those of the rear areas, being studded with lunettes and redans that created overlapping fields of fire.

SERGEANT W. R. EDDINGTON
97TH ILLINOIS INFANTRY, LANDRAM'S BRIGADE

To help relieve the tedium of siege warfare, the soldiers of both armies indulged in the bloodthirsty pastime of sniping at each other throughout the long, sultry Mississippi days. One Rebel asserted that "the chief aim of both combatants seemed to be concentrated in the invention of apparatus for taking human life." Eddington and his comrades even made crude periscopes to help them try to pick off their foes while staying completely under cover.

In making our breastworks we would dig our ditch about four feet wide and run them parallel with the Rebel line of works for miles in length. (Our line of battle was about 15 miles long.) We would put the dirt we got out of the ditch we dug up toward the rebel works. We would dig down about 3 feet then we would dig the top of the bank next to the rebels down about one foot and back far enough to make a comfortable seat, then we would take bags and fill them full of dirt (these we called sand bags) We would lay these bags along on top —end to end—of the loose dirt we had piled up out of the ditch we dug. As we laid up the first tier of bags we left about two inch space between each end of the bags. Now we would lay another tier of bags on top of this one and this would leave a small hole through which we would put our guns. We would lay more bags on top of these until we had them away over our heads so that we was entirely hid from the Rebels. Now we would get a small stick, sharpen one end of it and split the other end and put a small tin case looking glass in the split (most of the boys carried them) we would sit with our backs toward the Rebels and our guns stuck in the holes behind us, the muzzles pointed toward the Rebels, directly over the top of our heads, the guns cocked and our thumbs on the triggers. We would take the stick with the looking glass in it and stick it in the bank in front of us lining it up with the barrel of the gun levelled at the top of the Rebel breastworks then we would watch in the glass in front of us and whenever anything came across the gun in the glass we would pull the trigger.

"Now and then the little leaden messengers carried death with them rather than whispers of caution."

SERGEANT WILBUR F. CRUMMER
45TH ILLINOIS INFANTRY, LEGGETT'S BRIGADE

Though staff officers often were hit while relaying critical messages under fire, many enlisted men saw them as bombastic, cowardly "yellow dogs" and reveled in humiliating them whenever possible. Crummer's chances to participate in such practical jokes were cut short. On July 2, only two days before the surrender, he was severely wounded in the right breast. This injury prevented him from returning to active service before being discharged in 1864.

The boys in the ranks had no use for a "dude" officer. Gen. Mc-Pherson, who commanded our corps (a braver or finer gentleman never breathed), had on his staff a fine officer, but who was very fond of dress, and when he would ride along the line of march, in his velvet suit, the boys would guy him unmercifully. One day this Colonel came into the trenches, and, stopping opposite where I stood on the embankment behind the gabions, addressed one of our boys thus: "Sergeant, do you see the enemy from this point?" The Sergeant replied: "Yes, sir, by looking through this hole in the log, down that ravine you will occasionally see the enemy crossing." The Colonel got up, looked through the hole, and saw some Confederates crossing the ravine, and then he was moved to take a hand in the game, and turning 'round, said: "Sergeant, load your rifle and let me have a pop at those fellows." "All right, Colonel," and while he was still looking, the Sergeant at his rear, loaded the musket. The gun had been in use most of the day, and was pretty foul and if not held just right, would kick fearfully. Well, wicked sinner that the soldier was, he took two cartridges, using two charges of powder and one bullet, and loaded the Enfield rifle, put the percussion cap on and handed it to the Colonel and, stepping back into the trenches, awaited developments. The Colonel got ready, saw his man, pulled the trigger and—tumbled back into the trench. He handed the gun back, remarking: "Your gun, Sergeant, recoils considerable," and the innocent (?) soldier said, "Does it?" The Colonel did not ask for a second shot. I'll warrant he had a black and blue shoulder for a month.

Both sides at Vicksburg were so concerned about shellfire that they went to the extent of fortifying roads that passed through their positions. In the earthen walls lining this passageway are openings that one soldier, the artist Henry Dwight, called "cells of escape," which troops could duck into if fired upon.

PRIVATE HOSEA W. ROOD

12TH WISCONSIN INFANTRY, JOHNSON'S BRIGADE

Only 18 years old when he enlisted at Madison, Wisconsin, in December 1861, Hosea Rood came out of the army a grizzled veteran corporal when his enlistment expired in 1865. In his "Story of the Service of Company E, and of the Twelfth Wisconsin Regiment," published 30 years after the events at Vicksburg recounted here, Rood displays the veteran's wry, tongue-in-cheek sense of humor about the horrors of the bloody campaign. He not only recognized a good story when he heard it, he was a skilled raconteur in his own right.

We spent most of our time firing across the valley, and they over yonder busied themselves in the same way. It goes without saying that we did not expose ourselves to the view of the other fellows any more than was absolutely necessary, and it was indeed rare that we ever saw a head above the long line of yellow clay

on the other side. To all appearances the works of the Rebels were deserted; but a view behind the scenes would have revealed a great active army beyond them. The same on our side.

Some of my readers may wonder what we shot at, when nothing was to be seen. Well, we shot at various things. If a head did happen to show above the works we lost no time in sending a little leaden messenger over there as close as possible to the ears thereof to whisper a word of caution, the result being that the owner of said head always took it down unhesitatingly. So on our side. It must not be forgotten that now and then the little leaden messengers carried death with them rather than whispers of caution. If heads were not visible, and they seldom were, we fired at the upper part of their works, knowing that many heads were close to that line. Bullets thus aimed were not altogether harmless either to the enemy or to us; for there was an almost continual rain of them. None of us could very well take aim at the top of the works on the other side without getting at least one eye above our own defenses; and there was always a spice of uncertainty as to what might result from even a momentary exposure of that blessed organ of sight. More than one brave fellow was shot in the head while in the act of thus firing over the works. . . .

While we were tolerably safe in the pit, there was some danger in going to and returning from them. Whenever there was an exposed ridge to cross we fairly scampered over, not standing at all upon the order of our going. Some gentlemen came down from Wisconsin to see how a siege was carried on. While being shown about they were told that there was some danger from Rebel bullets while crossing these ridges. It was amusing to us to see the alertness they manifested in dodging imaginary bullets and bomb-shells while making 2:40 time for the shelter of the valleys beyond. Such motions as they made did not comport well with the dignity that naturally attaches to a silk hat.

Sometimes while passing to or from the works we became the objects of special Rebel attention, and the enemy scattered his shot and shell about our way right liberally. If we could not readily reach shelter at such a time, we lay down, flattened out as thin as we were able, and tremblingly waited for the firing to cease.

It was said one day that when some negro cooks were caught in such a shower of lead and iron the night before they so flattened themselves out on the ground that one of the boys coming along mistook them for rubber blankets, and picked one of them up to carry to camp. But I do not more than half believe the story.

Clouds of smoke issuing from hissing fuses mark the paths of cannonballs thrown by Confederate troops at an exposed Federal entrenching crew. The feverish efforts of Union troops, digging with shovels and picks toward the Rebel defenses, forced Pemberton's men to resort to this unconventional use of artillery shells when their fieldpieces could no longer be lowered sufficiently to bear on the Yankees.

CORPORAL EPHRAIM MCD. ANDERSON
2D MISSOURI (C.S.) INFANTRY, COCKRELL'S BRIGADE

Anderson, the son of a former midshipman on the U.S. Navy frigate Constitu-
tion, was captured when Vicksburg fell. The Missourian was exchanged in 1863
and promptly returned to duty, although he suffered from hepatitis through the
last years of the war. While recuperating at his home in Monroe County, Mis-
souri, after the conflict, he wrote a history of Cockrell's brigade, completing it in
1868. Anderson died in a Missouri Confederate soldiers home in 1916.

We found ourselves in close quarters with the enemy, and his contiguity was frequently evidenced by the throwing over into our lines of clods and hand-grenades; the former did no serious damage, but, on one occasion, Lieutenant Gillespie's nose was skinned in a pretty rough manner by a lump of clay that was dried hard in the sun. The hand-grenades were small shells about the size of a goose egg, filled with little bullets, probably larger than a buck-shot; they never exploded before striking the ground, and only then when hitting a hard place, as they were fired by friction, and not by fuses. They wounded several of the regiment in the legs, generally slightly, but killed no one within my knowledge, always bursting too low to strike a vital part.

In return for the hand-grenades, our regiment, whose position was more elevated than the enemy's, threw shells, varying from six to ninety pounds, into his works, many of which did great execution; but we did not know it at the time, and this sort of shelling was not kept up: it was only after the siege that we learned, if it had been sustained, especially with the heavy shells, the works there would have been untenable.

HOSPITAL STEWARD THOMAS H. BARTON
4TH WEST VIRGINIA INFANTRY, EWING'S BRIGADE

Although the Confederate and Federal forces battling at Vicksburg generally
tried to kill each other whenever possible, at times the desire for the food or
tobacco of their foes overcame the urge to shoot, and they would declare informal
truces in order to trade such items between the lines. This behavior, described by
Barton, took place in all the theaters of combat throughout the war and was
another incongruous feature of America's internal struggle.

One night . . . I went to the front and entered our works, which consisted of a trench four or five feet deep, and wide enough for four or five men to walk abreast in it. This trench ran in a zig-zag way, like an old fashioned rail fence. I followed it till I reached the front, where our pickets were stationed, about twenty yards from the Confederate lines. Here I had the pleasure of hearing the following conversation:

Reb.—"Hello Yank!"
Yank.—"What do you want?"
Reb.—"Have you plenty of bread on your side?"
Yank.—"Yes; have you plenty of tobacco?"
Reb.—"Will you give me bread for tobacco?"
Yank.—"Yes, I will—will meet you half way if you are willing."
Reb.—"Yes, I will."

They met midway between the lines like brothers, made the exchange, and returned to their respective stations. But on the ensuing day, it would have been dangerous for either of them to show his head above the ramparts, and if he did, he would be the target of half a score of rifles.

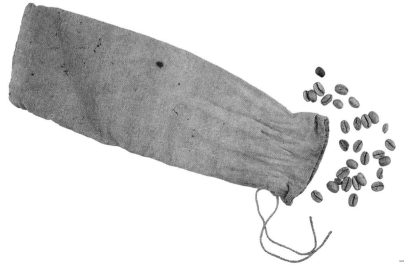

Coffee was highly desired by the worn down defenders of Vicksburg, and they
eagerly traded for it. A Tennessean named J. R. Taylor obtained this "poke bag"
of the coveted beans by exchanging tobacco with Yankee troops during the siege.

CORPORAL EPHRAIM MCD. ANDERSON
2D MISSOURI (C.S.) INFANTRY, COCKRELL'S BRIGADE

In June Confederate larders in Vicksburg began to run low, forcing the commissary to issue improvised rations. As Anderson relates, perhaps the most notorious of these experimental foodstuffs was "pea bread," a noxious combination made of beans known as cow peas, which local farmers grew for animal feed. Raw peas were also issued, although they were equally awful, causing one Rebel to grouse that they made a "very poor vegetable for the table."

There was a good supply of this pea in the commissariat at Vicksburg, and the idea grew out of the fertile brain of some official, that, if reduced to the form of meal, it would make an admirable substitute for bread. Sagacious and prolific genius! whether general or commissary—originator of this glorious conception! this altogether novel species of the hardest of "hard tack!" perhaps he never swallowed a particle of it. If he did, the truth and force of these comments will be appreciated.

The process of getting the pea into the form of bread was the same as that to which corn is subjected: the meal was ground at a large mill in the city, and sent to the cooks in camp to be prepared. It was accordingly mixed with cold water and put through the form of baking; but the nature of it was such, that it never got done, and the longer it was cooked, the harder it became on the outside, which was natural, but, at the same time, it grew relatively softer on the inside, and, upon breaking it, you were sure to find raw pea-meal in the centre. The cooks protested that it had been on the fire two good hours, but it was all to no purpose; yet, on the outside it was so hard, that one might have knocked down a full-grown steer with a chunk of it. The experiment soon satisfied all parties, and after giving us this bread for three days, it was abandoned. But it had already made a number of us sick. Peas were afterwards issued, boiled in camp, and still constituted about half our subsistence.

SERGEANT WILBUR F. CRUMMER
45TH ILLINOIS INFANTRY, LEGGETT'S BRIGADE

While Pemberton's Confederate troops in Vicksburg had ample quantities of rifles as well as abundant bullets and gunpowder—which the women of the city rolled into cartridges—they soon began to run low on percussion caps. Crummer tells how not only Rebel soldiers but also brave civilians of all ages volunteered for the risky work of acting as "couriers," or smugglers, and trying to sneak bagloads of caps into the city through the Yankee lines.

In front of the line of the 15th Illinois Regiment, near the picket line, was a low marshy sink, of about an acre in size, covered by brush and dense cane brakes. One night a boy of about 10 years of age came out of the brush towards the picket line, holding up his handkerchief as a sign that he wished to surrender. The sentinel told him to come in; he did, and the little fellow told a pitiful story; that he had been in Vicksburg visiting his aunt who was sick; that his mother lived in Jackson, and he wanted to go home. The story seemed plausible and he was allowed to go through the lines. Not long after, one night, the pickets in that same locality, heard a rustling in the bushes in the same swampy hole, and surmising that something was wrong, surrounded it, demanding the surrender of any one there on pain of being shot at once. To their surprise out came a half-dozen men, each with a bag over his shoulder containing 10,000 percussion caps. Gen. Johnston had sent the men and caps back, led by the same little boy, and they were trying to get into Vicksburg. They were marched to Gen. Grant's headquarters, and while waiting to be ushered into the General's presence, one of the prisoners said to the boy: "What do you suppose they will do with you, for you are the fellow that got us into this fix?" The little fellow, cocking one eye in a comical manner, replied: "Oh, I guess they won't hurt me much, coz I'se so little." The little fellow was not hurt much, but kept a prisoner until the surrender and then with the soldiers sent home.

Rebel troops, burdened with heavy knapsacks full of percussion caps provided for the beleaguered Vicksburg garrison by Confederate general Joseph E. Johnston, avoid a Union picket post by stealthily creeping through a dark, rocky, and vine-choked ravine in this engraving for the Illustrated London News. The dapper civilian Lamar Fontaine, pictured in the inset, is believed to have singlehandedly brought 18,000 caps into the city. Fontaine eschewed the overland route, hauling his precious cargo on a skiff no bigger than a "floating log" through the bayous north of the city.

PRIVATE JAMES K. NEWTON

14TH WISCONSIN INFANTRY, RANSOM'S BRIGADE

Only 17 when he enlisted, but already standing six feet tall and weighing 180 pounds, Newton, a schoolteacher, regularly wrote letters home like this one. Captured at the Battle of Corinth in 1862, Newton was paroled in time for the Vicksburg campaign. He reenlisted in December 1863 and left the army as a second lieutenant in 1865.

Head Quarters 14th Wis Vols
    In the Rear of Vicksburg
        My Dear Mother.

. . . Our Reg't was paid off a few days ago. As soon as possible I shall send some money home. I dont like to trust it in the mail, when it is so irregular as it is at the present time.

Since we were paid off a person cannot go five rods in any part of our camp without seeing someone gambling. The day after we were paid there were a good many of the boys to be found who had not a cent left of their two months pay. Every cent of it was gambled away. On the other hand there was some of the boys who had made *hundreds* of Dollars gambling. The orders are very strict against it, but that's all the good it does. If you should hear anything about persons belonging to the Co. sending more money home than some of the others do, you can *guess* how it is made. . . .

There was quite a little incident happened this forenoon. Dick Brighton was coming out of the rifle pits, where he had been sharp-shooting all day, and one of the rebels fired at him; the ball struck just at his feet and he stooped down and picked it up, remarking at the time to one of the boys that the "Rebs" would regret throwing their shot around in that way. In the after noon he went back into the pits again and loaded his gun with the ball that he had picked up. He soon had a good chance to fire, and he did so with such good aim that the Secesh

dropped, and Dick had the satisfaction of knowing that he had at least wounded a "Reb" with one of their own bullets.

Love to all the family
Your affectionate Son James

LIEUTENANT COLONEL ANDREW HICKENLOOPER

CHIEF ENGINEER, XVII CORPS

Hickenlooper was responsible for designing large sections of the Union saps and earthworks and supervising their construction. He did so well at this task that the XVII Corps' "Board of Honor" awarded him a gold medal at the conclusion of the siege. Here he tells of the activities of an eccentric Yankee sharpshooter known as Coonskin, who constructed a tower near the center of the Union lines from which to snipe at the Rebels.

He was an unerring shot and wore a cap made of raccoon fur. From this he was called "Coonskin" the Seventeenth Corps through, and wherever he was, woe to the Confederate head that appeared above a parapet. "Coonskin" went out once in the night-time, crept up toward the Confederate defenses and built himself a burrow in the ground, with a peep-hole in it. There he would frequently take provisions with him, and stay several days at a time, watching for Confederates. At length he built "Coonskin's Tower." The Jackson and Vicksburg railway had been torn up for miles in the rear of Vicksburg and railway iron and cross-ties lay all about. Taking advantage of the night hours, Coonskin built himself a tower of the loose railroad ties. Learned in backwoods lore, he knew how to construct the genuine pioneer log-cabin. Working several nights, he at length built the tower so high that by climbing toward its top he could actually look over the Confederate parapets. He could see the men inside the works. Then, taking aim through the chinks of the logs, he would pick off the enemy. The tower was a terror to the Confederates. They could not use their artillery against it, that having been already quite silenced by the Union batteries. All they could do was to fire musketballs at it, which whistled around its corners or buried themselves in the logs.

Standing in the doorway of his fortified tower, "Coonskin" poses for an artist's sketchpad. To the left of the structure, a squad of soldiers from the 20th Ohio fire at the Confederate fortifications, while artillerymen seek relief from the sun under a tarp spread over the trench. The large earthwork on the horizon is the 3d Louisiana Redan, the object of the XVII Corps' ill-fated attack of May 22.

From this fort, named Battery Hickenlooper after its builder, Union artillery kept up an almost constant fire against the Rebel works. To the left of the soldier lighting his pipe stands a stack of gabions. These large, open-ended, cylindrical woven baskets were filled with dirt and used in the construction of fortifications. Also visible is an infantryman who has placed a hat on his musket's ramrod in order to taunt Confederate snipers.

CHAPLAIN WILLIAM L. FOSTER
35TH MISSISSIPPI INFANTRY, MOORE'S BRIGADE

After suffering the embarrassing repulse of May 27, Admiral David Dixon Porter's riverine fleet contented itself with a long-range mortar shelling of the Confederate defenses. The huge rounds fired from boats moored beyond the reach of Vicksburg's batteries both terrified and amazed those trapped in the city. One resident even thought the projectiles were "beautiful, . . . scattering hither and thither . . . large, clear blue-and-amber stars" as they exploded.

The stillness & serenity of the twilight is now broken by an unusual sound. A dull heavy sound falls upon the ear. Every ear is directed now to the rear. Now a tremendous explosion takes place high above our heads. It is a mortar shell! The wide-throated mortar has opened upon us. In quick succession another follows & then another. The air is filled with them. Several mortar boats within easy range now shell the devoted city of hills. They cannot possess the place, so they will endeavor to destroy it. . . . These large mortar shells, thirteen inches in diameter & weighing about two hundred pounds, are sent clear across the peninsula & reach nearly to our lines in the rear, passing over a distance of four miles. Within their range was all our waggon trains, all our hospitals & even some of our arsenals. Their firing was directed to different parts of the town. Their fuses were shortened or lengthened so as to throw them in the heart of the city, or to throw them in the rear. The appearance presented by this bombardment at night was grand & terrific to the last degree. Directing the eye to the river you first see a small light about the size of a star, darting like a meteor through the air, ascending higher & higher in its progress. This you see before you hear the report, so much faster does light travel than sound. In a few seconds you hear a dull heavy report in the distance. The spark of light, which is caused by the burning of the fuse ascends higher & higher until it threatens to reach the very stars. Now it reaches the summit of its orbit & begins to descend on a curved line towards the earth. Nearer & nearer it approaches. Now a rushing sound greets your ear, like the coming tempest when the clouds roar with wind. The falling star now descends with fearful rapidity & the noise becomes more furious & terrible. It seems as if it will fall upon your head.

> "I suppose there never was a case before of a besieged town when the guns from front and back met and passed each other."

EMMA BALFOUR
RESIDENT OF VICKSBURG

Although Union gunners set their sights on military targets, the imperfect science of 19th-century artillery ensured that some of the deadly cannonballs would land in civilian areas, where citizens like Balfour could only hide out in caves or cellars and hope for the best. Like many other Americans of the period, Balfour believed that the sulfurous compounds released into the atmosphere by gunfire and the explosion of shells led to the onset of rainstorms.

There is no possibility of writing regularly. Several times I have attempted to write but have been compelled to stop. We have spent the last two nights in a cave, but tonight I think we will stay at home. It is not safe I know, for the shells are falling all around us, but I hope none may strike us. Yesterday morning a piece of a mortar shell struck the schoolroom roof, tore through the partition wall, shattered the door and then went into the door sill and down the side of the wall. Another piece struck in the same room and a third in the cement in front of the house. Such a large piece struck the kitchen also, but we see them explode all around us and as this is all the harm done to us yet, we consider ourselves fortunate. Mrs. Hawkes' house is literally torn to pieces, and Mrs. Maulin's was struck yesterday evening by a shell from one of the guns east of us and very much injured. In both of these houses gentlemen were sick and in neither case was any one hurt. It is marvelous. Two persons only that I have heard have been killed in town, and a little child. The child was buried in the wall by a piece of shell, pinned to it. Today a shocking thing occurred. In one of the hospitals where some wounded had just undergone operations a shell exploded and six men had to have limbs amputated. Some of them that had been taken off at the ankle had to have the leg taken off to the thigh and one who had lost one arm had to have the other taken off. It is horrible and the worst of it is we cannot help it. I suppose there never was a case before of a besieged town when the guns from front and back met and passed each other. . . .

In the midst of all this carnage and commotion, it is touching to see how every work of God save man, gives praise to Him. The birds are singing as merrily as if all were well, rearing their little ones, teaching them to fly and fulfilling their part in nature's program as quietly and happily as if this fearful work of man slaying his brother man was not in progress. The heaving firing gives us showers every day and nature is more lovely than usual. The flowers are in perfection, the air heavy with the perfume of jassmine and honeysuckle, and the garden bright and gay with all the summer flowers. The fruit is coming to perfection, the apricots were abundant and more beautiful than I ever saw them. Nature is all fair and lovely—"all save the spirit of man seems divine."

Freshly washed bed linens and the laundry of patients listlessly hang out to dry on clotheslines in the humid Mississippi air next to City Hospital. This structure and the Marine Hospital were the only two permanent infirmaries in Vicksburg. These facilities were quickly overwhelmed—there were nearly 10,000 sick and wounded soldiers in the city at siege's end—and several churches and large homes had to be quickly converted into temporary hospitals.

Determined to preserve some semblance of normal life to help soften the horrific and chaotic existence of the residents of the invested town, editor James W. Swords (above), an Ohio native, continued to print sporadic editions of the Vicksburg Daily Citizen, resorting to the use of wallpaper after he had expended his stock of newsprint. A Mississippi soldier stated that the "wall-paper . . . sheet" was "hailed with solicitude" by the troops at the front lines as a welcome diversion from the drudgery of trench life.

"During all this excitement there was a little baby boy born in the room dug out at the back of the cave; he was called William Siege Green."

LUCY MCRAE
RESIDENT OF VICKSBURG

By early June most of Vicksburg's citizens had taken shelter in caves designed to protect against anything but a direct hit from the Yankees' nearly continual bombardment. In one large cave holding some 200 people, Lucy, barely in her teens in 1863, endured the harrowing experience, feared by all, of being partially buried when a shell collapsed a portion of the roof.

way in a solid piece, catching me under it. Dr. Lord, whose leg was caught and held by it, gave the alarm that a child was buried. Mother reached me first, and a Mrs. Stites, who was partially paralyzed, with the assistance that Dr. Lord, who was in agony, could give, succeeded in getting my head out first. The people had become frightened, rushing into the street screaming, and thinking that the cave was falling in. Just as they reached the street over came another shell bursting just above them, and they rushed into the cave again. Then came my release. Mother had cried in distressing tones for help, so as soon as the men could get to me they pulled me from under the mass of earth. The blood was gushing from my nose, eyes, ears, and mouth. A physician who was then in the cave was called, and said there were no bones broken, but he could not then tell what my internal injuries were. Just here I must say that during all this excitement there was a little baby boy born in the room dug out at the back of the cave; he was called William Siege Green.

One night, soon after entering our cave home, mother fixed our beds for us, putting my brothers on a plank at one side, and putting me near Mary Ann; but, spoiled and humored child that I was, I decided not to stay near Mary Ann, so proceeded to tear up my bed. The Rev. Dr. Lord, of the Episcopal Church, and at that time rector of Christ Church, was suffering with a sore foot and leg, which was all bandaged and propped on a chair for comfort. He said, "Come here, Lucy, and lie down on this plank." Dr. Lord was almost helpless, but he assisted me to arrange my bed, my head being just at his feet. The mortars were sending over their shells hot and heavy; they seemed to have range of the hill, due, it was said, to some fires that a few soldiers had made on a hill beyond us. Every one in the cave seemed to be dreadfully alarmed and excited, when suddenly a shell came down on the top of the hill, buried itself about six feet in the earth, and exploded. This caused a large mass of earth to slide from the side of the arch-

The Reverend William W. Lord, who helped rescue Lucy McRae, later preached the gospel in the Confederate cities of Mobile, Alabama, and Charleston, South Carolina. After the war he returned to his former church in Vicksburg, although he eventually moved back to his native state of New York.

This wartime drawing by A. J. Volck shows Yankee shells bursting in Vicksburg's night sky over the head of a startled servant while a young woman in a cave home falls to her knees and prays for her safety. Although some families had cave dwellings that were mere burrows, others believed in "keeping house under ground," bringing into the caves the comforts of home. Volck, a Southern sympathizer living in Baltimore, Maryland, hoped to arouse pity for the city's beleaguered residents with this depiction of siege life.

MARYANN WEBSTER LOUGHBOROUGH

RESIDENT OF VICKSBURG

Before the trial by fire ended—by July 4, Admiral Porter's gunboats alone had hurled 22,000 rounds at Vicksburg—nearly 500 caves were dug within the encircled city, causing Union troops to call the town "Prairie Dog Village." Cave dweller Loughborough, the wife of a Confederate officer fighting in the town's defenses, survived the terrors and privations of the extended siege. Years later she became an author and ladies' magazine editor in Little Rock, Arkansas.

In the evening we were terrified and much excited by the loud rush and scream of mortar shells; we ran to the small cave near the house, and were in it during the night, by this time wearied and almost stupefied by the loss of sleep.

The caves were plainly becoming a necessity, as some persons had been killed on the street by fragments of shells. The room that I had so lately slept in had been struck by a fragment of a shell during the first night, and a large hole made in the ceiling. I shall never forget my extreme fear during the night, and my utter hopelessness of ever seeing the morning light. Terror stricken, we remained crouched in the cave, while shell after shell followed each other in quick succession. I endeavored by constant prayer to prepare myself for the sudden death I was almost certain awaited me. My heart stood still as we would hear the reports from the guns, and the rushing and fearful sound of the shell as it came toward us. As it neared, the noise became more deafening; the air was full of the rushing sound; pains darted through my temples; my ears were full of the confusing noise; and, as it exploded, the report flashed through my head like an electric shock, leaving me in a quiet state of terror the most painful that I can imagine—cowering in a corner, holding my child to my heart—the only feeling of my life being the choking throbs of my heart, that rendered me almost breathless. As singly they fell short, or beyond the cave, I was aroused by a feeling of thankfulness that was of short duration. Again and again the terrible fright came over us in that night.

I saw one fall in the road without the mouth of the cave, like a flame of fire, making the earth tremble, and, with a low, singing sound, the fragments sped on in their work of death.

Morning found us more dead than alive, with blanched faces and trembling lips.

SERGEANT EDWARD S. GREGORY
SIGNAL CORPS, ARMY OF NORTHERN VIRGINIA

Although officially assigned to the eastern theater, Gregory somehow ended up at Vicksburg "on extra duty . . . as an Operator," receiving "$.40/day extra pay" for his services with the Army of Vicksburg. The 20-year-old had a knack for finding himself under siege; by July 1864 he had been exchanged from post-Vicksburg captivity and was back on duty, relaying messages to the units of Robert E. Lee's hard-pressed army dug in outside Petersburg, Virginia.

The Signal Corps headquarters in the city was a room in the court-house, and its station was the cupola of the same. The court-house was set on the highest point of the town, and the cupola formed the most prominent feature of its river *facade*, except, perhaps, the soaring light spire and gold cross of the Catholic church, which was, I believe, never defaced by the fire of the enemy. Whether this was chance or intention is another study. I suspect Porter's Pats and Mikes didn't want to hurt it. Far otherwise with the Temple of Justice. The Federal papers say it was the general centre of their fire, and so say I, who was in it. The building and grounds were struck twenty-four times or more, and yet but one shell was fatal in its effects. *That* came at midnight, crushing through the roof, and, passing below to the marble pavement of the ground floor, exploded and flung two poor fellows against the wall with such mutilation that their mothers would not have known their dead darlings. They were Mississippi militiamen. Their comrades above suffered only less cruelly. The heavy shell passing through the court-room, which was packed with sleeping men, struck squarely a massive iron railing that inclosed the seats of the

lawyers and witnesses, and scattered its fragments on every hand. Legs were broken, heads crushed—all manner of injury inflicted. This one shell killed and disabled fourteen men; and, by strange fatality, two more men of those who went out to bury the two first killed, lost their lives on their way to the graveyard. This inclosure, also—the beautiful City Cemetery—was riddled by the plunging shot.

Completed in 1860, Vicksburg's Warren County Courthouse was built on a high ridge dominating the rest of the riverside city, and the cupola that was signalman Gregory's post was a familiar regional landmark. Although damaged, the Greek Revival-style building survived the conflict and still stands today.

"It is impossible," said General Dennis, "for men to show greater gallantry than the negro troops in that fight."

CHARLES A. DANA
ASSISTANT U.S. SECRETARY OF WAR

Dana, accompanying Grant's army as an observer dispatched by Washington, was impressed with the tenacity of the black troops of the so-called African Brigade at Milliken's Bend. They suffered more than 500 casualties in the battle, and even Confederate brigadier general Henry E. McCulloch, the officer who led the Rebel attack, lauded the "negro" for fighting with "considerable obstinacy."

The most serious attack from the west during the siege was that on June 7th, when a force of some two thousand Confederates engaged about a thousand negro troops defending Milliken's Bend. This engagement at Milliken's Bend became famous from the conduct of the colored troops. General E. S. Dennis, who saw the bat-

tle, told me that it was the hardest fought engagement he had ever seen. It was fought mainly hand to hand. After it was over many men were found dead with bayonet stabs, and others with their skulls broken open by butts of muskets. "It is impossible," said General Dennis, "for men to show greater gallantry than the negro troops in that fight."

The bravery of the blacks in the battle at Milliken's Bend completely revolutionized the sentiment of the army with regard to the employment of negro troops. I heard prominent officers who formerly in private had sneered at the idea of the negroes fighting express themselves after that as heartily in favor of it. Among the Confederates, however, the feeling was very different. All the reports which came to us showed that both citizens and soldiers on the Confederate side manifested great dismay at the idea of our arming negroes. They said that such a policy was certain to be followed by insurrection with all its horrors.

This engraving depicts the vicious hand-to-hand fighting that took place on June 7 between a Rebel force made up mostly of some 1,500 Texans and a Union army of one white and three black regiments at Milliken's Bend. Many of the black troops taken prisoner were returned to slavery, and stories circulated that some were hanged by the Confederates, who were enraged at their daring to fight.

PRIVATE WILLIAM H. TUNNARD
3D LOUISIANA INFANTRY, HÉBERT'S BRIGADE

To reduce the 3d Louisiana Redan, Union soldiers began tunneling toward it—protected by movable breastworks called "sap-rollers"—in the hope of exploding a charge of gunpowder beneath the strongpoint. As Tunnard recounts, however, their efforts in at least one case were dealt a temporary setback by the Confederates' ingenious use of improvised incendiary bullets.

The Federals procured a car-frame, which they placed on wheels, loading it with cotton bales. They pushed this along the Jackson road, in front of the breastworks held by the Third regiment. Protected by this novel, movable shelter, they constructed their works with impunity, and with almost the certainty of eventually

reaching our intrenchments. Rifles had no effect on the cotton bales, and there was not a single piece of artillery to batter them down. They were not a hundred yards from the regiment, and the men could only quietly watch their operations, and anxiously await the approaching hand-to-hand struggle. There was no shrinking or quailing; danger had long since ceased to cause any fear, and fighting was a recreation and pastime with the majority of the men. Exploding shells and whistling bullets attracted but little notice. Even death had become so familiar, that the fall of a comrade was looked upon with almost stoical indifference—eliciting, perhaps, a monosyllabic expression of pity, and most generally the remark, "I wonder who will be the next one." Men are not naturally indifferent to danger, nor do their hearts usually exhibit such stoical indifference to human agony and suffering; yet the occurrence of daily scenes of horror and bloodshed through which they passed, the shadow of the angel of death constantly hovering over them, made them undisturbed spectators of every occurrence, making the most of to-day, heedless of the morrow. Though constantly threatened with death, they pursued with eagerness limited occasions for amusement. The song and jest went around, fun actually being coined from the danger which some comrade escaped, or attempted to nimbly dodge.

The movable breastwork in front of the intrenchments of the Third Louisiana, became a perfect annoyance to the regiment, and various plans were proposed for its destruction, only to be declared unavailable. Some of the men actually proposed to make a raid on it and set it on fire, a plan which would have been the height of madness.

Lieutenant W. M. Washburn, of Company B, loaded a rifle, and fired a ball of cotton and turpentine into the hated object. Another and another blazing missile was sent on the mission of destruction, with apparently no satisfactory results, and the attempt was abandoned amid a general disappointment. The men, save those on guard, sought repose, and all the line became comparatively quiet. Suddenly some one exclaimed, "I'll be d——d if that thing isn't on fire!" The whole regiment was soon stirring about, like a hive of disturbed bees. Sure enough, smoke was seen issuing from the dark mass. The inventive genius of Lieutenant Washburn had proved a complete success, and the fire, which had smouldered in the dense mass of cotton, was about bursting forth. The men seized their rifles, and five companies were immediately detailed to keep up a constant and rapid fire over the top and at each end of the blazing mass, to prevent the enemy from extinguishing the flames. The Yankees could not understand how their movable breastwork was thus given to destruction under their very eyes.

LIEUTENANT COLONEL ANDREW HICKENLOOPER

Chief Engineer, XVII Corps

Having already spent about a month digging a quarter-mile-long trench, Hickenlooper describes the second phase of the mining of the 3d Louisiana Redan. Thirty-six experienced miners worked 12-hour shifts to dig the four-foot-wide-by-five-foot-high gallery beneath the Confederate position.

Each relief worked an hour at a time, two picking, two shoveling, and two handing back the grain-sacks filled with earth, which were deposited in the ditch until they could be carried back. The main gallery was carried in 45 feet, and then a smaller gallery extended in on the same line 15 feet, while from the end of the main gallery two others were run out on either side at angles of 45 degrees for a distance of 15 feet. The soil through which this gallery was driven was a reddish clay of remarkable tenacity, easily cut and requiring but little bracing. So rapidly was this work executed that on the morning of the 25th the miners commenced depositing the powder, 800 pounds at the extreme end of the main gallery and 700 pounds at the end of each of the lateral galleries, making a total of 2200 pounds. From each of these deposits there were laid two strands of safety fuse,—obtained, as was the powder, from the navy,—this duplication being made to cover the possible contingency of one failing to burn with the desired regularity and speed. These six strands were cut to exactly the same length, and having been carefully laid, the earth, which had been previously removed in grain-sacks, was carried back and deposited in the most compact manner possible, and well braced by heavy timbers, beyond the junction point of the three galleries. From this point out to the entrance it was more loosely packed in. The Confederate garrison, surmising the object in view, were active in efforts to thwart the purpose of the Union forces by throwing hand-grenades and rolling shells with lighted fuses over their parapet down into the trench in front of the fort. They also countermined in hopes of tapping the gallery. So near were they to the attainment of this object that during the last day the miners could distinctly hear the conversation and orders given in the counter-mine.

The powder was brought up in barrels and kept in the main sap at a safe distance from the enemy's hand-grenades and shells, and there opened and placed in grain-sacks, each one of which contained about 25 pounds. These were taken upon the backs of the miners, who made the run over the exposed ground during the intervals between the explosion of the enemy's shells; and so well timed were these movements that, although it required nearly one hundred trips with the dangerous loads, all were landed in the mine without a single accident.

UNIDENTIFIED SOLDIER

3d Louisiana Infantry, Hébert's Brigade

On June 25 Rebel fears were confirmed when blue-clad troops ignited 2,200 pounds of powder they had placed in the mine beneath the 3d Louisiana Redan. The explosion caused large sections of the fort to "commence an upward movement, gradually breaking . . . into an immense fountain of finely pulverized earth."

For several weeks it had been known to our Engineer Corps, that the enemy were gradually approaching our works by a series of zig-zag trenches, and that their objective point was the 3d Louisiana Redan on the left of the Jackson Road, occupied by the 3d Louisiana Infantry and a detachment of the Appeal Battery with a three inch rifle gun.

Having divined their object, it became necessary to guard against its consequences as far as practicable and to this end a perpendicular shaft was sunk near the centre of the redan in order that the force of the explosion when it came would break through the wall of the shaft and thus lessen the effects of the explosion.

For several days before it came the officers and men occupying the redan learned of the impending catastrophe and by lying down and placing the ear close to the ground one could distinctly hear the click of pick and spade at work beneath. And while we knew the explosion must come and that very soon we could not abandon the works. But in order to minimize the death list the troops with the exception of the necessary guards and the detail at work in the shaft were moved back a few steps down the hill but resting on their arms day and night so as to be ready for any emergency that might arise. The 25th of June came in as usual. The constant patter and ping of sharpshooters bullets kept up

After the blast, as Union infantrymen charged the smoking remains of the fractured redan, many of them hurled "Ketchum" hand grenades, like the one found at Vicksburg and shown here, as they ran toward the Confederate position.

souri Infantry led by the gallant Col Eugene Erwin came up the hill with a yell that sounded above the roar of battle and completed the overthrow of the enemy. But in the very instant of victory Col Erwin fell on the top of our works literally riddled with bullets. Immediately following their failure to make a breach in our lines, the enemy began throwing hand grenades over the works. These were about the size and shape of goose eggs with a flat heavy base on one end and a split stick with a white paper inserted in the other end. For a few minutes the air was so full of them that it looked like a miniture snow storm. But when they struck they were hot enough. Our men held blankets by the four corners and thus kept them from striking any hard substance then threw them back. We also broke the cartridges off our fixed ammunition and put paper fuses in lighted and threw them over among the enemy.

the same as it had for many days until about the middle of the day it perceptibly slackened and by two o clock had entirely ceased in our immediate front, and a strange stillness came over every thing that brought with it an uncanny feeling. Men looked inquiringly into each others faces and moved restlessly about as if vainly endeavoring to shake off this indescribable presetiment of impending evil.

Scanning the hills held by the enemy little groups of men could plainly be seen on every point that gave a clear view of our fortifications and as these groups grew larger and the stillness continued the awful truth was realized that we stood face to face with a disaster the extent of which we could hardly conjecture. The click of the spade could now no longer be heard and we knew the work was done—a fearful tragedy was about to be enacted. But no cheek paled. No lip quivered. Grasping their arms a little tighter grimly they waited a moment thus. Then suddenly the earth under our feet gave a convulsive shudder and with a muffled roar a mighty column of earth men poles spades and guns arose many feet in the air. About fifty lives were blotted out in that instant. And many of the survivors felt of themselves to find out if they were yet alive.

Before the debris had quit falling and while the air was yet darkened with dust, a furious cannonading commenced. But only for a few minutes when the enemys infantry column charged up the outer works of the redan. But the 3d Louisiana heroes every one of them led by Col Russell met them with a determination born of desperation. The 3 inch rifle of the Appeal Battery with double charges of canister swept the top of the works. The heavy columns of the enemy recoiled from the shock, faltered and began to retreat. Just at this moment the 6th Mis-

Commanding the 3d Louisiana during the siege, Major David Pierson quickly rallied his stunned men following the mine explosion. Disabled by a wound during this action, Pierson returned to duty late in the war, surrendering in 1865.

ENTRANCE OF THE MINE UNDER FORT HILL—REBEL HAND GRENADE EXPLODING.

UNDER FORT HILL.

THE SIEGE OF VICKSBURG—BLOWING UP THE REBEL FORT HILL.—SKETCHED BY MR. THEODORE R. DAVIS.—[SEE PAGE 478.]

The upper left panel of this engraving from Harper's Weekly depicts the entrance—located near Wexford Lodge—of the mine aimed at the 3d Louisiana Redan. The next picture shows Yankee "sappers," or miners, hard at work inside the fetid tunnel leading to Fort Hill, the Union's name for the redan. Despite the dramatic nature of the explosion, shown in the bottom illustration, only a handful of Confederate troops died in the blast.

"It seems to me, in looking back, a wonder that anyone in that hot place was left to tell the story."

SERGEANT WILBUR F. CRUMMER
45TH ILLINOIS INFANTRY, LEGGETT'S BRIGADE

Before detonating the mine, the Yankees unleashed a bombardment so intense that the concussion caused by the simultaneous firing of so many guns caused blood to "spurt from the nose and ears" of the artillerymen. Somehow the Rebels in the redan endured the shelling and hit Crummer's regiment with "volley after volley" as it led the Yankee attack. Despite the deadly fire, the Illinoisans held on, retiring only after their "guns were too hot for further use."

June, the 25th, a heavy artillery fire opened all along the line, and at 2:30 p.m., the explosion takes place. Huge masses of earth were thrown in the air, and the ground was shaken as by an earthquake. As soon as the earth was rent, a bright glare of fire issued from the burning powder, but quickly died away, as there was nothing combustible in the fort. A few Confederate soldiers were hurled into the air, one or two of whom came down inside our lines, and some were buried in the fort. . . . One negro boy fell among the men of our company. He gathered himself together, and looked around as though he thought the day of judgment had surely come. . . . When the smoke and dust had cleared away partly, a great saucer-shaped crater was seen, where before was the A-shaped Fort Hill. It was large enough to hold about 60 or 80 men. The 23rd Indiana and the 45th Illinois were in the trenches ready to charge; the command was given before the dust had fully settled; the 23rd Indiana charging to the left of the crater to the top of the works; the 45th Illinois up and into the crater. The enemy had come up behind the big pile of earth thrown out by the explosion, and as we went into the crater, they met us with a terrible volley of musketry, but on the boys went, up and over the embankment with a cheer, the enemy falling back a few paces to an inner or second line of breastworks, where are placed cannon loaded with grape and canister, and these cannon belched forth their death-dealing missiles, in addition to the heavy musketry fire, with such telling effect that many of the brave boys fall to rise no more; the line wavers, staggers, and then falls back into the crater. The enemy charge on us, but we repel them at the west bank of the crater, and a hand-to-hand conflict rages for hours; hand grenades and loaded shells are lighted and thrown over the parapet as you would play ball. These shells and hand grenades carry death, as many as a dozen men being killed and wounded at one explosion. It seems to me, in looking back, a wonder that anyone in that hot place was left to tell the story. I have witnessed our men grab these shells, at the risk of their exploding, and fling them back. Many a brave hero laid down his life in that death hole, or, as we most appropriately called it, "Fort Hell."

Perhaps the only slave ever blasted to freedom, this youth—like many so-called "contrabands"—was known only by his first name, Tom. Apparently inside the redan when the mine exploded, he sailed "300 feet in the air," according to one account, and landed unhurt in the Northern lines. Afterward, Tom worked for the U.S. Quartermaster Department.

PRIVATE STEPHEN C. BECK
124TH ILLINOIS INFANTRY, LEGGETT'S BRIGADE

Beck, a member of Company C, the color company of his regiment, managed to escape unharmed from the horrific fighting in the charnel house that was the June 25 crater. Left in Vicksburg with the provost force as a "commissary" and headquarters guard after the city's surrender, he became ill and was sent north to recuperate at Camp Douglas, Illinois. There he remained in the hospital until he left the army in August 1865.

On the morning of the 26th the 124th was ordered into the "Crater" or place of the mine explosion. This place as near as I can describe it was shaped like a large wash basin and was about fifty feet in diameter. There was next to the Rebels a bank of the fort perhaps eight feet higher than any other part of what was left of the fort after the explosion. There were eight Companies of our Regt. two of which were ordered into the Crater at a time, stayed in twenty minutes then were relieved by two other Companies. This was the order for the entire day. One third of the men were placed as near the top of this bank or crest of fort as they could get and not be seen by the Rebels for the purpose of firing the guns the other two-thirds of the men, who were lower down in the Crater, loaded and passed up to us. My position was up near the crest of the fort on the firing line. Those gun barrels became very hot, so much so that my left hand became seared or blistered in handling those hot guns. My duty was to poke the loaded gun over this bank and fire it off having no knowledge whether I was doing any execution or not. After firing passed the gun down to be reloaded. Perhaps we had been two or three times in this Crater when the Rebels began tossing six pound shells with lighted fuse over at us. They came directly over my head, could have reached those shells if so disposed. I knew too well their contents and what they meant for us if we happened to be in their way. I think it was the first one they threw over that rolled into Robert Vance's lap and exploded, he was sitting down about sixteen feet from where I was. He fell forward on his face mangled badly. In a few minutes another came over rolled to his side then exploded tearing the poor man into shreads. Soon another came over and exploded, mortally wounding George Grabendike and George Lanham. All three belonged to my Company and were married men. It was too much for mortal man to stand such destruction. Those men of that vicinity who could get away did so, leaving the Crater and went out into the trench. As the gunloaders had fled for safety, I made it my business to follow as I had no ammunition to work with. It was a very hot place to be in if we had had nothing to have done, no breeze could touch us. Then add those bursting shells that filled the air with dirt throwing it all over us. It simply can not be described. It was terrific. It was afterwards named "The Slaughter Pen."

PRIVATE WILLIAM H. TUNNARD
3D LOUISIANA INFANTRY, HÉBERT'S BRIGADE

As Tunnard and his mates staved off starvation by munching mule and rat meat, they were well aware that their well-fed foes were once again digging toward the 3d Louisiana Redan in another attempt to blow up the position. Set off on July 1, this second explosion heavily damaged the already battle-scarred fort. The Union high command, however, unwilling to suffer a repeat of the June 25 bloodbath, decided not to attempt another assault on the redan.

June 28th, orders were issued to select the finest and fattest mules within the lines, and slaughter them, for the purpose of issuing their flesh as food to the troops; a half pound per man was the ration of this new species of flesh. Several Spaniards belonging to the Texas regiments were busily occupied in jerking this meat for future consumption. This meat was also supplied to the citizens from the market, and sold for fifty cents a pound. Mule flesh, if the animal is in good condition, is coarse-grained and darker than beef, but really delicious, sweet and juicy. Besides this meat, traps were set for rats, which were consumed in such numbers that ere the termination of the siege, they actually became a scarcity. Hunger will demoralize the most fastidious tastes, and quantity, not quality of food, becomes the great desideratum. The author made a hearty breakfast on fried rats, whose flesh he found very good.

June 29th found the enemy once more undermining the works held by the Third Louisiana Infantry, and the men went spiritedly at work digging a counter mine. The laborers were so near each other that the strokes of the pickaxes could be distinctly heard, as well as the sound of their voices. Thus the deadly struggle went on, the brave boys never once dreaming of despairing or giving up, although fighting over a volcano which at any moment might burst forth and engulf them in a general ruin. The Federal sharpshooters very impudently wished to know how we liked mule meat, proving conclusively that they were constantly informed of every event which occurred within the lines. Their question, however, was responded to in not very flattering or complimentary language. At 2 P.M. the enemy exploded the mine beneath the works occupied by the Third Louisiana Infantry. A huge mass of earth suddenly, and with tremendous force and a terrific explosion, flew upwards, descending with mighty power upon the gallant defenders, burying numbers beneath its falling fragments, bruising and mangling them most horribly. It seemed as if all hell had suddenly yawned upon the devoted band, and vomited forth its sulphurous fire and smoke upon them. The regiment, at this time, was supported by the First, Fifth and Sixth Mis-

souri Infantry, and upwards of a hundred were killed and wounded. Numbers were shocked and bruised, but not sufficiently to more than paralyze them for a few moments. The scene that followed beggared description. At first there was a general rush to escape the huge mass of descending earth. Then the survivors, without halting to inquire who had fallen, hastened to the immense gap in the works to repel the anticipated assault. The enemy, taught by a dearly-bought experience, made no attempt to enter the opening, not daring to assault the intrepid defenders. An immense number of 12-pound shells, thrown from wooden mortars, by the Yankees, descended among the troops, doing fearful execution.

An artist positioned in the yard of Wexford Lodge drew this view of the Union's network of twisting, gabion-lined saps in front of the 3d Louisiana Redan the day after the July 1 explosion. At left, four Yankees rest as a column of men marches toward them on an unknown mission. At center, a wounded soldier is carried rearward on a stretcher, while at right, sharpshooters, supported by men loading weapons for them, keep up a harassing fire on the redan.

"Now I first seemed to realize that something worse than death might come; I might be crippled, and not killed."

ANONYMOUS WOMAN
RESIDENT OF VICKSBURG

Cooped up in dark caves and cellars, suffering from near starvation, fearing death or, worse yet, maiming by the nearly constant bombardment of the city, and anxious to keep her pro-Union sentiments secret from her neighbors, this young diarist let her fears and frustrations begin to dominate her emotions. Political sympathies aside, her account reflects the strain felt by the city's almost unanimously pro-Confederate residents as the terrible siege entered its sixth week.

A horrible day. The most horrible yet to me, because I've lost my nerve. We were all in the cellar, when a shell came tearing through the roof, burst upstairs, tore up that room, and the pieces coming through both floors down into the cellar. . . . On the heels of this came Mr. J——, to tell us that young Mrs. P—— had had her thigh-bone crushed. When Martha went for the milk she came back horror-stricken to tell us the black girl there had her arm taken off by a shell. For the first time I quailed. I do not think people who are physically brave deserve much credit for it; it is a matter of nerves. In this way I am constitutionally brave, and seldom think of danger till it is over; and death has not the terrors for me it has for some others. Every night I had lain down expecting death, and every morning rose to the same prospect, without being unnerved. . . . But now I first seemed to realize that something worse than death might come; I might be crippled, and not killed. Life, without all one's powers and limbs, was a thought that broke down my courage. I said to H——, "You must get me out of this horrible place; I cannot stay; I know I shall be crippled." Now the regret comes that I lost control.

CHAPLAIN WILLIAM L. FOSTER
35TH MISSISSIPPI INFANTRY, MOORE'S BRIGADE

Foster recounts a soldier's view of events leading up to the surrender. Pemberton, realizing that his weakening army could not defend the city much longer, and holding no hope of relief from Johnston, decided to ask for a truce on July 3 to discuss surrender terms. Ironically, Johnston, whose troops were posted near Jackson, was finally making plans to attack Grant by July 7. Pemberton did not learn of this crucial fact until after he had surrendered.

As I was walking down the river on a visit to the Marine Hospital I saw several men cutting up & dressing what I at first thought was beef. But near by I discovered a head with long ears—a veritable mules head. It was mule beef! This told a sad tale. Our provisions were running low. The sixth week had now closed & nothing from Johnson. Our fate seems to stare us in the face. Still we hear rumors that he is coming with a mighty army. O that we could hear his canon thundering in the rear! What a welcome sound. Cant our government send us relief Shall Vicksburg fall for the want of energy on the part of our government? Will all the blood shed be spilled in vain? For the first time dark doubts would cross my mind. Maybe Johnson cannot get suficient troops to come to our relief. Ever of a hopeful disposition, I would not listen to such fears, but would still believe that at the last hour, the long expected help will come. Visiting the lines frequently, I discovered that the men generally had almost given up hope of relief from without. They considered the place as lost, though they were willing to lie in the trenches another month if it would save the place.

On the 3d of July the firing begins to cease upon the lines. What can be the matter? A flag of truce is sent in from our General to the enemy. What is the meaning of this? Great excitement prevails throughout the garrison. Some suspect that a surrender of the town is in contemplation. At such a thought the indignation is universal & almost beyond control. Our brave men, who had endured so much from hunger, danger, exposure & fatigue could not endure the thought of loosing all their labor. The thought of yielding up their arms into the hands of a hated foe & becoming prisoners of war was beyond endurance. To calm this excitement & give the men time for sober second thought, so that mutiny & rebellion might be avoided, the rumor was circulated that the flag of truce was only to request permission for the removing of some citizens out of the enemies lines. . . .

Just before I reached the hospital where I was residing . . . I heard the shrill note of the artillery-man's bugle. It was the first time I had heard the blast of the bugle during the siege. In a moment our canon ceased firing. The enemy beyond the river also ceased & stillness again rested upon the peaceful bosom of the father of waters. Now for the first time for many long weeks, the sound of canon is not heard. At three o clock in the evening, Gen. Pemberton in person seeks an interview with Gen. Grant. This looks very suspicious. I visit the lines. The impression there prevails that a surrender will be made. Night approaches. All is still.

Captain Joseph Leonard of the 96th Ohio received the Rebel truce flag on July 3 while on picket duty with his company in the trenches forward of the XIII Corps' main line. Leonard quickly passed the Confederate party up the chain of command to his division's officer of the day.

This sketch shows General Grant on July 3 seated under the flag in front of his simple tent headquarters and reading Pemberton's request for a meeting. Grant's uniformed son Fred, holding a pony, chats with Charles A. Dana, both of whom are seemingly unaware of the momentousness of the occasion.

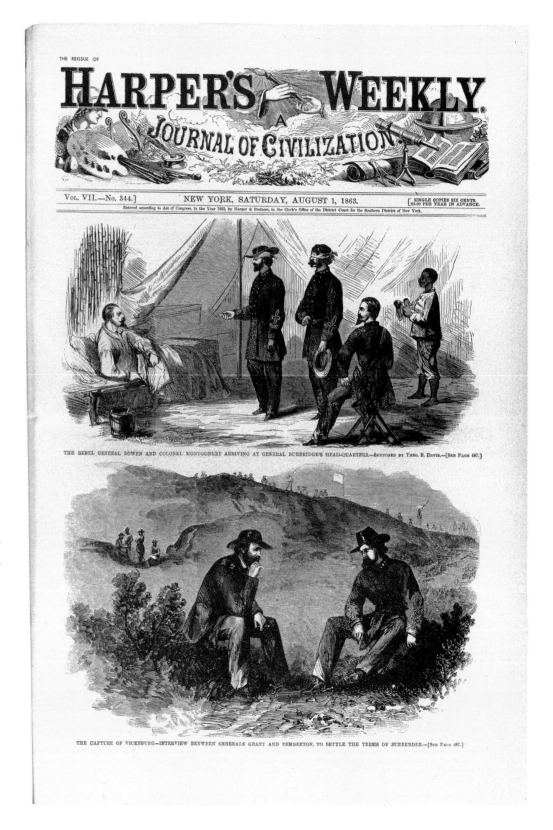

As could be expected, the "capitulation of Vicksburg" made welcome front-page news in the North's periodicals. Harper's Weekly ran this cover, along with Davis' account (next page), to report the final moments of the negotiated surrender. At top, the blindfolded Confederate emissaries General John Bowen and Colonel L. M. Montgomery present their mission to Brigadier General Stephen G. Burbridge, who had them forwarded up the line to Grant's headquarters. Below, Grant and Pemberton meet near the 3d Louisiana Redan at 3:00 p.m. to discuss terms of a surrender.

THEODORE DAVIS
SPECIAL ARTIST, HARPER'S WEEKLY

Although Pemberton and Grant knew each other from the Mexican War, their meeting was less cordial and more strained and difficult than Davis suggests. At one point, Pemberton rose and began to walk out in anger at Grant's demand of "unconditional surrender." Cooler heads prevailed, however, and the conference continued. Still, the generals were unable to agree to any terms, and the meeting adjourned with Grant promising to offer "final terms by ten o'clock that night."

The eyes of the gallant men in the rifle-pits in front of the Division of General A. J. Smith have been gladdened by the long-expected flag of truce that is, we hope, to close this eventful siege. The officers, General Bowen and Colonel Montgomery, were received by the "officer of the day" for the Division, Captain Joseph H. Green, of the Twenty-third Wisconsin Regiment, and by him conducted to the head-quarters of General Burbridge, Captain Green having first taken the precaution to blindfold the officers. At the quarters of General Burbridge, the General, who had been quite ill for some days, received them, with an apology for his inability to rise from his couch. The handkerchiefs were soon removed, and the message of which they were bearers was sent to General Grant, who returned word that he would meet General Pemberton at three o'clock in the afternoon, when the officers took their departure, blindfolded as before, walking out to the lines.

At three o'clock this afternoon the meeting of Generals Grant and Pemberton took place near the rebel work Fort Hill.

After a conference of some two hours, in the most quiet and courteous manner, the two officers parted with a hand-shake, that seemed most friendly.

Quietly seated upon the grassy slope near the rebel works, one could only look with the greatest interest upon the scene.

Meantime a conference was being had near by by Generals McPherson and Smith and General Bowen and Colonel Montgomery, the officers of the Generals' staffs being *en groupe*.

MAJOR GENERAL ULYSSES S. GRANT
COMMANDER, ARMY OF THE TENNESSEE

After 47 arduous days, the siege of Vicksburg finally and officially came to an end on the auspicious date of July 4, the day usually commemorated by both sides. Grant, in his memoirs, explained his reasons for the rather liberal parole he offered the Confederates. With the vital city lost to the Secessionist cause, the Union now controlled most of the Mississippi River, as only the Rebel stronghold at Port Hudson prevented the Confederacy from being split completely in two.

At three o'clock Pemberton appeared at the point suggested in my verbal message, accompanied by the same officers who had borne his letter of the morning. Generals Ord, McPherson, Logan and A. J. Smith, and several officers of my staff, accompanied me. Our place of meeting was on a hillside within a few hundred feet of the rebel lines. Near by stood a stunted oak-tree, which was made historical by the event. It was but a short time before the last vestige of its body, root and limb had disappeared, the fragments taken as trophies. Since then the same tree has furnished as many cords of wood, in the shape of trophies, as "The True Cross." . . .

. . . Had I insisted upon an unconditional surrender there would have been over thirty thousand men to transport to Cairo, very much to the inconvenience of the army on the Mississippi. Thence the prisoners would have had to be transported by rail to Washington or Baltimore; thence again by steamer to Aiken's—all at very great expense. At Aiken's they would have had to be paroled, because the Confederates did not have Union prisoners to give in exchange. Then again Pemberton's army was largely composed of men whose homes were in the South-west; I knew many of them were tired of the war and would get home just as soon as they could. A large number of them had voluntarily come into our lines during the siege, and requested to be sent north where they could get employment until the war was over and they could go to their homes.

The Father of Waters Unvexed

The Union forces still had important business to attend to after the surrender of Vicksburg. The town of Port Hudson, nearly 300 river miles to the south and the last Confederate stronghold on the Mississippi, had yet to be taken *(pages 146-159)*. More pressing for Grant was to deal with General Joseph Johnston, who, having belatedly decided to try to relieve Vicksburg, was advancing toward the Big Black River and the Union rear with four divisions—more than 31,000 men.

That rear was covered, of course, by General Sherman's blocking force of nearly 30,000. But Sherman and Grant had no intention of letting Johnston strike first if they could help it. Even as negotiations for the surrender were going on, Grant ordered Sherman to prepare to lash out as soon as Vicksburg was in Union hands. To make the task easier, Grant added 16,000 troops to those already under Sher-

Amid the crowd of Yankee celebrators, Vicksburg residents lament the raising of the Stars and Stripes at the courthouse on July 4, symbolizing Federal control of the town. One of Grant's first moves after the surrender was to send in food to the starved residents.

man's command. On the morning of July 4 the telegraph in Sherman's headquarters clicked out the news that Vicksburg had capitulated, and within minutes Sherman's army of 46,000, nearly two-thirds of Grant's entire command, moved against Johnston.

There would be no big battle, however. Johnston, cautiously reconnoitering Sherman's defenses on July 3 and 4, had become increasingly puzzled when he heard no artillery fire from Vicksburg. Then, on July 5, word of General Pemberton's surrender came through. Johnston began pulling his troops back toward the city of Jackson, knowing the Federals could now turn on him in overwhelming force.

Sherman pursued quickly, his three corps managing to get across the Big Black despite high water and bloody skirmishes with well-hidden Rebel troops. By July 9 his advance units were within five miles of Jackson.

Johnston's four divisions meanwhile had reached the city, the troops spending July 8 and 9 strengthening the ring of earthworks constructed back in May to fend off the first Federal attack. At 9:00 a.m. on July 10, Sherman's guns began shelling the Confederate defenses while Federal troops probed forward to test their strength.

Johnston's reply—return fire from a number of big rifled guns—quickly convinced Sherman that a head-on assault would be suicidal. Another siege was in order. To isolate the city, Sherman sent one of his corps around to the north and another to the south, while the third remained to the west. The Yankees then dug their own ring of rifle pits and gun emplacements about 1,000 yards from the Confederate works.

With that they sat down to wait—except for one probing action, which got badly out of hand. On July 12 troops of Colonel Isaac C. Pugh's brigade of Brigadier General Jacob G. Lauman's division, supposed to be merely testing the Confederates' south-facing positions, were mistakenly ordered to charge across a cornfield toward some woods—where they became entangled in a line of fallen timber. In minutes three Illinois regiments were cut to pieces by Rebel cannon and rifle fire, the Federals losing a total of 500 men out of the 1,000 engaged. Lauman was immediately relieved of duty and sent home to Iowa, never to command again.

The Confederate defenders also managed to throw back several Union probes from the north. Despite these evidences of his defensive strength, General Johnston soon decided that with only four divisions to face Sherman's nine, holding Jackson was hopeless. He ordered a withdrawal. By dawn on July 17 his infantry and artillery had silently slipped from their earthworks and were heading east for the bridges spanning the Pearl River.

Sherman, surprised to find the enemy gone, was at first slow to react, but by the afternoon of July 17 Federal troops had occupied Jackson, the men of the 35th Massachusetts geefully hoisting their regimental flag atop the golden dome of the capitol building of Confederate president Jefferson Davis' home state. Then, having ordered supplies of bread, flour, and bacon rushed to the hungry people of the desolate city, Sherman dispatched cavalry and other units to chase the fleeing Confederates.

The Union troops trudged eastward despite broiling summer heat, pursuing Johnston's army to the town of Canton and the village of Brandon. But the Rebels kept moving, finally falling back to Morton in the pinewood uplands of eastern Mississippi, a full 40 miles from Jackson. At that point Sherman called off the chase. The Confederates were now too far from Vicksburg to cause trouble. Besides, the Federals had made enemy operations impossible by ripping up every railroad line and bridge in the entire region. His task completed, Sherman turned his army around and headed back for Vicksburg.

There the Confederate surrender had been completed with astonishing calm and dispatch. On July 4 the entire garrison of Vicksburg, as Grant later wrote, "marched out of their works and formed line in front, stacked their arms and marched back in good order." While the ragged, beaten enemy gave up their weapons, the watching Federal troops, in a moving show of sympathy and restraint, kept strict silence. "Our whole army present," Grant recalled, "witnessed this scene without cheering."

The honor of leading the occupying troops into Vicksburg was given to General John "Black Jack" Logan, whose men had experienced much of the bloodiest fighting of the campaign. Grant then, with everything secure, ordered huge quantities of food shipped in to feed the half-starved Confederate troops and residents.

The behavior of the Yankee soldiers re-mained as exemplary as that of their commander. "No word of exultation was uttered to irritate the feelings of the prisoners," wrote a Confederate sergeant, William Tunnard. "On the contrary, every sentinel who came upon post brought haversacks filled with provisions, which he would give to some famished Southerner with the remark, 'Here, Reb, I know you are starved nearly to death.' "

When the time came for the Confederate prisoners who had signed their paroles to march out of Vicksburg, the scene was much the same. "Not a cheer went up, not a remark was made that would give pain," Grant remembered. "Really, I believe there was a feeling of sadness just then in the breasts of most of the Union soldiers at seeing the dejection of their late antagonists."

There was, of course, sadness and shock all across the South when news spread that the "Gibraltar of the West" had fallen. Now the two halves of the Confederacy, east and west, had been severed and an all-important supply line cut. "Absolute ruin seems our portion," wrote General Josiah Gorgas, ordnance chief in Richmond. "The Confederacy totters to its destruction."

Elation in the North equaled the despair in the South. Church bells rang in every town from Maine to Minnesota, and a half-dozen cities boomed with 100-gun salutes. Grant was hailed as a hero, the one Union commanding general who could and would fight. "I write," President Lincoln said in a letter to Grant, "as a grateful acknowledgement for the almost inestimable service you have done the country."

That service was not just military but political as well. After a seven-month string of almost unbroken disasters for the Union army, most recently the humiliating defeat of the Army of the Potomac under General Joseph Hooker at Chancellorsville in May, the Northern press and people had begun grumbling loudly against the Lincoln government's conduct of the war. But Grant's victory at Vicksburg, combined with the simultaneous defeat of Lee at Gettysburg and General William S. Rosecrans' recent success in gaining control of central Tennessee after the Tullahoma campaign, muted the voices of doom. At last it seemed the North might win the war. The sudden upswing in Federal fortunes doubtless helped Lincoln win reelection in 1864.

Grant went on to take over Rosecrans' army, bottled up in Chattanooga after its bloody reversal at the Battle of Chickamauga in September. Following close behind him was Sherman with a corps, then General McPherson and the troops that had garrisoned Vicksburg.

As for General McClernand, Grant had managed to rid himself of that troublesome and inept politico. After the May 22 Federal assault on the Vicksburg defenses, McClernand had issued an order congratulating his troops on their performance—and also claiming for himself the lion's share of the credit for virtually every success Grant's army had achieved. Grant seethed over this outrage but bided his time. It soon came.

McClernand stepped over the line when he had the self-congratulatory order—that "effusion of vain-glory and hypocrisy," as Sherman labeled it—published in a Memphis newspaper. This act violated a war department order forbidding such publication without approval by a commanding officer. Grant relieved McClernand of command and sent him home to Illinois—where he moldered until given a minor assignment late in the war.

SIEGE OF VICKSBURG CASUALTIES

FEDERAL

Killed	763
Wounded	3,746
Missing or Captured	162
Total	4,671

CONFEDERATE

Killed	805
Wounded	1,938
Missing or Captured	129
Subtotal	2,872
Surrendered on July 4	29,491
Total	32,363

"The rebels in their retreat polluted the branches they crossed by killing and throwing into the streams their worn-out horses and mules, hoping thus to strike a blow at us."

LIEUTENANT SETH A. RANLETT
36TH MASSACHUSETTS INFANTRY, BOWMAN'S BRIGADE

Ranlett enlisted as a private in August 1862 and rose quickly to become lieutenant in early December, just before the Battle of Fredericksburg. The 36th then moved west to Vicksburg and took a leading role in the march on Jackson. In the heat and rain Ranlett contracted a fever and was discharged in February 1864.

Upon reaching the Big Black River at Birdsong's Ferry on the 6th, our brigade was detailed to build a bridge. At this point the river was not very wide or deep, but the steep banks made it difficult to approach. Parties scattered in all directions and returned with timber and boards from farm buildings and fence rails. These were floated out and bound together with withes in such a way that a floating bridge was constructed strong enough to bear men and horses passing a few at a time. We worked all day and night of the 6th and until noon of the 7th on this bridge. The First Division had passed over it safely, and two brigades of the Second Division, when, as Durrell's Battery was crossing, the bridge suddenly broke and was swept away, cutting off Colonel Griffin's brigade, General Smith's division and most of the artillery. This was sent round to Messenger's Crossing and by means of rafts and a ferry-boat found sunk in the river and raised, the infantry was ferried over during the afternoon and night of the 7th. This accident greatly delayed the movement of the corps, which was forced to halt till the afternoon of the 8th for the delayed troops and artillery. The day we crossed the river the heat was something fearful and many of the men were overcome by it. Late in the afternoon there came up one of those thunder showers for which the Black River valley is famous. The lightning was appalling; the rain fell in torrents and the roads soon became little better than a quagmire. No orders came to halt and the troops plodded on as best they could. Some of the artillery became mired and badly hindered the movement of the infantry. Darkness came on and the storm continued, showing no signs of holding up. Finally, Colonel Norton's horse and my own became terrified and unmanageable, and we were forced to dismount and lead them, their plunging making it dangerous for the men around us. It was at this time that Quartermaster Hawes of the 35th Massachusetts was killed by a falling limb, and about nine o'clock in the evening Major Robert Parrett of the 100th Indiana in General Smith's division was also killed by a falling tree. It was a fearful night, and though our corps in its campaigning over six states saw some pretty tough times, no one has ever questioned the fact that that night "took the cake." At length the order came to go into bivouac, and our brigade marched into an old cotton-field, ankle-deep in mud, and stacked arms.

After much hard work some fires were started, and then followed a dipper of hot coffee, a good soldierly growl, a pipe, and—sleep.

PRIVATE ALEXANDER G. DOWNING

11TH IOWA INFANTRY, CHAMBERS' BRIGADE

When assigned to the kind of supply train escort duty described here, the 21-year-old Downing claimed that, "the men generally dreaded this kind of service for it was exceedingly dangerous. Then, too, much of the journey had to be made on the run—but it is a soldier's business to obey orders and do the best he can."

Saturday, 11th—The Eleventh Iowa started at sunup this morning for Jackson, Mississippi, as an escort for two hundred and forty-five wagons loaded with provisions and ammunition for General Sherman's army. By night we were within one mile of Clinton, where we went into bivouac, closely corralling the wagons. We rode on the wagons a part of the time during the journey. Whenever they came to a stretch of good roads, the teamsters would put the horses on the run, and in order to keep up we had to climb onto the loaded wagons. We suffered for lack of water today, for the rebels in their retreat polluted the branches they crossed by killing and throwing into the streams their worn-out horses and mules, hoping thus to strike a blow at us. Their march was marked by the buzzards flying above or feeding upon the carcasses of the slain animals.

Sunday, 12th—We started this morning at sunup and arrived at General Sherman's headquarters at 10 o'clock. Two regiments of Sherman's army came out to reinforce our train guard. They feared that the rebels' cavalry would make a raid on the train before we could reach the main army. We arrived safely without losing a single wagon. Cannonading is going on quite lively from both sides. Good water is very scarce here, and the few wells and cisterns which we can draw upon are crowded all the time; I stood with two canteens for more than an hour waiting for my turn.

CORPORAL LUCIUS W. BARBER

15TH ILLINOIS INFANTRY, HALL'S BRIGADE

Following the fall of Jackson, Barber came down with high fevers and dysentery, which put him out of action for several months, including 60 days of furlough home in Illinois in October and November 1863. Back in service by January of the following year, he was captured on October 4 at Ackworth after the Union victory at Atlanta. He spent almost two months in the notorious Andersonville prison before being paroled in late November, when he returned to his unit.

Much to our satisfaction, we now received orders to march to the front and join our division. Before night we had taken our position in line of battle. Johnson had made a stand at Jackson. Gen. Sherman concluded not to sacrifice the lives of his men by assaulting their works when a safer and surer method was open to him. So we commenced fortifying and gradually extending our lines toward the rear of the enemy with the purpose of surrounding him and cutting off his retreat. Our division-commander, Gen. Lauman, now made a blunder which lost him his command. In his strong desire for popularity and promotion, he overdid the thing. He misinterpreted an order to move forward our line for a charge on the rebel works. The charge was made and the rebels finding it unsupported, concentrated their whole available force against us. Unfalteringly we swept up to within a few rods of their works, but their fire was too terrific for flesh

Brigadier General Jacob Gartner Lauman, a merchant before the war, was relieved of his command by Ord and Sherman after the disastrous attack at Jackson mentioned by Barber. Grant sent him home to Iowa to await orders. Although Lauman never saw active duty again, he was brevetted a major general as of March 13, 1865, for "gallant and meritorious services during the war" and mustered out the following August.

and blood to stand. We were forced to retire with fully one-fourth of the boys placed hors de combat. A flag of truce was sent in asking permission to bury our dead. It was refused. They lay where they had fallen until the stench became so offensive to the rebels that they were forced to do something with them. So without any regard to decency, they scooped out shallow holes and rolled them in and left a great many arms and legs in sight.

PRIVATE DOUGLAS J. CATER
19TH LOUISIANA INFANTRY, D. W. ADAMS' BRIGADE

A skilled musician and music teacher when the war broke out, Cater took his violin along when he enlisted. He first served as a bugler in the 3d Texas Cavalry and then, in June 1862, transferred to the 19th Louisiana to fight beside his older brother, Rufus. The piano Cater mentions here was moved to the breastworks of Slocomb's battery from a house that was burned by the Confederate defenders of Jackson. The piano was saved and given to veterans of Slocomb's battery after the war.

*S*ome of our regiment had told the battery "boys" to send for me and that I would give them some good music on that piano. Slocumb sent for me, and brother Rufus went with me. We were enjoying the music, paying no attention to the shells and minnie balls which were passing over us when Capt. Slocumb, standing near the piano, caught the sound of the Federal yell, and looking over the breastworks, saw them coming on a charge. He was at his guns and brother Rufus and I were back at our posts with the regiment quicker than the time it has taken to write of this incident. We had reserved our fire until Slocumb's Battery opened fire on them. It seems that this was the signal for an attack all along the line but it met with such fearful slaughter that they retired out of the range of our guns.

Our brigade commander Gen. Dan Adams, mounted the breastworks and fired two rounds with a musket of one of our company men. Such is the indescribable enthusiasm which drives out fear in the storm of battle and sometimes causes our best generals to forget that too much depends on them to take such risks. . . . We took 150 prisoners in front of our brigade, who would not attempt to fall back under the fire of our muskets. After the firing ceased and quiet was restored, I went back to the piano and we had more music.

Major General Joseph E. Johnston (shown here in the colonel's coat he usually wore) urged Pemberton to bring his army out of Vicksburg and join forces to campaign actively against Grant's army in hopes of destroying the Union forces before they could be unified and reinforced. At the same time Confederate president Jefferson Davis was demanding that Pemberton defend the city at all costs. Unable to coordinate his strategy with the waffling Pemberton, Johnston finally marched against Grant's rear when it was too late; Vicksburg had already fallen. Johnston thereupon rushed his forces back to Jackson, where, after an eight-day siege, he was forced to abandon that city again, this time fleeing east.

Col. Z. R. Bliss. 10th Regt. R.V.V.

COLONEL ZENAS R. BLISS

7TH RHODE ISLAND INFANTRY, GRIFFIN'S BRIGADE

Bliss organized the 7th in Providence in September 1862. After fighting at Fredericksburg, it moved west to the sieges of Vicksburg and Jackson. Although he contracted "remittent fever" in Mississippi, Bliss continued in command off and on at the Wilderness, Spotsylvania, Cold Harbor, and Petersburg and in the pursuit of Lee in early April 1865. Here he recounts the dangers of picket duty around Jackson.

"About one o'clock in the morning, a shot was fired, and then came the most horrible scream that one could imagine, and all was still."

About one o'clock in the morning, a shot was fired, and then came the most horrible scream that one could imagine, and all was still. It was a very dark night, and in the very heavy woods and thick underbrush it was impossible to see anything distinctly. When the men went out to find that cause of the scream and the shot, they found a sentinel lying dead with his throat cut, and no other wounds on his body. Another man was put in his place and the relief turned and went back to the main line.

When they went around the next time to post sentinels, this man was missing.

He turned up during the day and told a remarkable story of his experience, which seems hardly credible, but was believed by the Officers to whom he told it. He said that soon after taking the Post of the man who had his throat cut, he heard a noise in the leaves near him, on the ground, but he could see nothing and stood perfectly still. In a few seconds he felt something press against his arm, and he moved his body slightly away from the pressure. In a few seconds he felt something press against his abdomen, and grabbed it with his hand. It was a sabre bayonet or a bowie knife tied to a pole. As he grabbed it, it made a quick lunge and cut his clothes across the body. He clubbed his musket and struck with all his might and hit somebody, and I believe they clinched. At all events he fell in a ravine with a Rebel on top of him.

Just at that time there were several shots fired, and the Rebel fell dead on top of him, being instantly killed by a shot from his own men. He laid still with the man on top of him, and soon all was quiet again. He crawled out from under the man, and went towards the Rebel line in the darkness, and passed through it, I believe, without being captured, at any rate he succeeded in getting away from them and working his way back into our lines.

There was a deep ravine immediately in front of the post of this picket, that our men did not know about, and it was supposed that the Rebels had a knife on a long pole; that they would make a noise with a stick in the leaves and when the sentinel fired in the direction of the noise, thinking someone was approaching in that direction, they would jump on him, and as they did with the first sentinel, cut his throat. His exact whereabouts being of course indicated, and he rendered plainly visible, from the flash of his rifle. As the second sentinel did not shoot at the noise, they attempted to stab him with the knife on the end of the pole.

I think the sentinel after being stabbed or after having his clothes cut, fired his piece and seeing a man near him clubbed his rifle and struck, and then they clinched, with the result as above stated.

In corroboration of his story, the man had his trouser cut across the abdomen, and his breast was soaked in blood, as he said, from the man who was killed, when on top of him.

PRIVATE JOHN W. GREEN

9TH KENTUCKY (C.S.) INFANTRY, HELM'S BRIGADE

Green's journal entries outline the siege of Jackson. Green went on to fight at Chickamauga and Chattanooga and in the Atlanta campaign. Captured at Jonesboro, Georgia, in the summer of 1864, he was soon exchanged and rejoined his now mounted unit. They harassed Sherman's flank during his March to the Sea.

The enemy appeared in our front on July the 9th. The next morning the fireing between the opposing forces was quite brisk but they made no charge upon our works. July 11th some pretty sharp fiting. The artillery being pretty active [and] the extreme right of our line being pretty hard pressed we went to Lorings assistance and repulsed the ennemy.

The line of battle ran right through the yard of Col Withers, an old man, probably nearly 70. One of the soldiers was killed & the old gentleman buckled on the dead mans cartridge box & took his gun & began deliberately to pick off the enemy. Our boys would lie down & load & then rise to their knees & fire at the enemy, but he stood erect in plain view of them, loading & firing with deadly aim, completely ignoring our calls to him to lie down to load. He was fighting for his fire side & the fire of battle was in his eye but in a few minutes the deadly bullet felled him & he expired with the remark, "There they've got me." We repulsed this charge & burried him & the others who were killed in his yard & returned that night to our rifle pits on the extreme left.

July 12th. Fighting again brisk. Our good commisary Seargent Henry E Hughes brought to us the days cooked rations. We had hardly broken our fast before the enemy made a furious attack on our Brigade but we were fixed for them & when they were in close range we opened Capt Cobbs battery on them, which to this time had been masked, & the slaughter was dreadful. We killed two hundred & fifty of them in less than a half hour. They had been repulsed in every attack thus far.

July 14th. A truce has been arranged to bury the dead, the stench has become terrible. All Our dead have been buried as the deaths occured, we having held our lines without fail; it is therefore their dead we are helping to bury.

July 15th. Brisk musketry & artillery fire.

July 16th. More quiet today. Some sharp shooting but no charge & only occasional artillery fire; at midnight we are ordered to fall into line & be very quiet; we soon find out we are in retreat for we cross Pearl river. Great quiet was preserved until we got across the river, when the pontoon bridge was burnt. It was important to keep the enemy in ignorance of our movements, otherwise they would have rushed upon us while we were crossing the river & caught our forces divided. Genl Johnston found they had gotten heavy reenforcements & were preparing to flank us.

Our Brigade covered the retreat in such a soldierly manner as to receive the praise of Genl Johnston. We marched 14 miles & bivouacked near Brandon Miss.

LIEUTENANT COLONEL ADEN G. CAVINS

97TH INDIANA INFANTRY, COCKERILL'S BRIGADE

The 97th had done only light picket duty near Jackson until the July 16 attack, in which Cavins describes being stunned when his horse was killed by artillery fire. He went on to fight at Missionary Ridge and in the Atlanta campaign. A graduate of the Indiana University School of Law before the war, he returned to his Bloomfield, Indiana, hometown after mustering out in 1865 to set up a law practice with his brother, E. H. Cavins, who had commanded the 14th Indiana Infantry.

Jackson, Miss., July 17, 1863.
My Dear Matilda:
Our regiment entered Jackson about sunrise this morning. I am completely worn out, so stunned and jarred by concussion from cannon balls that I have not a sound limb; with headache, backache and every muscle in my body sore.

On yesterday at 11 o'clock a.m., our regiment and the Sixth Iowa were ordered to storm the rebel works covering a front of over one-half

"He was fighting for his fire side & the fire of battle was in his eye."

mile. The Ninety-seventh went in most beautifully, passing through a storm of grape and cannister until within about two hundred yards of the rebel fortifications, when we stopped, having the cover of a little elevation about two feet high rounding over so as to make but a slight swell in the field. We held our position, picking off the rebel gunners until 4 o'clock p.m., with the shell bursting over us and in our faces, and the grape and cannister raking over us, missing our men about one foot. Twenty or thirty shell burst in from four feet to thirty feet of me, and sometimes almost burying me in the earth. The rebels sent out three brigades and drove the Sixth Iowa so as to turn our flanks and we retreated through the terrific fire to our original lines.

We lost over thirty, killed and wounded. One shell that burst about four feet from me stunned me so much that the news passed along the line that I was killed. I could not hear anything in my left ear for four or five hours. When flanked and all our support gave way, I ordered the right wing to fall back. They went on a run through the grape and cannister, and solid shot, and occasionally musketry, and rallied on our old line. I was so stunned that I had to walk through it, but did not get a scratch though covered all over with dirt.

Our boys behaved heroically. Old officers compliment us and say we were in the worst fire they ever saw. Col. Catterson says he never saw anything like it. I cannot imagine how any of us ever got back. The rebels evacuated the place this morning or last night, and, believing the place deserted, we, being the skirmishers of our division, started off this morning early and soon placed our flag on the rebel works. But I must stop. In the hottest of the work I thought of your last letter. How much suffering your connection with me had inflicted on you. I have felt more or less of sadness ever since I got that letter and hope your next will be more cheerful.

CAPTAIN GEORGE WASHINGTON WHITMAN
51ST NEW YORK INFANTRY, FERRERO'S BRIGADE

Whitman had risen quickly from private to captain. Slightly wounded at Fredericksburg, he otherwise fought unscathed through many of the bloodiest battles of the war until he was captured during the siege of Petersburg. His somewhat prosaic diary was less than the "perfect poem of the war" his older brother first called it, but it probably contributed to the realism of Walt Whitman's Civil War poetry.

The enemy did not pretend to make a stand, untill they got behind their entrenchments at Jackson, this City you know is the Capitol of the state and is built on the bank of the Pearl river, their earthworks started from the river above the town and ran along the outskirts untill they struck the river again just below the city, makeing a line of about 3 miles in length. The enemy were supposed to be from 25 to 30,000 strong and on the afternoon of July Tenth we drove their skirmishers, inside of their entrenchments, and we threw forward a heavy line of skirmishers, reaching nearly the whole length of the ene-

After surrendering his Army of Vicksburg on July 4, Lieutenant General John C. Pemberton (left) was accused by many Southerners of having divided loyalties because he was a native of Pennsylvania. Actually, years of prewar duty in the South and the influence of his Virginia-born wife had given him a devotion to the region. Rather than being treasonous, as some claimed, Pemberton, harassed and bewildered by Grant's brilliant maneuverings and by conflicting orders from Jefferson Davis and Joseph Johnston, was outgeneraled. In May 1864 he resigned his general's commission and served the rest of the war as a lieutenant colonel and inspector of artillery. His sword and scabbard are shown below.

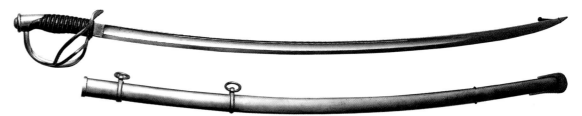

mys line, and within easy rifle range of the enemys works. Each Brigade had a certain part of the line, and the regts, relieved each other every 24 hours that is, the ones that were up to the front one day, were moved back a short distance, the next, and held in reserve, but had to be ready, at any moment to fall in and sometimes when we heard heavy fireing, we had to fall in two or three times during the night. It seemed very curious fighting to me, and very different from what we had been used to. There was no general engagement but during the day, and sometimes during the night, quite a brisk fire was kept by sharpshooters on each side, Each party kept themselvs concealed as much as possible, the enemy behind their earthworks, and our side behind trees, and by laying flat on the ground, and the moment anyone showed themselvs there was two or three rifles pointed at them. I expected Gen. Sherman (who I believe had command on our side) intended to skirmish with them, and keep them buisy on this side of the river, while someone crossed the river, and made an attack on the rear, which of course would have cutt off their retreat, but for some probably good reason (that I know nothing about) nothing of the kind was attempted, as far as I can hear. The skirmish was kept up untill about daylight on the morning of the 17th when a white flag was run up, by some citazens on one of the rebel works and we soon found that the whole rebel force had skedaddled during the night, and we went in and occupied the place.

ANONYMOUS WOMAN
RESIDENT OF VICKSBURG

This unnamed pro-Union diarist recounts what she heard and saw of the surrender of Pemberton's force on July 4. She learned of the capitulation in a conversation with a Rebel who came to her doorstep to ask for scraps to eat. Thus alerted, she and her husband (designated only as H—— in the diary) climbed to an upper balcony to witness the subsequent events, which were as glorious and joyous in their eyes as they were tragic and hope-destroying to their neighbors.

*I*s it true about the surrender?"

"Yes; we have had no official notice, but they are paroling out at the lines now, and the men in Vicksburg will never forgive Pemberton. An old granny! A child would have known better than to shut men up in this cursed trap to starve to death like useless vermin. . . . Haven't I seen my friends carted out three or four in a box, that had died of starvation! Nothing else, madam! Starved to death because we had a fool for a general."

"Don't you think you're rather hard on Pemberton? He thought it his duty to wait for Johnston."

"Some people may excuse him, ma'am, but we'll curse him to our

"The men in Vicksburg will never forgive Pemberton."

dying day. Anyhow, you'll see the blue-coats directly."

Breakfast dispatched, we went on the upper gallery. What I expected to see was files of soldiers marching in, but it was very different. The street was deserted, save by a few people carrying home bedding from their caves. Among these was a group taking home a little creature, born in a cave a few days previous, and its wan-looking mother. About eleven o'clock a man in blue came sauntering along, looking about curiously. Then two followed him, then another. . . .

Soon a group appeared on the court-house hill, and the flag began slowly to rise to the top of the staff. As the breeze caught it, . . . it sprang out like a live thing exultant. . . . In an hour more a grand rush of people setting toward the river began. . . .

"Oh," said H——, springing up, "look! It is the boats coming around the bend."

Truly, it was a fine spectacle to see that fleet of transports sweep around the curve and anchor in the teeth of the batteries so lately vomiting fire.

ALEXANDER ST. CLAIR ABRAMS
NEWSPAPERMAN, VICKSBURG WHIG

Abrams describes the triumphal entry of Union forces into Vicksburg and then launches into an emotional and highly dubious diatribe alleging outrageous Federal depredations throughout the city and holding the Yankees responsible for behavior "beyond all expression" by freed slaves. Most other Southern eyewitnesses expressed wonder at the respect for life and property shown by the Yankees, as well as the kindnesses and care extended to the soldiers and civilians of the conquered city.

On Saturday, at twelve o'clock, M., Logan's division of McPherson's corps, of the Federal army, commenced entering the city, and in a quarter of an hour Vicksburg was crammed with them. Their first act was to take possession of the court house, on the spire of which they hoisted the United States flag, amid the exultant shouts of

This first national pattern Confederate flag, the so-called Stars and Bars, flew over one of the garrisons in Vicksburg during the siege. Federal soldiers of the 83d Indiana Infantry captured this flag on July 4 and held it as a trophy. It was not returned to Vicksburg until 1962.

their comrades, and a deep feeling of humiliation on the part of the Confederate soldiers who witnessed the hauling up of the flag which they had hoped never to see floating over the city they had so long and proudly boasted impregnable, and never to be taken by the enemy of the South.

After the enemy's forces had stacked their arms, they scattered over the city, and then commenced a scene of pillage and destruction which beggars all description. Houses and stores were broken open, and their contents appropriated by the plunderers. The amount of money and property stolen in this way was enormous, and the Yankee soldiers appeared to glory in their vandalism. . . . In reply to a remonstrance on the part of a gentleman whose residence they had broken open, they said, "we have fought hard enough to capture Vicksburg, and now we have got it, we intend to plunder every house in the d——d rebel city." . . .

The conduct of the negroes, after the entrance of their "liberators," was beyond all expression. While the Yankee army was marching through the streets, crowds of them congregated on the sidewalks, with a broad grin of satisfaction on their ebony countenances. The next day, which was Sunday, witnessed a sight, which would have been ludicrous had it not galled our soldiers by the reflection that they were compelled to submit to it. There was a great turn out of the "contrabands," dressed up in the most extravagant style imaginable, promenading through the streets, as if Vicksburg had been confiscated and turned over [to] them. In familiar conversation with the negro wenches, the soldiers of the Federal army were seen, arm-in-arm, marching through the streets, while the "bucks" congregated on the corners and discussed the happy event that brought them freedom.

Accorded the honor because of its pivotal role throughout the campaign, especially at Raymond and Champion's Hill and in the fighting around the 3d Louisiana Redan, Major General John A. Logan's division leads the march into Vicksburg on July 4. Logan (inset) went on to command the XV Corps and briefly the Army of the Tennessee through the Atlanta, Georgia, and Carolinas campaigns. After the war, he served as a U.S. congressman and senator for several years but was unsuccessful as Cleveland's vice presidential running mate in 1884. He campaigned successfully to have Memorial Day established as a national holiday.

PRIVATE WILLIAM H. TUNNARD
3D LOUISIANA INFANTRY, HÉBERT'S BRIGADE

This description of the rage and frustration felt by the soldiers of Tunnard's regiment at the surrender order, contrasted with the subsequent friendly fraternization between old enemies, first appeared in Tunnard's "A Southern Record: A History of the Third Regiment Louisiana Infantry." Published in 1866, and based on private letters, journals, newspaper accounts, official reports, and personal observances, Tunnard's was one of the first Civil War unit histories.

The receipt of this order was the signal for a fearful outburst of anger and indignation seldom witnessed. The members of the Third Louisiana Infantry expressed their feeling in curses loud and deep. Many broke their trusty rifles against the trees, scattered the ammunition over the ground where they had so long stood battling bravely and unflinchingly against overwhelming odds. In many instances the battle-worn flags were torn into shreds, and distributed among the men as a precious and sacred memento that they were no party to the surrender. The Federals who marched into the place had more the appearance of being vanquished than the unarmed Confederates, who gazed upon them with folded arms and in stern silence, a fierce defiance on their bronzed features, and the old battle fire gleaming in their glittering eyes. During all the events of the surrender, not one had been seen, and afterward no word of exultation was uttered to irritate the feelings of the prisoners. On the contrary, every sentinel who came upon post brought haversacks filled with provisions, which he would give to some famished Southerner, with the remark, "Here, reb., I know you are starved nearly to death." . . .

When the Federal soldiers entered the city they mingled freely with the Confederates, and expressed their sympathy with their deplorable situation by every possible means in their power. They were now no longer deadly combatants, but mortals of similar feelings. . . .

July 5th, rations for five days were issued to the Confederates from the Commissariat of the Federals. These rations consisted of bacon, hominy, peas, coffee, sugar, soap, salt, candles and crackers. How the famished troops enjoyed such bounteous supplies it is needless to state. For once the brave boys were objects of their enemy's charity. They grew jovial and hilarious over the change in their condition. The Yankees came freely among them, and were unusually kind. They asked innumerable questions, and were horrified at the fact of the men eating mules and rats, and openly expressed their admiration for the unfaltering bravery of the Confederates.

In addition to the rations mentioned by Tunnard, the Federals also provided a herd of cattle to be slaughtered to feed the soldiers and citizens of Vicksburg. Captain Elijah H. Clark of Company D, 42d Georgia Infantry, shown above, right as a private early in the war, saved one of the cow's horns (right). He eventually inscribed his name and July 4, 1863, on it and kept it as a souvenir.

"Soon there was a general mingling of gray coats and blue coats, as if there were no differences between them and never had been."

PRIVATE ROBERT L. BACHMAN
60TH TENNESSEE (C.S.) INFANTRY, VAUGHN'S BRIGADE

Bachman's camp was captured in the Federal attacks on May 19. He later wrote, "We lost everything: knapsacks, extra blankets, books and photographs. We did not have a stitch of clothes except those we had on. . . . I did not have a change of clothes for forty-seven days and nights." Provisioned by the Federals after the siege, he wrote, "How good the bread and meat and hard-tack and coffee and sugar all tasted to us hungry, almost starved men, may well be imagined."

Soon there was a general mingling of gray coats and blue coats, as if there were no differences between them and never had been. I remember talking to a soldier of the 9th Iowa Regiment. I said something to him about our regimental camp having been captured, and the loss of our soldier belongings. He said: "Our regiment has occupied that camp." Then I described to him my little dog, "Bob Hatton," named for General Bob Hatton, of Tennessee. He said to me, "I am quite sure from your description that I got that dog." I asked, "What did you do with him?" He said, "I sent him home." I replied, "As I could not have him, I am glad you have him." So it appears that little "Bob Hatton" had a long ride on a steam boat up the Mississippi, and found a good home in Iowa.

The Ammons brothers of the 1st Tennessee Heavy Artillery posed with pistols and Bowie-style knives sometime before they were taken in the surrender at Vicksburg. Benjamin (right), having broken his left knee at Island No. 10 the year before, had served as a cook. He did not fight again after Vicksburg. Radford joined the 18th Tennessee Cavalry after his exchange and continued fighting until losing an arm near Atlanta a year later.

LIEUTENANT JOSEPH W. WESTBROOK
4TH MISSISSIPPI INFANTRY, BALDWIN'S BRIGADE

This was the second of three times that Westbrook fell into enemy hands during the war. The first was at Fort Donelson in March 1862. Exchanged in September of that year, he went to Vicksburg only to be taken again. The third time he was in a hospital in Nashville recuperating from an amputation of his left leg just above the knee after being wounded at the Battle of Franklin in late November 1864.

All this 47 days, we were looking and hoping for relief by Joseph E. Johnson, but alas, on the morning of July 4th. we were surrendered, this was my second capture by Grant. This time however we were paroled and allowd to go home.

I was 125 miles from home, and as soon as paroled, which was about the 7 of July, my two brothers Jim and Gainey and others of the Company struck the road for home on foot. On the last night out, we put up at Sprawls hotel on the side of the R.R. 6 miles south of Canton, and 52 miles from home We agreed among ourselves to see home the next

night, at 12 o clock that day, We roasted some roasting ears out of a field, ate them and went on our way rejoicing. At dusk we were at Kosciuska 8 miles from home.

We pressed on and when near by we raised a song, and the good old faithful dogs, from whom we had been away so long, recognized our voices and ran full tilt to meet us, and of corse the family rose hurriedly, and we had a great meeting, which lasted all night.

LIEUTENANT SAMUEL H. M. BYERS
5TH IOWA INFANTRY, MATTHIES' BRIGADE

Byers recounts the camaraderie shown by both sides as Confederates were marched toward parole camps in Alabama and Mississippi. Most of the prisoners were paroled before reaching the camps. Many took off for their homes, feeling that with the fall of Vicksburg the cause was already lost. These men would never fight again. Others, however, following proper exchanges in the coming months, would return to fight on stubbornly until wounded or killed or until the war was over.

The Vicksburg prisoners were to go back to a camp of parole, and for days we marched along the country road side by side—lines of the "blue" and lines of the "gray." It was a strange sight—those two armies that only a few hours before had been hurling destruction and death at each other, now walking in silence, side by side; they to prison, we in pursuit of their retreating comrades; we glowing in victory, they saddened in defeat. There were no jeers as we marched along; no reproaching, no boasting, and no insults. On the contrary, we recognized an honorable foe, crippled but not dead; and many were the little kindnesses received on that strange and silent march, by Pemberton's men, from the boys of Grant's army. Many a ration was divided, many a canteen filled, and many were the mutual, sympathizing wishes that the cruel war might soon be over. I recall how a soldier, observing one of the prisoners footsore, weary with the march, and almost fainting, relieved him by taking from him his heavy burden, and fastening it on top of his own, carrying it for miles. The prisoners, seeing the incident, cheered, and I think more than one honest, kindly man of that stranger train was touched to tears.

Captain Toby Hart, 8th Louisiana Heavy Artillery, shown along with his gauntlets and the remains of his kepi, was among those prisoners marched to a parole camp in Enterprise, Mississippi. Hart and his men had manned four large guns guarding the Vicksburg waterfront. After being exchanged in 1864, he served with the 1st Louisiana Heavy Artillery until war's end.

"Let us tak Fresh Courige. We will acheve our inDipendans aftere awhile."

Some of the 172 Confederate cannon captured at Vicksburg, with their caissons and limbers, line an artillery park in the town. In addition to the cannon, large quantities of ammunition and more than 60,000 stands of arms fell into Federal hands. These small arms were a boon to the soldiers of Grant's army, most of whom had been issued various calibers of obsolescent smoothbore muskets converted from flintlocks to percussion caps and Belgian muskets imported early in the war—"Almost as dangerous to the person firing," Grant wrote, "as to the one aimed at." The Yankees soon exchanged their old weapons for the newer, uniform-caliber Confederate arms, primarily rifled Enfields of British make that had been run through the blockade.

PRIVATE F. M. CAYLOR
CAVALRY BATTALION, WAUL'S TEXAS LEGION

Written on July 27 in one of the Mississippi parole camps, this letter home by Caylor to his brother sums up the mixed feelings of many Confederate veterans by midsummer 1863. Humiliated by defeat, exhausted by long campaigning, wounded in body and spirit, and longing for home and family, Caylor, like many others, still possessed an undying optimism about the ultimate outcome of the Southern struggle and a fierce determination to fight it out to the end.

This July 27, 1863
My very Dear Brother

It is threw the kind Merces of an unerring Providence I am still in the Land among the living and enjoying good health which I feel very thankful to almity for his kind preservation. I am well as to health But LaBoring under a very severe wound. Though I Do not think it will prove Fatel. . . .

Well George, I have seen a very Misarible hard time Since I saw you. Since we left Gran gulf and come up here we have had to fight the Cussifiered yanks evry Few Days and the Damned Sons of Bitches Fights like Hell at Beating Tann Bark. But we have stood our ground and with the exception of one time they repulsed us and Drove us 65 miles. We turned Right around and followed them Back to our old Stamping ground. Well George I Cant tell you anything about my difacultys with my pen so I will say nothing about them. I guess you know enuff about Difacultis. . . . I want to hear From home so Bad, I am Nearly Frose. I use to think if the yanks ever Captured vicksburg Tha whiped me But it only aDDed Fuel to the Flame. I Fellt more Like Fighting them Than ever. Let us tak Fresh Courige. We will acheve our inDipendans aftere awhile. Geo. Dont get discouraged. the Lord is on our Side. we will come out all wright. My light is gone up so I will Close Remaining your affectionate Brother untill Death F. M. Caylor

Subduing the Last Bastion

The job of capturing the sole remaining Confederate stronghold on the Mississippi, Port Hudson, Louisiana, fell to Nathaniel P. Banks, the erstwhile bobbin boy in a Massachusetts textile mill who had become governor of the state, Speaker of the U.S. House of Representatives—and a Union major general. Badly outfoxed and outfought by Stonewall Jackson during the 1862 Shenandoah Valley campaign and again at Cedar Mountain during the Second Manassas campaign later that year, Banks had been sent south to see what he could do there. In spring 1863 he went about his new task manfully enough—but for months he met with an even more resounding lack of success.

The main problem was that Port Hudson, like Vicksburg, was a natural fortress. Located on 80-foot-high bluffs looming over a sharp bend in the river, it was ringed inland by bayous, swamps, creeks, and heavy stands of timber. On the bluffs facing the river the Confederates had emplaced 19 heavy guns—including one fearsome 10-inch Columbiad called the Old Demoralizer. To the north, south, and east they had built an arc of trenches, redans, redoubts, and gun platforms that was protected by impenetrable tangles of downed trees and undergrowth. It was, said a Rebel private with fine understatement, "a place hard to get at."

The Confederates, moreover, were dead set on holding the town at any cost. Port Hudson's big guns not only choked off the Mississippi to Federal ships but also offered a measure of protection to traffic on the nearby Red River, a prime avenue for supplies flowing to the Confederacy from the West. Most determined of all to defend the place was its combative commanding officer, Major General Franklin Gardner, a 40-year-old West Pointer who, though born in New York, had married a Louisiana girl and chosen to fight for the South. Manning Port Hudson's formidable earthworks Gardner had a garrison of 16,000 troops who were well armed and equally ready to fight.

In March Banks agreed to move some 12,000 troops, about one-half of his Army of the Gulf, to Port Hudson for a land attack on the city in support of an attempt by Admiral David Farragut to make another of his runs up the river. The entire affair was a disaster. Farragut's flotilla blasted away in a furious, and fruitless, duel with Port Hudson's batteries. Of the seven vessels involved, only two succeeded in getting past the hilltop fortress. In addition, Banks' force arrived too late to do anything more than witness the fiery spectacle.

But then in early May the strategic situation appeared to turn markedly in Banks' favor. General Pemberton in Vicksburg, desperate for help to turn back Grant's army, ordered Gardner to send more than half of Port Hudson's garrison marching north, leaving behind only about 7,000 troops. Banks, who had been campaigning in southern Louisiana, seized the opportunity. He reunified his command and shipped the whole force, now numbering about 24,000 men, across the Mississippi on May 23 and 24, landing north of Port Hudson. Then, after spending a couple of days deploying his force, he attacked, mounting an all-out assault on the morning of May 27. The result was a nightmare for the Federals—followed by six weeks of dreadful suffering and bloodshed for both sides.

Attacking from the north, the divisions of Brigadier Generals Godfrey Weitzel and Cuvier Grover immediately became entangled in the ravines and felled trees on the outward faces of the Rebel works. Pinned down, the Federals were then cut to pieces by rifle fire from the defenders, who were commanded by Colonels I. G. W. Steedman and W. R. Miles, and by grapeshot and canister from Confederate guns. Federal assaults on other parts of the enemy defenses were also bloodily thrown back. "It was difficult not only to move but even to see," recalled a Union officer. "The affair was a gigantic bushwhack."

Learning little from the disaster, Banks ordered another attack on June 14, spearheaded by the divisions of Brigadier Generals William Dwight and Halbert E. Paine. Again it was a fiasco, the Union troops being blasted back almost before they got started. Once more Federal casualties were horrendous, Banks' force losing 1,792 killed, wounded, and missing—to a Confederate toll of 47.

Meanwhile, some 7,000 Union troops had become ill with dysentery or had been felled by sunstroke in the area's pestilential swamps. "The heat, especially in the trenches, became almost insupportable, the stenches quite so," said a Union colonel as the blazing June sun caused the bayous to become "festering ooze."

The same ills and worse also afflicted the defenders, who, desperately short of food and water, were reduced to eating rats and drinking from stagnant pools. Still General Gardner would not give up, convinced that by holding out he kept Union troops busy that would otherwise join in attacking Vicksburg.

In desperation, Banks bombarded the Confederates night and day with his 90 guns and had his troops dig tunnels within yards of the enemy works, hoping to plant mines that would blow holes big enough for the Federal infantry to rush through—the same tactic that Grant had twice tried at Vicksburg and that twice had ended in dismal, bloody failure.

Before Banks could touch the first mine off, word came on July 7 that Vicksburg had surrendered. General Gardner at first refused to believe the news, shouted at his outposts from the Federal lines. But on July 8, under a flag of truce, Banks sent in a copy of Grant's dispatch.

The following day Gardner surrendered. With Vicksburg gone, holding Port Hudson was not only hopeless but also useless. As the firing stopped, weary troops from both sides struggled from their trenches to shake hands. Banks, in generous recognition of a courageous foe, returned the sword that Gardner had surrendered.

The news, which was telegraphed to Washington, set off renewed celebrations. The Vicksburg campaign was over; Union forces at last controlled all 2,000 miles of the Mississippi. Wrote a joyous President Lincoln: "The Father of Waters again goes unvexed to the sea."

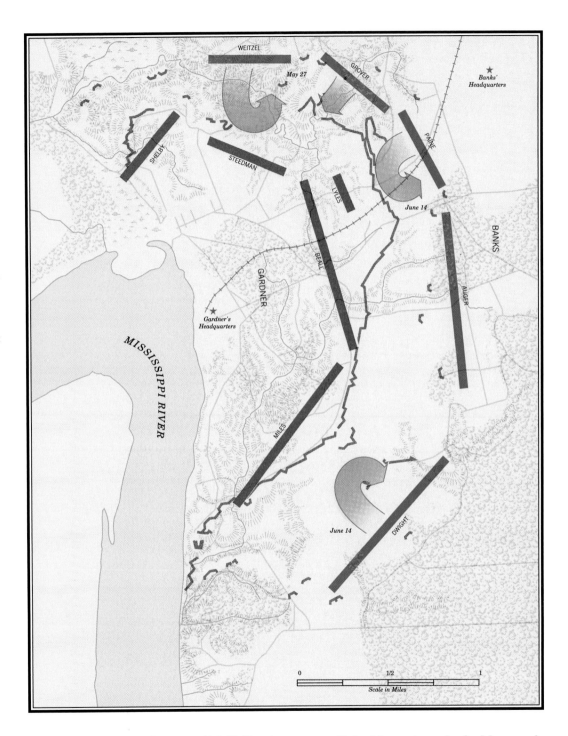

Like Vicksburg, Port Hudson sat on high bluffs and was protected inland by rough terrain. On May 27 and June 14 Federals attacked the town but were easily repulsed. Nevertheless, the large Rebel garrison was suffering from sickness and starvation, and it surrendered on July 9 after word came that Vicksburg had fallen.

ANONYMOUS CORRESPONDENT
New York Herald

This account of the first Union attack on Port Hudson appeared in Harper's Weekly with the engraving below. The correspondent claimed, "We were literally muzzle to muzzle, the distance between us and the enemy's guns being not more than twenty yards. . . . In fact, the Battle of Port Hudson has been pronounced by officers and seamen who were engaged in it . . . as the severest in the naval history of the war."

And now was heard a thundering roar, equal in volume to a whole park of artillery. This was followed by a rushing sound, accompanied by a howling noise that beggars description. Again and again was the sound repeated, till the vast expanse of heaven rang with the awful minstrelsy. It was apparent that the mortar-boats had opened fire. Of this I was soon convinced on casting my eyes aloft. Never shall I forget the sight that then met my astonished vision. Shooting upward at an angle of forty-five degrees, with the rapidity of lightning, small globes of golden flame were seen sailing through the pure ether—not steady, unfading flame, but corruscating, like the fitful gleam of a fire-fly—now visible, and anon invisible. Like a flying star of the sixth magnitude, the terrible missile—a 13-inch shell—nears its zenith, up and still up—higher and higher. Its flight now becomes much slower, till, on reaching its utmost altitude, its centrifugal force becomes counteracted by the earth's attraction; it describes a parabolic curve, and down, down, it comes, bursting, it may be, ere it reaches *terra firma*, but probably alighting in the rebel works ere it explodes, where it scatters death and destruction around. . . .

. . . The action now became general. The roar of cannon was incessant, and the flashes from the guns, together with the flight of the shells from the mortar boats, made up a combination of sound and sight impossible to describe. To add to the horrors of the night, while it contributed toward the enhancement of a certain terrible beauty, dense clouds of smoke began to envelop the river, shutting out from view the several vessels and confounding them with the batteries. It was very difficult to know how to steer to prevent running ashore, perhaps right under a rebel battery or into a consort. Upward and upward rolled the smoke, shutting out of view the beautiful stars and obscuring the vision on every side. Then it was that the order was passed, "Boys, don't fire till you see the flash from the enemy's guns." That was our only guide through the "palpable obscurity." Intermingled with the boom of the cannonade arose the cries of the wounded and the shouts of their friends, suggesting that they should be taken below for treatment. So thick was the smoke that we had to cease firing several times, and, to add to the horrors of the night, it was next to impossible to tell whether we were running into the *Hartford* or going ashore, and, if the latter, on which bank, or whether some of the other vessels were about to run into us or into each other. All this time the fire was kept up on both sides incessantly. It seems, however, that we succeeded in silencing the lower batteries of field-pieces.

BOMBARDMENT OF PORT HUDSON BY ADMIRAL FARRAGUT'S FLEET, MARCH 14–15, 1863.—Sketched by Mr. Hamilton.—[See Page 250.]

On March 14, 1863, before Grant crossed the Mississippi at Bruinsburg, Farragut tried to steam upriver, bombarding Port Hudson. Its defenses proved too much for the Union fleet. In mid-May, however, Farragut's mortar boats would silence several of the Confederate batteries. By May 27 Nathaniel Banks would have 24,000 men encircling the city.

This emplacement for Captain Richard Duryea's Battery F, 1st U.S. Artillery, sits in broken ground just outside Port Hudson. Once the position was attained in the May 27 assault, as described by Paine, Duryea's men fortified it with logs, cotton bales, and whatever else was at hand. The battery would remain here for the duration of the siege.

BRIGADIER GENERAL HALBERT E. PAINE

Division Commander, Army of the Gulf

Paine describes the bloody fighting on the Union right during the assault of May 27. Although he lost a leg to a wound received during the next assault on June 14, he continued to serve for the remainder of the war. He then represented Wisconsin for three terms in Congress, maintained a private law practice, and served as U.S. Commissioner of Patents, introducing typewriters into the Federal bureaucracy.

The attack was a huge bushwhack. The rebels availed themselves of the thickets, trees, fallen timber ridges, ravines, and also of rifle pits and breastworks of earth and logs constructed at convenient points, and being concealed and protected themselves gave us a most destructive rifle fire, retreating rapidly from point to point. From favorable positions, their light artillery fired upon us grape, shell, and canister, and for a few minutes with comparative immunity, on account of our momentary uncertainty as to the position of Dwight's troops, resulting from the darkness of the morning, the underbrush and the smoke; but we pushed on until we drove the rebels within their works, capturing many prisoners, but suffering heavily in killed and wounded. At length we reached a ridge two hundred yards from their fortifications and the enemy met us with a concentrated artillery and infantry fire. With admirable celerity the pioneers opened up the roads and Capt. Duryea brought up the division artillery, and within fifteen minutes after driving him in, our batteries were answering his guns from two commanding points, which positions were retained until the surrender. While we were waiting for Augur's and Sherman's guns, Grover, whose division joined our left, took command of the right wing. Positions were gained within one hundred yards of the parapet and kept in those hazardous places by frequent reliefs until the assault of June 14th.

"The Government will find in this class of troops effective supporters and defenders."

CHIEF CLERK THOMAS R. MYERS
QUARTERMASTER'S DEPARTMENT, PORT HUDSON

Although Myers grossly exaggerates the numbers in Ullmann's command, which he mistakenly calls Wellman's, his description of the impossible task given the black troops of the 1st and 3d Louisiana Native Guards is quite accurate. Ordered to attack the heavily fortified Confederate left in an effort to relieve pressure on another front, the brigade's 1,000 men suffered nearly 50 percent casualties in charging the Rebel works. The Confederate defenders suffered no casualties.

One bright, hot morning a brigade of negro soldiers of about 4000, commanded by General Daniel Wellman of New York, came out of the heavy cotton wood forest about 3/4 of a mile in front of the bluff we were on, formed a beautiful line and struck a double quick pace for the bluff. . . . This broad, extended plateau was level and had the appearance of a smooth, clean sea beach. The bluff was almost abrupt and along its whole line, bristled with heavy Confederate artillery. It also had rifle pits and light artillery stations. It was astounding that this negro brigade would assault such a place. But they came on in splendid form, bayonets glistening like silver in the bright June sun, uniforms spic and clean and the Commanding Officers riding close behind them. When they got within 150 yards of the foot of the bluff, every cannon, heavy and light, double shotted, and every rifle turned loose on them. They stopped and at once fell to pieces in this terrific fusilade playing havoc and death among them. They stampeded, and every man, not on the ground, took to his heels for the woods; the guns, meanwhile playing on them, and after the ones fortunate enough to escape reached the heavy timber, the 100 cannon continued to pour a volcano of shot and shell into the timber producing a terrible crashing noise. About 500 or 600 of the negro Federals were left dead or wounded on the ground which they traversed. . . . No other attack was made on the bluff side than the one related.

MAJOR GENERAL NATHANIEL P. BANKS
COMMANDER, DEPARTMENT OF THE GULF

Banks, who praises the role of his black troops in the May 27 assault, had proved himself an able military administrator but a poor tactician in the eastern theater. In the West, his moment of glory came with the surrender of Port Hudson after a protracted siege, but his success brought frustration, as Port Hudson was always treated as a sideshow to the siege of Vicksburg.

On the extreme right of our line I posted the First and Third Regiments of negro troops. The First Regiment of Louisiana Engineers, composed exclusively of colored men, excepting the officers, was also engaged in the operations of the day. The position occupied by these troops was one of importance, and called for the utmost steadiness and bravery in those to whom it was confided. It gives me pleasure to report that they answered every expectation. In many respects their conduct was heroic. No troops could be more determined or more daring. They made during the day three charges upon the batteries of the enemy, suffering very heavy losses and holding their position at nightfall with the other troops on the right of our line. The highest commendation is bestowed upon them by all the officers in command on the right. Whatever doubt may have existed heretofore as to the efficiency of organizations of this character, the history of this day proves conclusively to those who were in condition to observe the conduct of these regiments that the Government will find in this class of troops effective supporters and defenders. The severe test to which they were subjected, and the determined manner in which they encountered the enemy, leaves upon my mind no doubt of their ultimate success.

Major General Christopher C. Augur (seated with cane) poses in camp surrounded by members of his headquarters staff. Severely wounded at Cedar Mountain in August 1862, Augur moved west later that year to serve as Banks' second in command of the Department of the Gulf. In the attack of May 27, Augur's men faced blistering artillery and rifle fire as their advance foundered in a tangle of logs and branches cut and strewn about by the Confederates for a distance of about a mile outward from their lines.

PRIVATE WILLIAM H. HAYWARD
ATTACHED TO HEADQUARTERS, AUGUR'S DIVISION

Because he was detached from his regiment, the 52d Massachusetts, Hayward escaped the bloody fighting on May 27 but saw perhaps more than his share of the horrors of battle. At Augur's headquarters he was charged with keeping a record of the dead and wounded for the division. His estimate for total Union losses in the assault was too low. Banks' official report claimed 293 killed, 1,545 wounded, and 157 missing. Confederate losses numbered only 350.

Brigadier General Thomas W. Sherman, commanding the 2d Division at Port Hudson, was so slow in initiating an attack on the strong Confederate works on May 27 that he was relieved of command by Banks after a heated exchange between the two. Before his replacement could arrive, however, Sherman, possibly reinforced by drink, mounted up and led his troops in a costly charge. His horse was shot from under him, but he continued on foot, only to be felled by artillery fire, losing a leg.

In Camp near Port Hudson
May 28, 1863
My Darling Wife
As I have a chance to send to Baton Rouge today, I will write a few lines. I came up here Monday and was assigned the duty of taking the Record of the Wounded that are brought in and you may judge how busy I am kept when I tell you that yesterday between four and nine P.M. over *three hundred* were brought in. You will understand that my duty is with our own Augur's Division. There are three other Divisions here, Grover's, Weitzel's and Sherman's. The fight began Tuesday with Artillery and up

"Just as I jumped down, the rebels opened up and the air was full of bullets, but just a moment too late to do me any harm."

to yesterday at 3 o'clock the cannonading was terrific. Then a general assault was made by the Infantry along the entire line, but it was unsuccessful. The loss in killed, wounded and missing yesterday was probably 1000. My friend Lt. Col. O'Brien 48 Mass was killed and several other officers that I knew as well. The fight will commence again this afternoon.

I am well and *am in no* danger so you must not worry about me at all. My letters will now of neccessity be short but will write frequently. . . .
I am as ever and always,
Your Devoted and Loving
Will

Two Union soldiers gaze downward at the saps leading to one of the two mines dug under the Confederate works at Port Hudson. It was Banks' plan to explode the mines as precursors to frontal attacks, much as had been tried, unsuccessfully, at Vicksburg. The longer one under Priest's Cap in the northern part of the lines was destroyed by a Rebel countermine. The one shown here, under the Citadel on the extreme southern end of the lines, was still being excavated when Port Hudson surrendered.

PRIVATE WILLIAM L. S. TABOR
15TH NEW HAMPSHIRE INFANTRY, DOW'S BRIGADE

Tabor describes the dangers of the mining operations against the Citadel at the southern end of the Confederate defenses. The constant bombardments and sniping led both sides to develop ingenious methods of wounding or killing their opponents. Tabor was eventually awarded the Medal of Honor for his role in thwarting the effect of the Rebel trough mentioned here.

LIEUTENANT SYLVESTER B. SHEPARD
91ST NEW YORK INFANTRY, HOLCOMB'S BRIGADE

In his last letter to his sister, Shepard describes the siege of Port Hudson and the preparations for Banks' second direct assault on the city. Ironically, Shepard wears a mourning badge on his left sleeve, presumably to honor fallen comrades. He was killed in action the next day.

During the siege of Port Hudson in 1863, it was necessary to undermine the enemy's works, and for this purpose a large number of negroes was set to work digging a trench under the rebel fortifications, and protected by our sharpshooters who were supplied with hand-grenades, to be thrown over the parapets. The sand from the trench was thrown over the breastworks, for there was no place to dispose of it on our side. This exposed our men to the fire of the rebels, and I was one of the men detailed as sharpshooters to prevent the rebels from doing further damage. We were under a scathing fire all this time, as the enemy were enabled to enfilade our ranks, and with their shot and shell did much damage. One of their contrivances for throwing shells amongst our men, was to place short fuse shells into a trough, constructed of planks, lift up one end of it, thus lowering the other end over our works, and drop the shells into our ranks.

The first time they attempted this they succeeded in killing and wounding 125 men, mostly negroes, who were engaged in shovelling. Just as they were putting a second shell in the trough, I jumped up on the sand bags which formed our breastworks, slipped a noosed rope around the trough, and jerked it into our lines.

This resulted in throwing the shell the other way, falling among the rebels and exploding there. While slipping the rope around the trough I was necessarily exposed to the full view of the rebel sharpshooters but I did it so quickly and unexpectedly, that for a moment not a shot was fired. Just as I jumped down, the rebels opened up and the air was full of bullets, but just a moment too late to do me any harm.

In front of Port Hudson, La
Saturday June 13, 1863.
My dear Sister

The general assault upon Port Hudson did not take place upon Tuesday last, as we were anticipating it would, and now we know as little of it, or when it will take place as we did at my last writing. We have for almost three weeks had them completely surrounded with our troops and artillery, and have from the latter fired upon them upon an average of at least once in ten minutes, the damage done them must be great. Still they hold out, and will undoubtedly until some general attack is made.

Our troops under personal superintendence of Maj. Genl. Banks are daily preparing for the encounter, which judging from the preparations is expected to be a desperate one. Yesterday three regiments were notified to hold themselves in readiness to make a charge upon their works. The three notified were the 12th Conn, 75th and 91st N.Y. We are all to be armed with what is called a hand grenade—besides our muskets. A hand grenade is a cast iron shell, made about egg shape and weigh three and five pounds each. They have in the smallest end a dart which guides them and in the largest a plunger which is so made that immediately after being thrown from the hand and striking an object, the shell bursts into hundreds of pieces and must necessarily scatter death and consternation all around. They are truly the worst instrument that I have yet seen and if they are brought to execution, their work is terri-

ble. I do not fear the charge, but still I wish it were over, as until that time comes, there will be no quiet or rest for any of us.

We have now been over three months without our tents, have marched nearly eight hundred miles, and have been exposed to all the inclemancies of the wind and climate, and are now (although still patriotic) become tired and worn. Is it surprising that we should wish rest?

6:00 P.M.—This afternooon a sharp bombardment took place from both sides and Genl. Banks sent a flag of truce demanding the surrender of the place. Genl. Gardner (the rebel commander) refused to surrender and replied that his duty as an officer demanded that he hold the place, and that he should do his duty to the last. We have since received orders to be ready at daybreak tomorrow, and we are consequently expecting to be the first in the fight tomorrow. If it must come, the sooner the better, we can do our best and hope for the best.

Will write again as soon as the action is over. Give my love to all. . . . Write me often and ever believe me

Your loving brother,
Bub.

LIEUTENANT COLONEL RICHARD B. IRWIN
ASSISTANT ADJUTANT GENERAL, XIX CORPS

Even more detrimental to the health and welfare of opposing Federals and Confederates than the sniping and cannonades was illness caused by the stifling heat, the lack of water, and the foul swamps described by Irwin. The Rebels also suffered from food shortages even worse than those experienced by the defenders of Vicksburg. Partially because he feared the debilitation of his forces by disease, Banks had tried to end the siege with the second attack on June 14.

On the 14th of June, time still pressing, the lines being everywhere well advanced, the enemy's artillery effectually controlled by ours, every available man having been brought up, and yet our force growing daily less by casualties and sickness, Taylor menacing our communications on the west bank of the Mississippi, and the issue of Grant's operations before Vicksburg in suspense, Banks ordered a second assault to be delivered simultaneously at daybreak on the left and center, preceded by a general cannonade of an hour's dura-

Under the watchful eye of an officer, members of the 1st Indiana Heavy Artillery (left) pose at the ready with one of their siege guns at Port Hudson. Here, at the point where the Union and Confederate lines were so close that the combatants threw messages back and forth, the Hoosiers built imposing parapets of baled cotton to protect themselves and their guns. At least one of the men found sufficient free time to carve the image of a house in the tree in the left foreground.

After the siege, the section of defense line on the northeastern side of Port Hudson, called Fort Desperate by the Confederates, is a shambles of wrecked timbers and cannon (right). General Gardner's Rebels survived bombardment by heavy Union artillery by burrowing bombproofs deep into the earth that protected against all but a direct hit. When the surrender finally came, the men from both sides crawled from their trenches and redoubts and shook hands.

tion. Dwight's attack on the left was misdirected by its guides and soon came to naught. Paine attacked with great vigor at what proved to be the strongest point of the whole work, the priest-cap near the Jackson road. He himself almost instantly fell severely wounded at the head of his division, and this attack also ended in a disastrous repulse, our men being unable to cross the crest just in front of the work, forming a natural glacis so swept by the enemy's fire that in examining the position afterward I found this grass-crowned knoll shaved bald, every blade cut down to the roots as by a hoe.

Our loss in the two assaults was nearly 4000, including many of our best and bravest officers. The heat, especially in the trenches, became almost insupportable, the stenches quite so, the brooks dried up, the creek lost itself in the pestilential swamp, the springs gave out, and the river fell, exposing to the tropical sun a wide margin of festering ooze. The illness and mortality were enormous. The labor of the siege, extending over a front of seven miles, pressed so severely upon our numbers, far too weak for such an undertaking, that the men were almost incessantly on duty; and as the numbers for duty diminished, of course the work fell the more heavily upon those that remained. From first to last we had nearly 20,000 men of all arms engaged before Port Hudson, yet the effective strength of infantry and artillery at no time exceeded 13,000, and at the last hardly reached 9000, while even of these every other man might well have gone on the sick-report if pride and duty had not held him to his post.

SERGEANT MARCUS A. HANNA
50TH MASSACHUSETTS INFANTRY, DUDLEY'S BRIGADE

On July 4 the 50th was ordered into the rifle pits without a chance to fill their haversacks or canteens. "The day was intensely hot and by noon the men were suffering from thirst," Hanna wrote. "How to get water was a problem, with the enemy on the alert and posted on works but a short distance from and considerably higher than our position." Hanna's Medal of Honor, awarded years later, was inscribed, "Voluntarily exposed himself to a heavy fire to get water for comrades in rifle pits."

At about 2 or 3 o'clock P.M. the thirst of our men had become almost unbearable and Lieutenant William H. Hurd, in command of our company, gave some of us permission to go to the rear for water. Orderly Sergeant Blatchford and myself were the only sergeants present that day. I at once volunteered to go, and asked for a file of men to assist me. No one responded. I decided to try it alone. I took twelve or fifteen canteens—all I could conveniently carry—hung them about my neck, and placed them about my body to afford protection from rebel bullets. A dummy, made by rigging up a musket with a blouse and cap, was prepared, the idea being to raise it above our pit and, if possible, draw the fire of the enemy, and then, before they had time to reload, I was to take my chances. Carefully we raised the dummy until the cap only could be seen, then we ducked it out of sight, to hoist it again at once, this time showing the head and body. The deception was a success, for at once there came a heavy volley, and before the smoke had cleared away, I was up and off as rapidly as my light but bulky load would permit. I steered across the level plains for the nearest cover some 500 yards away, but I had not gone far, before I could hear the patter of bullets all around me, and knew that I was within sight and range. Yet, I kept on my course, until half the distance was covered when I realized that I could not escape being hit, and bethought myself of the ruse of throwing myself prostrate, as if killed or badly wounded. The trick was successful. The firing ceased, and, after lying prone until I was well rested, I sprang to my feet and ran like a deer for the blackberry hedge. In this second race, no further shots were sent after me by the enemy.

I went about half a mile further to a spring, filled my load of canteens, not one of which, in spite of the firing, had been punctured, and began cautiously to work my way back to my company in the rifle-pits. Instead of making a bee-line for the pit, I made a detour to the left, in order to bring one of our batteries between myself and the enemy. After I had reached the battery I had still some sixty or seventy yards to go to the right, wholly exposed to the enemy's fire. However, I covered this distance unmolested. Lieutenant Hurd and the men warmly congratulated me, and expressed gratitude for the partial relief I had brought them.

LIEUTENANT COLONEL RICHARD B. IRWIN
ASSISTANT ADJUTANT GENERAL, XIX CORPS

In writing after the war, Irwin praised the "heroic defense" of Port Hudson by the besieged, and then stated, "But, stout as the defense had been, the besiegers had on their part displayed some of the highest qualities of the soldier: among these valor in attack, patient endurance of privations, suffering, and incredible toil, and perseverance under discouragement."

At last on the 7th of July, when the sap-head was within 16 feet of the priest-cap, and a storming party of 1000 volunteers had been organized, led by the intrepid Birge, and all preparations had been made for springing two heavily charged mines, word came from Grant that Vicksburg had surrendered. Instantly an aide was sent to the "general-of-the-trenches" bearing duplicates in "flimsy" of a note from the adjutant-general announcing the good news. One of these he was directed to toss into the Confederate lines. Some one acknowledged the receipt by calling back, "That's another damned Yankee lie!" Once more the cheers of our men rang out as the word passed, and again the forest echoed with the strains of the "Star-spangled Banner" from the long-silent bands. Firing died away, the men began to mingle in spite of everything, and about 2 o'clock next morning came the long, gray envelope that meant *surrender.*

Formalities alone remained; these were long, but the articles were signed on the afternoon of the 8th; a moment later a long train of wagons loaded with rations for the famished garrison moved down the Clinton road, and on the morning of the 9th a picked force of eight regiments, under Brigadier-General George L. Andrews, marched in with bands playing and colors flying; the Confederates stacked arms and hauled down their flag, and the National ensign floated in its stead. By General Banks's order, General Gardner's sword was returned to him in the presence of his men in recognition of the heroic defense—a worthy act, well merited.

LIEUTENANT JAMES FRERET

STAFF, MAJOR GENERAL FRANKLIN GARDNER, PORT HUDSON

Freret, assistant engineer at Port Hudson, was wounded during the siege while he superintended repairs on the Citadel. Even before the official surrender took place, according to Freret, "Soldiers swarmed from their places of concealment on either side and met with each other in the most cordial and fraternal spirit. . . . Federal soldiers vied with each other in courtesy. . . . Not a single case occurred in which the enemy exhibited a disposition to exult over their victory."

Shortly after dark a train of wagons brought in a liberal supply of provisions for the garrison from the enemy's commissariat. They were issued to the troops during the night-time, and early the next morning our men enjoyed the first good meal they had partaken of for a long time.

At seven o'clock on the morning of the 9th, our line was formed in a field back of the railroad depot, near the landing, every man not too sick to be confined in the hospital being in the ranks. As General Gardner rode along the line, with his staff, he was enthusiastically cheered by the men who had served so faithfully under him, and whose affection and confidence he had permanently gained during days and weeks of trial.

The enemy's column, marching down the road to the landing, approached the right of our line, preceded by General Andrews and staff.

When Brigadier-General Andrews approached, General Gardner advanced with his sword drawn and presented the hilt to General Andrews with the following words:

"Having thoroughly defended this position as long as I deemed it necessary, I now surrender to you my sword, and with it this post and its garrison."

To which General Andrews replied:

"I return your sword as a proper compliment to the gallant commander of such gallant troops—conduct that would be heroic in another cause."

To which General Gardner replied as he returned his sword, with emphasis, into the scabbard:

"This is neither the time nor place to discuss the cause."

The order was given along our line to ground arms, which was obeyed, and our men stood in line while the enemy had marched from right to left until they had formed in line before us, when they hoisted their flag upon the bluff, fired a salute, and the ceremony was over.

Brigadier General George L. Andrews, Banks' chief of staff, accepts the surrender of Port Hudson from Confederate commander Franklin Gardner on July 9, 1863, in this engraving from Harper's Weekly. Of this event Lieutenant Colonel Irwin wrote, "It is unjust to say that Port Hudson surrendered only because Vicksburg had fallen. The simple truth is that Port Hudson surrendered because its hour had come. The garrison was literally starving. . . . With the post, there fell into our hands 6340 prisoners, 20 heavy guns, 31 field pieces, about 7500 muskets, and two river steamers."

THE FORMAL SURRENDER OF PORT HUDSON.—Drawn by Mr. J. R. Hamilton.

Shown with his kepi, General Gardner had led a cavalry brigade at Shiloh against his old West Point classmate, Grant. Like Pemberton, Gardner was a Northerner by birth but a Southerner by sentiment and had a Southern wife. And like Pemberton he was condemned by some for surrendering his garrison. But, as one Union officer observed, "With less than 3,000 famished in line, powerful mines beneath the salients, and a last assault about to be delivered at 10 paces, what else was left to do?" Gardner spent his postwar years in Louisiana as a planter.

MAJOR GENERAL ULYSSES S. GRANT
COMMANDER, ARMY OF THE TENNESSEE

Grant's second in command, William Tecumseh Sherman, asserted, "The campaign of Vicksburg, in its conception and execution, belonged exclusively to General Grant, not only in the great whole, but in the thousands of its details." In his memoirs, Grant placed the Vicksburg victory into the context of the greater war.

The capture of Vicksburg, with its garrison, ordnance and ordnance stores, and the successful battles fought in reaching them, gave new spirit to the loyal people of the North. New hopes for the final success of the cause of the Union were inspired. The victory gained at Gettysburg, upon the same day, added to their hopes. Now the Mississippi River was entirely in the possession of the National troops; for the fall of Vicksburg gave us Port Hudson at once. The army of northern Virginia was driven out of Pennsylvania and forced back to about the same ground it occupied in 1861. The Army of the Tennessee united with the Army of the Gulf, dividing the Confederate States completely.

ABRAHAM LINCOLN
PRESIDENT OF THE UNITED STATES

Unable to attend a meeting of Union supporters in his hometown of Springfield, Illinois, Lincoln sent this letter instead. In it he expresses satisfaction over the progress of the war to date, while cautioning that a long struggle still faced the Union. Indeed, more than a year and a half of bloody fighting remained.

Executive Mansion, Washington, August 26, 1863. Hon. James C. Conkling My Dear Sir.

The signs look better. The Father of Waters again goes unvexed to the sea. Thanks to the great North-West for it. Nor yet wholly to them. Three hundred miles up, they met New-England, Empire, Key-Stone, and Jersey, hewing their way right and left. The Sunny South too, in more colors than one, also lent a hand. On the spot, their part of the history was jotted down in black and white. The job was a great national one; and let none be banned who bore an honorable part in it. And while those who have cleared the great river may well be proud, even that is not all. It is hard to say that anything has been more bravely, and well done, than at Antietam, Murfreesboro, Gettysburg, and on many fields of lesser note. Nor must Uncle Sam's Web-feet be forgotten. At all the watery margins they have been present. Not only on the deep sea, the broad bay, and the rapid river, but also up the narrow muddy bayou, and wherever the ground was a little damp, they have been, and made their tracks. Thanks to all. For the great republic—for the principle it lives by, and keeps alive—for man's vast future,—thanks to all.

Peace does not appear so distant as it did. I hope it will come soon, and come to stay; and so come as to be worth the keeping in all future time. It will then have been proved that, among free men, there can be no successful appeal from the ballot to the bullet; and that they who take such appeal are sure to lose their case, and pay the cost. And then, there will be some black men who can remember that, with silent tongue, and clenched teeth, and steady eye, and well-poised bayonet, they have helped mankind on to this great consummation; while, I fear, there will be some white ones, unable to forget that, with malignant heart, and deceitful speech, they have strove to hinder it.

Still let us not be over-sanguine of a speedy final triumph. Let us be quite sober. Let us diligently apply the means, never doubting that a just God, in his own good time, will give us the rightful result. Yours very truly   A. LINCOLN

"The Father of Waters again goes unvexed to the sea."

OPENING OF THE MISSISSIPPI—VIEW OF THE REBEL BATTERIES AT PORT HUDSON.—From a Sketch by our Special Artist, Fred. B. Schell.

OPENING OF THE MISSISSIPPI—OVATION OF THE INHABITANTS TO THE SALLIE LIST, DESCENDING THE MISSISSIPPI.—From a Sketch by our Special Artist, Fred. B. Schell.

On this page from Frank Leslie's Illustrated Newspaper dated August 15, 1863, the Stars and Stripes fly over Port Hudson's bluffs (top) as civilian and Union naval boats sit at quayside. At bottom, with the river at last under Union control, the Sallie List steams down the Mississippi. It is saluted by ex-slaves from a riverside plantation, who, it was reported, viewed her as "a token of emancipation and hope." While the Unionists celebrated their successes along the Father of Waters, those events seemed to spell doom for the Confederates. "Yesterday we rode on the pinnacle of success," wrote one Rebel general, "today absolute ruin seems our portion. The Confederacy totters to its destruction."

GLOSSARY

adjutant—A staff officer assisting the commanding officer, usually with correspondence.

bastion—A projecting portion of a fort's rampart into which artillery is placed. Or any fortified place.

battery—The basic unit of artillery, consisting of four to six guns. Or an emplacement where artillery is mounted for attack or defense. A battery is generally open or lightly defended in the rear.

bivouac—A temporary encampment, or to camp out for the night.

bombproof—A shelter from mortar or artillery attack, usually made with walls and a roof of logs and packed earth.

breastwork—A temporary fortification, usually of earth and about chest high, over which a soldier could fire.

brevet—An honorary rank given for exceptional bravery or merit in time of war. It granted none of the authority or pay of the official rank.

buck and ball—A round of ammunition consisting of a bullet and three buckshot.

caisson—A cart with large chests for carrying artillery ammunition; connected to a horse-drawn limber when moved.

canister—A tin can containing lead or iron balls that scattered when fired from a cannon. Used primarily in defense of a position as an antipersonnel weapon.

cap—Technically a percussion cap. A small, metal cover, infused with chemicals and placed on the hollow nipple of a rifle or revolver. When struck by the hammer the chemicals explode, igniting the powder charge in the breech.

clubbed musket—A musket swung like a club in hand-to-hand combat.

Columbiad—A large cast-metal, smoothbore cannon adopted for all U.S. seacoast defenses in 1860.

contraband—A slave who sought the protection of Union forces.

corduroy road—A road with a surface of logs laid together transversely.

Dutchmen—A term, often pejorative, for Union soldiers of German descent.

Enfield rifle—The Enfield rifle musket was adopted by the British in 1853, and the North and South imported nearly one million to augment their own production. Firing a .577-caliber projectile similar to the Minié ball, it was fairly accurate at 1,100 yards.

enfilade—Gunfire that rakes an enemy line lengthwise, or the position allowing such firing.

fatigues—Work uniform worn by military personnel while doing manual or menial labor.

flank—The right or left end of a military formation. Therefore, to flank is to attack or go around the enemy's position on one end or the other.

forage—To search for and acquire provisions from nonmilitary sources. To soldiers of the Civil War it often meant, simply, stealing.

forage cap—The standard-issue soft woolen cap, having a short leather bill and a round, high, flat-topped crown.

gabion—An open-ended, cylindrical basket of brush or metal strips woven on stakes and usually filled with dirt or cotton. Used to create or reinforce earthworks.

garrison—A military post, especially a permanent one. Also, the act of manning such a post and the soldiers who serve there.

glacis—The outer rim of the defensive ditch protecting a fort's rampart. It usually sloped down toward the enemy.

grapeshot—Iron balls (usually nine) bound together and fired from a cannon. Resembling a cluster of grapes, the balls broke apart and scattered on impact. Although references to grape or grapeshot are numerous in the literature, some experts claim that it was not used on Civil War battlefields.

haversack—A shoulder bag, usually strapped over the right shoulder to rest on the left hip, for carrying personal items and rations.

lanyard—An artillerist's cord with a handle on one end and a clip connector for a friction primer on the other. The friction primer was inserted into the touchhole on an artillery piece. When the gunner jerked the lanyard, friction in the touchhole ignited powder in the breech, firing the weapon.

limber—A two-wheeled, horse-drawn vehicle to which a gun carriage or a caisson was attached.

lunette—A crescent-shaped fortification, usually for artillery.

masked battery—Any concealed or camouflaged battery of artillery.

Minié ball—The standard bullet-shaped projectile fired from the rifled muskets of the time. Designed by French army officers Henri-Gustave Delvigne and Claude-Étienne Minié, the bullet's hollow base expanded, forcing its sides into the grooves, or rifling, of the musket's barrel. This caused the bullet to spiral in flight, giving it greater range and accuracy. Appears as minie, minnie, and minni.

musket—A smoothbore, muzzleloading shoulder arm.

oblique—At an angle.

orderly—A soldier assigned to a superior officer for various duties, such as carrying messages.

parallel—A trenchwork for artillery dug parallel to the face of an enemy fortification in order to cover an advancing siege party.

parapet—A defensive elevation raised above a fort's main wall, or rampart.

parole—The pledge of a soldier released after being captured by the enemy that he would not take up arms again until he had been properly exchanged.

Parrott guns—Muzzleloading, rifled artillery pieces of various calibers made of cast iron, with a unique wrought-iron reinforcing band around the breech. Patented in 1861 by Union officer Robert Parker Parrott, these guns were more accurate at longer range than their smoothbore predecessors.

picket—One or more soldiers on guard to protect the larger unit from surprise attack.

pioneers—Construction engineers.

prime—To pour gunpowder into the touchhole or vent of a cannon or musket.

rampart—The main wall of a fort, usually a mound of earth with a flattened top.

ration—A specified allotment of food for one person (or animal) per day. The amounts and nature of rations varied by time and place throughout the war. *Rations* may also refer simply to any food provided by the army.

redan—A V-shaped defensive earthwork, usually projecting from a fortified line.

redoubt—An enclosed, defensive stronghold, usually temporary.

rifle—Any weapon with spiral grooves cut into the bore, which give spin to the projectile, adding range and accuracy. Usually applied to cannon or shoulder-fired weapons.

rifle pits—Holes or shallow trenches dug in the ground from which soldiers could fire weapons and avoid enemy fire. Foxholes.

salient—That part of a fortress, line of defense, or trench system that juts out toward the enemy position.

sap—A narrow trench dug by a besieging party so that it approaches the enemy's fort or strongpoint. Or to dig such a trench.

section of artillery—Part of an artillery battery consisting of two guns, the soldiers who manned them, and their supporting horses and equipment.

shrapnel—An artillery projectile in the form of a hollow sphere filled with metal balls packed around an explosive charge. Developed by British general Henry Shrapnel during the Napoleonic Wars, it was used as an antipersonnel weapon. Also called spherical case.

skirmisher—A soldier sent in advance of the main body of troops to scout out and probe the enemy's position. Also, one who participated in a skirmish, a small fight usually incidental to the main action.

small arms—Any hand-held weapon, usually a firearm.

solid shot—A solid artillery projectile, oblong for rifled pieces and spherical for smoothbores, used primarily against fortifications and matériel.

spherical case—See shrapnel.

spike—To render a piece of artillery unserviceable by driving a metal spike into the vent.

Springfield rifle—The standard infantry shoulder arm of both sides; named for the U.S. arsenal at Springfield, Massachusetts, which produced it in 1861, 1863, and 1864 models. The term eventually referred to any similar weapon regardless of where it was made.

stack arms—To set aside weapons, usually three or more in a pyramid, interlocking at the end of the barrel with the butts on the ground.

trail arms—To grasp a musket at about midpoint and carry it at one's side, roughly parallel to the ground.

withe—Any tough, flexible twig or osier, suitable for binding items together. Used in making gabions.

ACKNOWLEDGMENTS

The editors wish to thank the following for their valuable assistance in the preparation of this volume: Eva-Maria Ahladas, Museum of the Confederacy, Richmond; James Baughman, U.S. Army Military History Institute, Carlisle Barracks, Pa.; Pam Cheney, U.S. Army Military History Institute, Carlisle Barracks, Pa.; Gordon Cotton, Old Courthouse Museum, Vicksburg, Miss.; Jeff Giambrone, Old Courthouse Museum, Vicksburg, Miss.; Randy W. Hackenburg, U.S. Army Military History Institute, Carlisle Barracks, Pa.; Christine Harvey, Confederate Museum, New Orleans; Michael Hennan, Mississippi Department of Archives and History, Jackson; Mary Ison and Staff, Library of Congress, Washington, D.C.; Elizabeth Joyner, Vicksburg National Military Park, Vicksburg, Miss.; David Keough, U.S. Army Military History Institute, Carlisle Barracks, Pa.; Mary Lohrenz, Old Capitol Museum, Jackson, Miss.; Robert A. McCown, University of Iowa, Iowa City; Shaner Magalhães, State Historical Society of Iowa, Iowa City; Vann Martin, Madison, Miss.; Mary L. Sluskonis, Museum of Fine Arts, Boston; Richard Sommers, U.S. Army Military History Institute, Carlisle Barracks, Pa.; Jennifer Songster, Ohio Historical Society, Columbus; Ellen Sulser, State Historical Society of Iowa, Des Moines; Michael J. Winey, U.S. Army Military History Institute, Carlisle Barracks, Pa.; Terrence Winschel, Vicksburg National Military Park, Vicksburg, Miss.

PICTURE CREDITS

The sources for the illustrations are listed below. Credits from left to right are separated by semicolons, from top to bottom by dashes.

Dust jacket: front, Chicago Historical Society; rear, Sharon and Bob Humble, Balfour House, Vicksburg, Miss., copied by Henry Mintz.

All calligraphy by Mary Lou O'Brian/Inkwell, Inc.

6: Gift of Maxim Karolik, courtesy Museum of Fine Arts, Boston. 8: Library of Congress, Neg. No. LC-USZ 62-5473. 11, 14: Map by R. R. Donnelley & Sons Co., Cartographic Services. 16: Massachusetts Commandery, Military Order of the Loyal Legion and the U.S. Army Military History Institute (MASS-MOLLUS/USAMHI), copied by Robert Walch; National Portrait Gallery, Smithsonian Institution, Washington, D.C./Art Resource. 17: Hargrett Rare Book and Manuscript Library, University of Georgia Libraries, Athens; Vicksburg National Military Park, copied by Henry Mintz. 18: Chicago Historical Society. 19: Karl Sundstrom Collection, copied by Richard A. Baumgartner. 20, 21: L. M. Strayer Collection, Dayton; Frank and Marie-Thérèse Wood Print Collections, Alexandria, Va. 22: Frank and Marie-Thérèse Wood Print Collections, Alexandria, Va. 23: MASS-MOLLUS/USAMHI, copied by A. Pierce Bounds. 24: From *Autobiography of Dr. Thomas H. Barton: The Self-Made Physician of Syracuse, Ohio,* by Thomas H. Barton, West Virginia Printing Co., Charleston, 1890, copied by Philip Brandt George—Old Courthouse Museum, Vicksburg, Miss. 25: Ohio Historical Society, Columbus. 26: U.S. Naval Historical Center, Washington, D.C. 27: Library of Congress, Neg. No. LC-USZ62-65084. 28: Frank and Marie-Thérèse Wood Print Collections, Alexandria, Va. 29: Chicago Historical Society. 30: Frank and Marie-Thérèse Wood Print Collections, Alexandria, Va. 33: Map by William L. Hezlep. 35: Map by Walter W. Roberts. 36: Ohio Historical Society, Columbus. 37: Frank and Marie-Thérèse Wood Print Collections, Alexandria, Va. 38: Museum of the Confederacy, Richmond, photographed by Katherine Wetzel. 39: Confederate Memorial Hall, New Orleans, photographed by Claude Levet. 40: From *Battles and Leaders of the Civil War,* Vol. 3, edited by Robert Underwood Johnson and Clarence Clough Buel, Century, New York, 1887, copied by Philip Brandt George. 41: Old Courthouse Museum, Vicksburg, Miss., copied by Henry Mintz; Mike Paul Collection, photo at U.S. Army Military History Institute (USAMHI), copied by A. Pierce Bounds. 43: Vann Martin Collection, copied by Henry Mintz. 44, 45: Lloyd Ostendorf Collection—Department of Archives and Manuscripts, Louisiana State University Library, Baton Rouge.

46: Vicksburg National Military Park, copied by Henry Mintz—Blue Acorn Press. 47: Frank and Marie-Thérèse Wood Print Collections, Alexandria, Va. 48: Library of Congress, Neg. No. LC-B811-2430. 49: Vann Martin Collection, copied by Henry Mintz; Melville J. Boucher Collection at USAMHI, copied by A. Pierce Bounds. 50: Vann Martin Collection, copied by Henry Mintz. 52: Ohio Historical Society, Columbus. 53: Library of Congress, Neg. No. LC-USZ62-14963. 54: Old Courthouse Museum, Vicksburg, Miss., photographed by Gil Ford Photography. 55: Frank and Marie-Thérèse Wood Print Collections, Alexandria, Va. 56: Vann Martin Collection, copied by Henry Mintz. 57: Gift of Maxim Karolik, courtesy Museum of Fine Arts, Boston. 58: Frank and Marie-Thérèse Wood Print Collections, Alexandria, Va. 59: L. M. Strayer Collection, Dayton. 60: Ohio Historical Society, Columbus. 61: Vann Martin Collection, copied by Henry Mintz. 62: University of Iowa Special Collections, Iowa City; Vicksburg National Military Park, photographed by Henry Mintz. 63: State Historical Society of Missouri, Columbia. 64: From *The Photographic History of the Civil War,* Vol. 10, Review of Reviews, New York, 1911, copied by Philip Brandt George. 65: Old Courthouse Museum, Vicksburg, Miss., photographed by Henry Mintz; Vann Martin Collection, copied by Henry Mintz. 67: L. M. Strayer Collection, Dayton. 68, 69: Frank and Marie-Thérèse Wood Print Collections, Alexandria, Va.; William Schultz Collection, photo at USAMHI, copied by A. Pierce Bounds. 70, 71: Vann Martin Collection, copied by Henry Mintz. 72: Courtesy Virginia Easley, State Historical Society of Missouri, Columbia. 73: Frank and Marie-Thérèse Wood Print Collections, Alexandria, Va. 74: L. M. Strayer Collection, Dayton, photographed by Patterson Graphics, Inc. 75: Library of Congress. 76: From *A Soldier's Story of the Siege of Vicksburg, from the Diary of Osborn H. Oldroyd,* H. W. Rokker, Springfield, Ill., 1885—Library of Congress, Neg. No. LC-B8184-10195. 77: Sharon and Bob Humble, Balfour House, Vicksburg, Miss., copied by Henry Mintz. 78: Frank and Marie-Thérèse Wood Print Collections, Alexandria, Va. 81: Map by Walter W. Roberts. 84: Vicksburg National Military Park, Vicksburg, Miss. 85: Chicago Historical Society. 87: MASS-MOLLUS/USAMHI, copied by A. Pierce Bounds; Vicksburg National Military Park, photographed by Henry Mintz. 88: Gregory Coco Collection, photographed by Mike Brouse. 89: Richard K. Tirrals Collection, photo at USAMHI, copied by A. Pierce Bounds. 90: State Historical Society of Iowa, Iowa City. 91: Vann Martin Collection, copied by Henry Mintz. 92: Paul Crawford Collection, copied by Henry Mintz. 94: Confederate Memorial

Hall, New Orleans, photographed by Claude Levet. 95: Old Courthouse Museum, Vicksburg, Miss., photographed by Henry Mintz. 96: Old Courthouse Museum, Vicksburg, Miss. 97: State Historical Society of Iowa, Iowa City. 98: Library of Congress, Neg. No. LC-B813-6554. 99: Museum of the Confederacy, Richmond, copied by Katherine Wetzel. 100: Ohio Historical Society, Columbus. 101: MASS-MOLLUS/USAMHI, copied by A. Pierce Bounds. 102: Ohio Historical Society, Columbus. 103: Wisconsin Veterans Museum, Madison. 104: Frank and Marie-Thérèse Wood Print Collections, Alexandria, Va. 105: Museum of the Confederacy, Richmond, photographed by Katherine Wetzel. 107: Vicksburg National Military Park, copied by Henry Mintz—Frank and Marie-Thérèse Wood Print Collections, Alexandria, Va. 108: State Historical Society of Wisconsin, Madison. 109: Ohio Historical Society, Columbus. 111: Vann Martin Collection, copied by Henry Mintz. 112: Vicksburg National Military Park, photographed by Henry Mintz (2); Old Courthouse Museum, Vicksburg, Miss., copied by Henry Mintz. 113: Courtesy Guy B. Montgomery—from *Vicksburg: 47 Days of Siege,* by A. A. Hoehling. 114: Library of Congress. 115: Vann Martin Collection, copied by Henry Mintz. 116, 117: Frank and Marie-Thérèse Wood Print Collections, Alexandria, Va. 118: Roger D. Hunt Collection at USAMHI, copied by A. Pierce Bounds. 119: Old Courthouse Museum, Vicksburg, Miss., photographed by Henry Mintz—Vann Martin Collection, copied by Henry Mintz. 120: Frank and Marie-Thérèse Wood Print Collections, Alexandria, Va. 121: Thomas Smith Collection, courtesy L. M. Strayer, Dayton. 123: From *Battles and Leaders of the Civil War,* Vol. 3, edited by Robert Underwood Johnson and Clarence Clough Buel, Century, New York, 1887, copied by Philip Brandt George. 125: L. M. Strayer Collection, Dayton—from *Battles and Leaders of the Civil War,* Vol. 3, edited by Robert Underwood Johnson and Clarence Clough Buel, Century, New York, 1887, copied by Philip Brandt George. 126: Frank and Marie-Thérèse Wood Print Collections, Alexandria, Va. 128: Albert Shaw Collection, Review of Reviews, *Photographic History of the Civil War,* copied by Larry Sherer. 132: MASS-MOLLUS/USAMHI, copied by A. Pierce Bounds. 133: From *Downing's Civil War Diary,* by Alexander G. Downing, Historical Department of Iowa, Des Moines, 1916—from *The Photographic History of the Civil War,* Vol. 10, Review of Reviews, New York, 1911, copied by Philip Brandt George. 134: National Archives, Neg. No. 111-B-1782. 135: USAMHI, copied by A. Pierce Bounds. 136: Orphan Brig. Kinfolk Collection, USAMHI, copied by A. Pierce Bounds. 137: Trent Collection, Special Col-

BIBLIOGRAPHY

BOOKS

Anderson, Ephraim McD. *Memoirs: Historical and Personal; Including the Campaigns of the First Missouri Confederate Brigade.* Dayton: Press of Morningside Bookshop, 1972 (reprint of 1868 edition).

Arms and Equipment of the Confederacy (Echoes of Glory series). Alexandria, Va.: Time-Life Books, 1991.

Arms and Equipment of the Union (Echoes of Glory series). Alexandria, Va.: Time-Life Books, 1991.

Barber, Lucius W. *Army Memoirs of Lucius W. Barber: Company "D," 15th Illinois Volunteer Infantry.* Chicago: J. M. W. Jones Stationery and Printing, 1894.

Barton, Thomas H. *Autobiography of Dr. Thomas H. Barton.* Charleston: West Virginia Printing, 1890.

Basler, Roy P., ed. *The Collected Works of Abraham Lincoln,* Vol. 6. New Brunswick, N.J.: Rutgers University Press, 1953.

Battles and Leaders of the Civil War, Vol 3. Ed. by Robert Underwood Johnson and Clarence Clough Buel. New York: Thomas Yoseloff, 1956.

Bearss, Edwin Cole:
Decision in Mississippi. Jackson: Mississippi Commission on the War between the States, 1962.
Grant Strikes a Fatal Blow, Vol. 2 of *The Campaign for Vicksburg.* Dayton: Morningside, 1986.
The Siege of Jackson: July 10–17, 1863. Baltimore: Gateway Press, 1981.
Three Other Post-Vicksburg Actions. Baltimore: Gateway Press, 1981.
Unvexed to the Sea, Vol. 3 of *The Campaign for Vicksburg.* Dayton: Morningside, 1986.
Vicksburg Is the Key, Vol. 1 of *The Campaign for Vicksburg.* Dayton: Morningside, 1985.

Bearss, Edwin Cole, and Warren Grabau. *The Battle of Jackson: May 14, 1863.* Baltimore: Gateway Press, 1981.

Bell, Lucy McRae. "A Minie Ball Passed through His Whiskers." In *Yankee Bullets, Rebel Rations,* by Gordon A. Cotton. Vicksburg, Miss.: Office Supply, 1989.

Blanchard, Ira. *I Marched with Sherman: Civil War Memoirs of the 20th Illinois Volunteer Infantry.* San Francisco: J. D. Huff, 1992.

Boatner, Mark Mayo, III. *The Civil War Dictionary.* New York: David McKay, 1959.

Byers, S. H. M.:
"Some Recollections of Grant." In *The Annals of the War: Written by Leading Participants, North and South.* Philadelphia: Times, 1879.
With Fire and Sword. New York: Neale, 1911.

Carter, Samuel, III. *The Final Fortress: The Campaign for Vicksburg, 1862–1863.* New York: St. Martin's Press, 1980.

Cater, Douglas John. *As It Was: Reminiscences of a Soldier of the Third Texas Cavalry and the Nineteenth Louisiana Infantry.* Austin, Tex.: State House Press, 1990.

Cavins, Aden G. *War Letters of Aden G. Cavins: Written to His Wife Matilda Livingston Cavins.* Evansville, Ind.: Rosenthal-Kuebler Printing, 1980.

Chambers, William Pitt. *Blood & Sacrifice: The Civil War Journal of a Confederate Soldier.* Ed. by Richard A. Baumgartner. Huntington, W.Va.: Blue Acorn Press, 1994.

Coggins, Jack. *Arms and Equipment of the Civil War.* Wilmington, N.C.: Broadfoot, 1962.

Crummer, Wilbur F. *With Grant at Fort Donelson, Shiloh and Vicksburg.* Oak Park, Ill.: E. C. Crummer, 1915.

Dana, Charles A. *Recollections of the Civil War: With the Leaders at Washington and in the Field in the Sixties.* New York: D. Appleton, 1902.

Davidson, W. J. "Diary of Private W. J. Davidson: Company C, Forty-first Tennessee Regiment." In *The Annals of the Army of Tennessee and Early Western History,* Vol. 1. Ed. by Edwin L. Drake. Nashville: A. D. Haynes, 1878.

Deeds of Valor: How America's Heroes Won the Medal of Honor, Vol. 1. Ed. by W. F. Beyer and O. F. Keydel. Detroit: Perrien-Keydel, 1903.

Downing, Alexander G. *Downing's Civil War Diary.* Ed. by Olynthus B. Clark. Des Moines: Historical Department of Iowa, 1916.

Force, Manning F. "Personal Recollections of the Vicksburg Campaign." In *Sketches of War History, 1861–1865: Papers Read before the Ohio Commandery of the Military Order of the Loyal Legion of the United States, 1883–1886,* Vol. 1. Wilmington, N.C.: Broadfoot, 1991 (reprint of 1888 edition).

Foster, William Lovelace. *Vicksburg: Southern City under Siege.* New Orleans: Historic New Orleans Collection, 1980.

Freret, James. "Fortification and Siege of Port Hudson." In Southern Historical Society Papers, Vol 14. Wilmington, N.C.: Broadfoot, 1990.

Grant, Frederick Dent. "With Grant at Vicksburg." In *Crucial Moments of the Civil War.* Ed. by Willard Webb. New York: Fountainhead, 1961.

Grant, Ulysses S. *Personal Memoirs of U. S. Grant.* New York: Charles L. Webster, 1894.

Green, Johnny. *Johnny Green of the Orphan Brigade: The Journal of a Confederate Soldier.* Ed. by A. D. Kirwan. Lexington: University of Kentucky Press, 1956.

Gregory, Edward S. "Vicksburg during the Siege." In *The Annals of the War: Written by Leading Participants, North and South.* Philadelphia: Times, 1879.

Harwell, Richard B., ed. *The Confederate Reader.* New

York: David McKay, 1976 (reprint of 1957 edition).

Hewitt, Lawrence Lee. *Port Hudson, Confederate Bastion on the Mississippi.* Baton Rouge: Louisiana State University Press, 1987.

Hoehling, A. A. *Vicksburg: 47 Days of Siege.* Mechanicsburg, Pa.: Stackpole Books, 1996.

Hopkins, Owen Johnston. *Under the Flag of the Nation: Diaries and Letters of a Yankee Volunteer in the Civil War.* Ed. by Otto F. Bond. Columbus: Ohio State University Press, 1961.

Howell, H. Grady, Jr. *Hill of Death: The Battle of Champion Hill.* Madison, Miss.: Chickasaw Bayou Press, 1993.

Illustrated Atlas of the Civil War (Echoes of Glory series). Alexandria, Va.: Time-Life Books, 1991.

Jones, Jenkin Lloyd. *An Artilleryman's Diary.* Madison: Wisconsin History Commission, 1914.

Jones, J. H. "The Rank and File at Vicksburg." In *Publications of the Mississippi Historical Society,* Vol. 7. Ed. by Franklin L. Riley. Oxford: Mississippi Historical Society, 1903.

Jones, Samuel C. *Reminiscences of the Twenty-second Iowa Volunteer Infantry.* Iowa City, Iowa: n.p., 1907.

Kellogg, J. J. *War Experiences and the Story of the Vicksburg Campaign: From "Milliken's Bend" to July 4, 1863.* Washington, Iowa: Evening Journal, 1913.

Korn, Jerry, and the Editors of Time-Life Books. *War on the Mississippi: Grant's Vicksburg Campaign* (The Civil War series). Alexandria, Va.: Time-Life Books, 1985.

Lee, Stephen D. "The Campaign of Vicksburg, Mississippi, in 1863—From April 15 to and Including the Battle of Champion Hills, or Baker's Creek, May 16, 1863." In *Southern Historical Society Papers,* Vol 21. Wilmington, N.C.: Broadfoot, 1990 (reprint of 1893 edition).

Loughborough, Mary Ann Webster. *My Cave Life in Vicksburg: With Letters of Trial and Travel.* Spartanburg, S.C.: Reprint, 1976.

Morris, W. S., L. D. Hartwell, and J. B. Kuykendall. *History, 31st Regiment Illinois Volunteers.* Herrin, Ill.: Crossfire Press, 1991.

Newton, James K. *A Wisconsin Boy in Dixie: The Selected Letters of James K. Newton.* Ed. by Stephen E. Ambrose. Madison: University of Wisconsin Press, 1961.

Oldroyd, Osborn H. *A Soldier's Story of the Siege of Vicksburg.* Springfield, Ill.: H. W. Rokker, 1885.

Porter, D. D. *Incidents and Anecdotes of the Civil War.* New York: D. Appleton, 1885.

Ranlett, Seth A. "The Capture of Jackson." In *Civil War Papers: Read before the Commandery of the State of Massachusetts, Military Order of the Loyal Legion of the United States,* Vol. 1. Boston: F. H. Gilson, 1900.

Rood, Hosea W. *Story of the Service of Company E, and of the Twelfth Wisconsin Regiment of Veteran Volunteer Infantry, in the War of the Rebellion.* Milwaukee: Swain and Tate, 1893.

Sherman, William Tecumseh:

Home Letters of General Sherman. Ed. by M. A. DeWolfe Howe. New York: Charles Scribner's Sons, 1909.

Memoirs of General William T. Sherman. Bloomington: Indiana University Press, 1957.

The Sherman Letters: Correspondence between General and Senator Sherman from 1837 to 1891. Ed. by Rachel Sherman Thorndike. New York: AMS Press, 1971 (reprint of 1894 edition).

Tunnard, W. H. *A Southern Record: The History of the Third Regiment Louisiana Infantry.* Dayton: Morningside Bookshop, 1970 (reprint of 1866 edition).

United States War Department:

The War of the Rebellion: A Compilation of the Official Records of the Union and Confederate Armies, Series 1, Vol. 24, Part 3—Correspondence. Harrisburg, Pa.: National Historical Society, 1971 (reprint of 1889 edition).

The War of the Rebellion: A Compilation of the Official Records of the Union and Confederate Armies, Series 1, Vol. 24, Parts 1 and 2—Reports. Harrisburg, Pa.: National Historical Society, 1971 (reprint of 1889 edition).

The War of the Rebellion: A Compilation of the Official Records of the Union and Confederate Armies, Series 1, Vol. 26, Part 2—Correspondence—Confederate. Harrisburg, Pa.: National Historical Society, 1971 (reprint of 1889 edition).

The War of the Rebellion: A Compilation of the Official Records of the Union and Confederate Armies, Series 1, Vol. 26, Part 1—Reports—Union and Confederate, Correspondence—Union. Harrisburg, Pa.: National Historical Society, 1971 (reprint of 1889 edition).

Warner, Ezra J.:

Generals in Blue: Lives of the Union Commanders. Baton Rouge: Louisiana State University Press, 1964.

Generals in Gray: Lives of the Confederate Commanders. Baton Rouge: Louisiana State University Press, 1959.

Wheeler, Richard. *The Siege of Vicksburg.* New York: Thomas Y. Crowell, 1978.

Whitman, George Washington. *Civil War Letters of George Washington Whitman.* Ed. by Jerome M. Loving. Durham, N.C.: Duke University Press, 1975.

Williams, T. J. "The Battle of Champion's Hill." In *Sketches of War History, 1861-1865: Papers Prepared for the Commandery of the State of Ohio, Military Order of the Loyal Legion of the United States, 1896-1903,* Vol. 5. Wilmington, N.C.: Broadfoot, 1992 (reprint of 1903 edition).

Willison, Charles A. *Reminiscences of a Boy's Service with the 76th Ohio.* Huntington, W.Va.: Blue Acorn Press, 1995 (reprint of 1908 edition).

Winschel, Terrence J., ed. *Alice Shirley and the Story of Wexford Lodge.* Conshohocken, Pa.: Eastern National Park and Monument Association, 1993.

Yeary, Mamie, comp. *Reminiscences of the Boys in Gray: 1861-1865.* Dayton: Morningside, 1986.

PERIODICALS

Camp, Raleigh S. " 'What I Know I Know, and I Dare Express It': The History of the 40th Georgia Infantry in the Vicksburg Campaign," *Civil War Regiments: A Journal of the American Civil War,* Vol. 5, No. 1, 1996.

Cheavens, Henry Martyn. "A Missouri Confederate in the Civil War." *Missouri Historical Review,* October 1962.

Longacre, Edward G. "Port Hudson Campaign." *Civil War Times Illustrated,* February 1972.

Wilcox, Charles E. "With Grant at Vicksburg." Ed. by Edgar L. Erickson. *Journal of the Illinois Historical Society,* January 1938.

"A Woman's Diary of the Siege of Vicksburg." *Century Magazine,* September 1885.

OTHER SOURCES

Bachman, Robert Lucky. "Reminiscences of Childhood and the Civil War." Unpublished manuscript, n.d. Vicksburg, Miss.: Old Courthouse Museum.

Balfour, Emma. Diary. Jackson: Mississippi Department of Archives and History.

Beck, S. C. "A True Sketch of His Army Life." Unpublished manuscript, n.d. Vicksburg, Miss.: Old Courthouse Museum.

Bliss, Zenas R. Manuscript, n.d. Carlisle Barracks, Pa.: U.S. Army Military History Institute.

Boucher, John Vincent. Letter, May 6, 1863. Carlisle Barracks, Pa.: U.S. Army Military History Institute.

Caylor, F. M. Letter, n.d. Vicksburg, Miss.: Old Courthouse Museum.

Eddington, W. R. Diary, n.d. Carlisle Barracks, Pa.: U.S. Army Military History Institute.

Farwell, Sewall S. Papers, 1852-1911. Iowa City: State Historical Society of Iowa.

Hayward, William H. Letter, May 28, 1863. Carlisle Barracks, Pa.: U.S. Army Military History Institute.

Hollingsworth, W. F. Diary, n.d. Vicksburg, Miss.: Old Courthouse Museum.

Morgan, Henry T. Letter, March 28, 1863. Carlisle Barracks, Pa.: U.S. Army Military History Institute.

Renyolds, A. H. Unpublished manuscript, n.d. Vicksburg, Miss.: Vicksburg National Military Park.

Shannon, Anne. Crutcher-Shannon Papers, April 27, 1826-

March 30, 1929. Jackson: Mississippi Department of Archives and History.

Shepard, Sylvester. Letter, June 13, 1863. Carlisle Barracks, Pa.: U.S. Army Military History Institute.

Smith, George. Letter, May 6, 1863. Vicksburg, Miss.:

Old Courthouse Museum.

Spencer, James G. Letter, September 18, 1910. Vicksburg, Miss.: Vicksburg National Military Park.

Westbrook, Joseph W. Letter, n.d. Carlisle Barracks, Pa.: U.S. Army Military History Institute.

INDEX

TIME® Time-Life Books is a
LIFE division of Time Life Inc.
BOOKS

TIME LIFE INC.

PRESIDENT and CEO: George Artandi

TIME-LIFE BOOKS

PRESIDENT: Stephen R. Frary
PUBLISHER/MANAGING EDITOR: Neil Kagan

VOICES OF THE CIVIL WAR

MARKETING DIRECTOR: Pamela R. Farrell

VICKSBURG

EDITOR: Paul Mathless
Deputy Editors: Philip Brandt George (principal),
Harris J. Andrews, Kirk Denkler
Art Directors: Ellen L. Pattisall (principal),
Barbara M. Sheppard
Associate Editor/Research and Writing: Annette Scarpitta
Senior Copyeditor: Judith Klein
Picture Coordinator: Lisa Groseclose
Editorial Assistant: Christine Higgins

Initial Series Design: Studio A

Special Contributors: James Michael Lynch, Dana B. Shoaf,
David S. Thomson (text); Paul Birkhead, Connie Contreras,
Charles F. Cooney, Robert Lee Hodge, Todd Miller, Henry
Mintz, Dana B. Shoaf (research); Roy Nanovic (index).

Correspondents: Christina Lieberman (New York).

Director of Finance: Christopher Hearing
Director of Book Production: Marjann Caldwell
Director of Publishing Technology: Betsi McGrath
Director of Photography and Research: John Conrad Weiser
Director of Editorial Administration: Barbara Levitt
Production Manager: Marlene Zack
Quality Assurance Manager: James King
Chief Librarian: Louise D. Forstall

Consultants

Richard A. Baumgartner, a former newspaper and magazine
editor, has written, edited, or published 16 books dealing with
Civil War and World War I history, including *Blue Lightning:
Wilder's Mounted Infantry Brigade in the Battle of Chickamauga*. A longtime student of the Civil War's western theater, he
served as editor of *Blood & Sacrifice: The Civil War Journal of
a Confederate Soldier* and coedited *Yankee Tigers* and two volumes in the award-winning Echoes of Battle series: *The
Atlanta Campaign* and *The Struggle for Chattanooga*. Focusing
on the experiences of the common soldier, he has written
numerous articles for several military-history journals.

Larry M. Strayer, an editor with Blue Acorn Press, has written
or contributed to more than a dozen books on the war's western theater, including *Yankee Tigers* and the award-winning
Echoes of Battle volumes on the Atlanta and Chattanooga
campaigns. Well known in living-history circles, he currently
serves as adviser to Accuracy Historical Productions. Focusing on the common soldier, his next publication will photographically chronicle Ohio's involvement in the Civil War.

First printing. Printed in U.S.A.
School and library distribution by Time-Life Education,
P.O. Box 85026, Richmond, Virginia 23285-5026.

TIME-LIFE is a trademark of Time Warner Inc. U.S.A.

Library of Congress Cataloging-in-Publication Data
Vicksburg / by the editors of Time-Life Books.
    p. cm.—(Voices of the Civil War)
    Includes bibliographical references and index.
    ISBN 0-7835-4713-7
    1. Vicksburg (Miss.)—History—Siege, 1863.
    I. Time-Life Books. II. Series.
E475.27.V57 1997
973.7'344—dc21   97-25385
                                                    CIP

OTHER PUBLICATIONS:

HISTORY
The Civil War
The American Indians
Lost Civilizations
The American Story
Mysteries of the Unknown
Time Frame
Cultural Atlas

SCIENCE/NATURE
Voyage Through the Universe

DO IT YOURSELF
The Time-Life Complete Gardener
Home Repair and Improvement
The Art of Woodworking
Fix It Yourself

TIME-LIFE KIDS
Library of First Questions and Answers
A Child's First Library of Learning
I Love Math
Nature Company Discoveries
Understanding Science & Nature

COOKING
Weight Watchers® Smart Choice Recipe Collection
Great Taste~Low Fat
Williams–Sonoma Kitchen Library

For information on and a full description of any of the Time-
Life Books series listed above, please call 1-800-621-7026
or write:

Reader Information
Time-Life Customer Service
P.O. Box C-32068
Richmond, Virginia 23261-2068